Thinking about the Environment

Thinking about the Environment

Our Debt to the Classical and Medieval Past

Edited by
Thomas M. Robinson
and Laura Westra

LEXINGTON BOOKS
Lanham • Boulder • New York • Oxford

LEXINGTON BOOKS

Published in the United States of America
by Lexington Books
A Member of the Rowman & Littlefield Publishing Group
4720 Boston Way, Lanham, Maryland 20706

12 Hid's Copse Road
Cumnor Hill, Oxford OX2 9JJ, England

British Library Cataloguing in Publication Information Available

Library of Congress Cataloging-in-Publication Data

Thinking about the environment: our debt to the classical and medieval past / edited by Thomas M. Robinson and Laura Westra.
p. cm.
Essays in English and Italian.
Includes bibliographical references.
ISBN 0-7391-0420-9 (cloth: alk. paper)
1. Environmentalism—History. 2. Philosophy, Ancient. 3. Philosophy, Medieval. 4. Nature in literature. I. Robinson, T. M. II. Westra, Laura.

GE50.T48 2002

2002066133

Printed in the United States of America

™ The paper used in this publication meets the minimum requirements of American National Standard for Information Sciences—Permanence of Paper for Printed Library Materials, ANSI/NISO Z39.48–1992.

To Katie Paris, in admiration of her work in this vineyard

—— Thomas M. Robinson

To Father Joseph Owens, truly "il Maestro di colore che sanno"

—— Laura Westra

CONTENTS

II. Medieval Christianity

III. Medieval Islam

IV. Medieval Judaism

V. Then and Now

FOREWORD

Alan Holland

The papers in this collection are the product of a conference whose venue, in the central regions of Italy, was preeminently suited to its subject. Culture and nature, literature and landscape, have intermingled here over many centuries. Here, contemporary place-names speak of the blood and bones of the Roman soldiers slaughtered by Hannibal at the battle of Lake Trasimene. But here too, both Vergil and Horace spoke of their love and joy of the countryside.

But why should the work of the ancients and the medievals, so far as it relates to nature, still be an interest and an inspiration to us now? Aren't our relations with the natural world, and our understanding of those relations, now so transformed that the earlier world and the earlier understandings of that world are no longer relevant? In medieval times, a sow might be hanged for murder and moles given safe conduct whilst being moved from an area where they were causing damage—with an extra fourteen days grace being allowed for pregnant females and their young. The worldview lying behind such practices might seem to have little bearing on today's concerns. True, this has not prevented some modern writers from delving into the past in hope of explaining—and even excusing—our present environmental predicament. But is this the only way to conceive of "relevance"? And how far is it plausible to blame elements of both ancient and medieval worldviews for the way we live now?

The contributions to this volume point to the possibility of quite different forms of illumination. These arise not from the attempt to trace (narrow) causal relationships but from a wider view of what it is to make sense of events and use that illumination to inform current practice. Hence we find at least three areas of illumination. The first is the area of meaning, for we frequently under-rate the strength of our quest for meaning, both within the span of our own individual lives and in the sequence of events in which our lives are interwoven. The more we can uncover a meaningful trajectory of relationships between then and now, the more meaningful our own span becomes. Continuity and contact with the past is important both in culture and in nature—hence the appeal to nativeness and venerability in nature conservation. And one of the delights and privileges of scholarship, of course, is to try to contribute to and to enrich this meaningful relation with our past. Through this we learn that to destroy nature is to destroy meaning.

The second form of illumination lies in our being awakened to contrasting sensibilities. The ordinary citizen of the pre-modern world, for example, lived much closer than we do now to earth, air, fire, and water and would feel, in a visceral sense, the contrast between hot and cold, wet and dry. Accordingly, their sensibilities would be different from ours, and it is important to learn how they would be different. In other cases we encounter sensibilities that we still share but risk losing in light of changing beliefs and circumstances. It might be important to learn how we could retain those sensibilities. Nor should we forget the sensibilities that may be reawakened. When John Keats wrote:

> My heart aches, and a drowsy numbness pains
> My sense, as though of hemlock I had drunk

he had open before him Horace's fourteenth Epode:

> Why a soft numbness drenches all my inmost senses
> With deep oblivion.

Through this we learn that to destroy nature is to destroy sensibility.

The third form of illumination is through the generation of varieties of understanding—(a term preferable to "enlightenment" with its *pro*gressive and *ag*gressive resonance). To examine ancient and medieval "work"—understood in the broadest sense to include literature, labour, and the institutions and forms of organiszation through which these are expressed—provides context through which we better understand how we have reached our present situation. It further provides us with contrasts which serve to illuminate and show up in relief features of our present situation of which we otherwise would remain unaware. It also provides samples—possibly quaint and parochial—for external reflection, reminding us of how we too will seem to the gaze of others.

In short, by reading and interpreting the literature, the land, the texts, and the textures, we gain meaningful contact and contrast between then and now along many dimensions—relating to the sense of control or lack of control, the sense of responsibility or lack of responsibility, of defiance or acceptance, gratitude or ingratitude, attachment or alienation. Through this we learn that to destroy nature is to destroy understanding.

And so, the editors of this collection deserve both our praise and our thanks for inspiring a project that affords us, the readers, this opportunity for enrichment of our sense of meaning, our sensibilities, and our understanding.

INTRODUCTION

Thomas M. Robinson and Laura Westra

In an earlier volume, *The Greeks and the Environment*, we edited a series of essays, one major purpose of which was to show that the writings of classical Greek thinkers, and in particular the writings of Plato and Aristotle, were far less inimical to current environmental ideas than is often supposed and that in certain critical respects they constitute the historical basis for a number of them. This present volume continues in the same vein, though this time the range is broader, extending from classical antiquity and earlier to the medieval epoch and beyond.

The discussion begins just about as far back in antiquity as one can go, with Mesopotamian mythology, which Michael Herren spends time comparing with Greek mythology. His conclusion, after an examination of the evidence, is that both of them had the effect of ensuring that civilization and culture would progress, but largely at the cost of a retreat from nature. Early Greek philosophers, by contrast, especially Anaximander and Heraclitus and Plato, with their commitment to the notion of justice and balance within the natural world, have, as Hideya Yamakawa shows, proved to be a useful counterbalance to such a vision. In the same vein, Giovanni Casertano stresses the importance of Empedocles as an exponent of the view that there is a commonality between ourselves and all living things, and how there will never be true peace on earth until this is accepted; and Helen Karabatzaki describes how not simply the Stoics but also the Epicureans and the Skeptics stressed the inherent goodness of all animate and inanimate nature. Finally, moving very effectively from theory to practice, Livio Rossetti tells the remarkable story of the first known ecological edict in the west, stemming from Athens in the fifth century B.C.E.

The thinking of classical Latin writers is represented by Vergil in the early Roman Empire and St. Augustine in the late. For Lorina Quartarone, Vergil's poetry offers clear evidence of his negative feelings for human ignorance and insensitivity towards nature. For Madonna Adams, St. Augustine is a very praiseworthy exponent of the goodness of the natural world and of our obligation, when using it, to establish such use on a basis of need, not of "greed, luxury, or waste."

Medieval Christian views on the natural world and our relationship to it are represented in essays on the attitude of various writers from Poland, from Germany (the author of *Parzifal*), and from Italy (Aquinas); and, in the same vein as the essay of Rossetti on fifth-century Athens, by an essay on the attitude of the enlightened leaders of the Commune of Perugia toward the preservation of Lake Trasimene. For Teresa Kwiatkowska, there are clear differences between the views of various medieval Polish poets towards nature and the views of less romantically inclined chroniclers. But all, she finds, are, despite their differences, imbued with a common sense of wonder at the natural beauty of their homeland. For Rosmarie Morewedge, *Parzifal* is an account of how, in the grail, two conflicting views of nature become, by agreement, a powerful, unified one. For Laura Westra, the foundational role of the laws of nature in Aristotle is necessary for a proper understanding of natural law in Aquinas; because of its roots, natural law must be understood as a universal rather than a sectarian doctrine. Finally, Valentina Vincenti tells the heartening story of how the forward-looking leaders of Perugia introduced a number of excellent pieces of legislation to protect the fragile ecosystem of Lake Trasimene and tells how such legislation indeed succeeded in protecting the lake for years into the future.

Medieval Arabic views are represented in essays by Parviz Morewedge and by Lynda Clarke. For Morewedge, a central feature of medieval Arabic thought is the remarkable fact that the person is deemed to be inseparable from nature; it is in fact an *essential dimension* of the person. For the Sufi mystic Jalál al-Dín Rúmí, of whom Clarke speaks in detail in her essay, the natural world is harmonious, purposive, and good. But, unlike the world as seen by the Greeks, it is not a world that is subject to mechanistic law; it is, rather, along occasionalist lines, forever being created anew and sustained by God at every moment.

Medieval Jewish views are represented in essays on Maimonides and Nachmanides and in the implications of the accounts of the origins of the universe as seen in the book of Genesis and Plato's *Timaeus*. The first of these, by Edward Halper, is a detailed account of how two major thinkers disagreed over the interpretation of the famous injunction at Deuteronomy 22.6-7 that a mother bird was never to be taken away with her young. The second essay, by Emilie Kutash, argues that ecologically sounder consequences are more likely to stem from the Genesis account than from the *Timaeus* account of the world's origins.

The volume concludes with an essay by Daryl Tress on the breakdown between science and value in contemporary ecological thought and on how a second look at Greek thought, which in large measure avoids such a breakdown, is urgently called for.

Our thanks, finally, to the Department of Philosophy at the University of Toronto for financial aid toward the publishing of the book.

Toronto, March 3, 2002

I. Greece and Rome

I

NATURE AND CULTURE IN MESOPOTAMIAN AND GREEK MYTHS

Michael W. Herren

The world may have moved past Max Müller and his idea, founded in shaky linguistic theory, that all myths are nature allegories.[1] But out of the ashes of this discarded image rises the phoenix of Claude Levi-Strauss's notion, founded in Hegelian dialectic, that the "privileged theme" of myths is the conflict between nature and culture and the search for resolution in mediation.[2] In structuralist theory, the nature-culture conflict projected onto the screen of the human imagination is a reflection of the very instrument that projects it. The human being belongs to nature, yet does not. The same creature that is governed by the iron laws of hunger, thirst and lust is capable of soaring heavenwards. There the human mind beholds not the chaotic world of burning gasses and meteors that we choose to call nature, but a panorama of abstract forms, coexisting in perfect harmony, and governed by the motions of divine beings, or perhaps angels.

That the ancient Greeks were aware of a deep fissure between the way things are ("the nature of things") and the way humans want them to be is transparent in Plato's theory of ideas. For Plato, all that we experience through our senses can only approximate (as a portrait approximates its model) the truer, deeper reality which it is said to resemble. This reality, expressed as non-sensible ideas or forms, is equated with perfection—a perfection that is never attainable in this world (represented by Plato's cave or Augustine's land of exile), yet, paradoxically, must be striven for ceaselessly. Whence came the strange notion that there might be a better world somewhere else? Music may transport us, as Schubert's lovely "Ode to Music" promises, but in what sense "in eine bess're Welt"? Are those animals which do not read Plato able to conceive of qualitatively better pasture, or do they simply desire to roam where there is more of the same? Did the human quest for a perfect world begin with the realization of the imperfections of the nature of things, "things as they are"? But, if so, how and under what circumstances did humans recognize such imperfections, if they had no prior knowledge of perfection?

It is not our intention here to explore the mystery of the origin of human dissatisfaction with the way things are, that is, with nature. It is, for our purposes, enough to assert the fact of its existence from time unremembered. Whether we regard myths as "prephilosophical", it is clear that, in many cases, they preserve and transmit deeply rooted ideologies to posterity. In the myths and myth-systems that have been influential on western thought it is possible to discover formative views on a number of crucial subjects. These include a belief in cosmic purpose and the possibility of progress; that progress is achieved through the evolution of a male line of gods; that "the feminine" is unpredictable and constitutes an impediment to progress unless stabilised by male intervention. These ideologies, supported by a belief in a patriarchal sky god,[3] constitute the core of the "codifying myths"[4] that lie at the basis of western thinking. Developing from these central ideas is the association of nature (=repetition without development) with the female principle, and culture (=progress) with the male.

The mythology of Mesopotamia, beginning with the Sumerian myths, lies at the source of much of the mythology and ideology of the Hebrews and Greeks, who built the foundations of western civilization.[5] Certainly we find there the "core ideas" noted above that condition western attitudes towards nature. The cosmological conflict among generations of male gods that resolves itself in the victory of the youngest and cleverest (who goes on to shape and govern the universe) is first found there.[6] In the version of the myth transmitted in the Babylonian poem *Enuma Elish*, development of the male line is represented in the change from a sleepy, barely conscious (and hence, practically female) male principle Apsu, who closely resembles phenomena of the natural world, to a fully anthropomorphic hero-god (Marduk), who blends brawn with brains and is capable of overcoming and destroying the terrifying and destructive female principle (Tiamat). Although Marduk possesses the requisite masculine courage, his victory over untrammeled female nature is accomplished by the application of cunning and technology (a net). To make the destruction of the female hegemony complete, Tiamat's consort Kingu, accused as an instigator, is executed: an example to all males who dared to place their intellectual talents in the service of the female principle. With this disposition of the impediments to cosmic progress, it becomes possible to create new forms of life, namely human beings; the first man is fashioned out of the blood of Kingu.[7] By contrast, the carcass of the slaughtered Tiamat is used to create the foundations of the inanimate (and unthinking) universe.[8]

In Hesiod's *Theogony*, the earliest extant Greek cosmogony, the Sumero-Akkadian first principles of salt and fresh water, partially anthromorphosized, are replaced by a curious assortment of unconscious phenomena—Chaos, "wide-bosomed Earth", and Eros, the personified sex-impulse. These three principles are required to start things up. The basis of their selection, however, remains obscure, and why three elements are needed—in place of a primal couple—is by no means clear. Moreover, the precise meaning of "Chaos" is problematic. Does the name refer to primal matter, or to the abyss, or "watery deep"?

In the latter case it would correspond to Apsu of the *Enuma Elish*, and possibly also to the abyss of Genesis 1:2. At all events, parthenogenesis was the order of the day. Chaos and Earth began creating things of their own accord, then some of the creations mated with each other. Earth produced Heaven, "to cover her on every side,"[9] and later mated with him to create Ocean and the host of Titans. None of these early birthings or matings appears to have been very well thought out. Indeed, if we interpret correctly, all was driven by Eros, "who overcomes the mind and wise counsels of all gods and all men."[10] Generation, the coming into being of all that exists, occurred more or less haphazardly. No god planned creation—the gods belong to a later stage of generation—nor is there any hint of a disembodied rational principle at work in the process. The Hesiodic account of "coming into being" appears to be purely chaotic in the modern sense of the word.

While Hesiod's account contains layers of complexity that we do not find in the *Enuma Elish*, it resembles the latter in its basic structure: in both works the process of generation, or the coming into being of things, is partially accomplished before the appearance of the gods. It is true that the Hesiodic gods are more concerned with establishing law and order while Marduk of the *Enuma Elish* is directly involved in the process of creation, like the Jewish god of the Book of Genesis. Yet Marduk came late to the scene, as did Hesiod's Zeus. Both accounts agree in the essential point that the cosmic planning process begins with the advent of a masculine god. Before this event there were only haphazard happenings—chaos (again, in the modern sense). This determination of a turning point in cosmic history simultaneously determined the belief that all that is purely natural is mindless. Nature can only acquire value when it is subjected to a purpose, and all purpose is perforce the product of the divine male mind.

The Mesopotamians and the Greeks built the concept of evolution into their cosmogonies, and sought to establish a "missing link" between unconscious natural forces and gods, in somewhat the same way as modern evolutionary theorists have searched for a link between monkey and man. The Hesiodic account posits an intermediate race known as the Titans, who possessed tremendous strength, at least one of them with remarkable intelligence. This last was Prometheus, whose name means "Forethought". That the whole race of Titans was not endowed with great mental ability is shown in Prometheus's brother Epimetheus, whose name means "Afterthought". The Sumerian counterpart of Prometheus is Enki, represented as Ea, the father of Marduk, in the *Enuma Elish*. Both are tricky characters and both possess a special relationship to the human species, as we shall see presently. Neither of these intermediate beings is able to attain permanent rule: Ea delegated the fight against Tiamat to his son Marduk, thereby abdicating, while Prometheus underwent eternal torment after a failed revolt against Zeus. Both are witnesses to the truth that sheer cunning is not enough to establish lasting hegemony. Physical might and the "will to power" are indispensable.

A remarkable feature common to the *Enuma Elish* and the *Theogony* is the myth of the separate origin of mankind. In the Hesiodic account humans mysteriously appear. They are not reckoned as part of the grand evolutionary process that begins with the virgin birthings and indiscriminate matings of the primal forces. In contrast to the account in Hesiod's other work *Works and Days,* in which generations of men are described as the creation of the gods, in the *Theogony* they simply appear without explanation in the section of the work that deals with the crimes and revolt of Prometheus.[11] Other sources record that Prometheus created men from clay and taught them the arts.[12] Thus, the human race is neither the result of "natural" evolution nor the direct creation of the ruling class of gods. Rather, it might be termed a "rogue race"—the product of neither nature nor true divinity, but the work of a sort of "rebel angel" who served as its teacher and guardian. This (reconstructed) myth of the origin of man was not devised by the Greeks. It reached them, through lost intermediaries, from the Mesopotamian world. It corresponds to the account in the *Enuma Elish*, in which Ea, who, like Prometheus, belonged to an earlier generation of divine beings who did not succeed to permanent rule, created man at Marduk's behest.[13] It is perhaps worth noting that in the Babylonian account mankind was created from the blood of the rebel, Kingu, the "vizier" of Tiamat. Thus, in both accounts mankind assumes his origin from rebels. Human beings, made *by* rebels or *out of* rebels, endowed with a spark of divine intelligence, are neither wholly natural nor wholly supernatural. This myth lies at the base of Gnostic teaching. God delegated the creation of man to the archons; the first and greatest of these, Ialdabaoth, made Adam and set him in the garden.[14]

Humans in their precarious condition, physically weak and subject to death, needed a great deal of help to be competitive in an environment controlled by the immortal gods. The Serpent of the Book of Genesis, descendant of Ea and distant relative of Prometheus, was a willing partner to Adam and Eve, eager to get them out of the Garden of Torpor and on their way to a dangerous and thrilling apotheosis. Little did the first couple realize that some generations later their offspring would be building a skyscraper to heaven to overthrow the *elohim.*[15] Six millennia after that, in the calculations of Bishop Ussher, they would be engaged in cloning their own race, thereby ending the divine monopoly on creation. Their first gift was fire, given them by the rebel Prometheus, not as an object of worship, but as a means of changing nature into culture, initially used to cook food, then to transform the metals of the earth and make weapons. Zeus was exceedingly angry over Prometheus's theft of fire and his giving it to mankind, for fire was the token of the celestial monopoly on technology and know-how. Yahweh was no less apoplectic about the theft from the tree of the knowledge of good and evil. He didn't give a fig for the tree of life. Life, at least mortal life, was widely available, but knowledge was password-protected.[16]

The concept of *mankind* is full of pitfalls. In the first Genesis account of creation it is an inclusive term: "Male and female he created them."[17] But the second account, doubtless older and more "mythical", offers a startlingly different picture. God made a man, but woman was "Epimethean"—an afterthought.[18] In the second Genesis account she is formed from the rib of Adam, arguably making her unequal but yet not wholly separate. Even so, God was not able to come up with the ideal partner for man right off the bat. He experimented at first with matching Adam to the animals (to whom Adam gave names), "but for the man himself no partner had been found".[19] The myth of the creation of women in the *Theogony* is indeed different, but it derives from the same impulse: a deep-seated belief that women are not really of the same race as men ("Men are from Mars, Women from Venus").

The original company of men who ate beef with the gods were males only, nor were their bodies exploited for the creation of women. Contrary to the second creation account in Genesis, one cannot find the slightest trace of the notion in either of Hesiod's poems that women were missed, or that men needed some kind of partner. However, one may conclude that the creation of the "race of women" in the *Theogony*, along with the parallel account in Hesiod's *Works and Days*, is related to the account of the creation of women in the Book of Genesis. In both the Greek and the Jewish accounts, the giving of women to men is directly connected to the removal of man from his primitive condition to a state of culture. Eve accomplishes this by giving Adam the fruit of the tree of the knowledge of good and evil, the consequence of which is the expulsion from the garden and the beginning of a life dependent upon human arts. Hesiod records a very similar story:

> For ere this the tribes of men lived on earth remote and free from ills
> and hard toil and heavy sickness which brings the Fates upon men;
> for in misery men grow old quickly.[20]

But there is at least a glimmer of recognition in Hesiod that women were in some way connected to the art of agriculture: the gods gave women as both gift and bane to "men who eat grain."[21] In the hands of the divine male gods Zeus and Yahweh, the female principle is transformed from its original unconscious condition, capable only of generation, to a purposeful catalyst of transformation from nature to culture. We shall return to this motif shortly.

The charter myths of the western world show that the human species, whose origin might be described as "other than natural," never wished to accommodate itself to the laws of nature, but rather to subdue nature and subjugate it. Even the first Genesis account of creation, in which humans are described as being fashioned directly by God and created together "male and female", accords them a distinction not given to the rest of creation: "So God created man in his own image."[22] It is this image of the divine that provides humans with the entitlement to rule over the natural kingdom: "Let us make man in our image and likeness to rule the fish in the sea, the birds of heaven, the cattle, all wild things on earth, and all reptiles that crawl upon the earth."[23] And to this was added the command: "Be fruitful and increase, fill the earth and subdue it."[24] It might be observed that humans, who throughout history studiously ignored the decalogue, fulfilled this pristine commandment to the letter.

The Genesis account of man's creation in the likeness of God and his superiority over the natural world is almost certainly not the invention of Jewish theologians, but is doubtless inherited from the Mesopotamian civilization that influenced Jewish thought and literature in numerous ways. The Babylonian tale of Adapa, the first man, of which our earliest copy dates to the fourteenth century B.C.E., begins with a description of the hero's relation to the god Ea:

> In those days, in those years long ago at Eridu, the city which stands on the sweet lagoon, there was a man. He was wise like one of the gods. When he gave an order it was as though Ea, the master himself, that subtle god, had spoken; for Ea is the master of subtlety, and he also controls the waters. Ea had made him a leader, a man to be followed. He gave him sagacity and intelligence enough to comprehend the design of the world; but he made him a dying man.[25]

Here we find man likened to the gods in wisdom and a charter delegating to man the right to give commands in the name of the gods. Adapa was the deputy of Ea.

Absent from the mythology of the Mesopotamians and the Greeks is the idea that men came from animals or that they lived in a primal paradise in harmony with animals.[26] There are, of course, many stories about humans who are changed into animals, but rarely, if ever, do such stories represent the fulfillment of a happy wish. Indeed, descent into animal form is nearly always the result of some offence against the gods and is to be deeply dreaded. Circe is abhorrent precisely because she has the power to change men into swine. The opposite of apotheosis was theriomorphosis—the best condition contrasted with the worst. Nor did paradisiacal fantasies include a communal life with animals. Animals were for eating (if the relevant covenant allowed), or for human uses such as agriculture and the manufacture of clothing. Adam named the animals, he did not mate with them. Hesiod's golden folk under Chronos enjoyed partying with their own kind.[27]

Man's consciousness of his superiority to nature, so clearly reflected in myths of Mesopotamian and Greek origin, is buttressed by the construction of a series of subhuman sports and monsters that must be dreaded, hated, and ultimately rooted out and destroyed because of their association with nature. Animals might be fearsome, but men had the ability to tame them or hunt them. However, creatures that looked like men but acted like animals were another matter altogether. The Graeco-Roman Stoic ideal of "following nature as a guide" had nothing to do with living instinctually, while the attempt of the Cynics to validate "a dog's life" was met with revulsion and scorn. The belief that a man had to be demonstrably rational in order to enjoy the rights of a man has a long history. Aristotle's notion that some men were fitted by their nature to be slaves resurfaced in the debates of sixteenth-century Spain over the claimed rights of the *conquistadores* to enslave Indians on the ground that they did not possess rational souls.[28] The Mesopotamians and the Greeks (before Aristotle) clearly had conducted similar discussions. Whether wild men should be educated and tamed or dealt with more harshly was clearly an important question, as it arises in three myths, two of which are Mesopotmian, the other, Greek.

The tale "The Coming of Enkidu", attached to great Sumero-Akkadian *Epic of Gilgamesh,* is paradigmatic. Enkidu, who was to become the boon companion of the hero Gilgamesh, began life as a wild man:

> His body was rough; he had long hair like a woman's it waved like the hair of Nisaba, the goddess of corn. His body was covered with matted hair like Samuqan's, the god of cattle. He was innocent of mankind; he knew nothing of the cultivated land. Enkidu ate grass in the hills with the gazelle and lurked with wild beasts at the water-holes; he had joy of the water with the herds of wild game.[29] (Gilgamesh, 63)

One might gain the impression that this is a tale about a first man living close to nature. But this is deceptive. Civilization has already been established, and Enkidu does not fit into it. Indeed, he has become a dreadful nuisance, since his companionship with the wild animals has induced him to fill in the pits and ruin the snares of the trappers. One way or another he must be dealt with. None of the local men is strong enough to take him on physically, so a clever plan is devised. A messenger is sent to King Gilgamesh to dispatch a harlot "from the temple of love" to seduce him and deprive him of his strength. The plan works to perfection: after Enkidu has sex with the harlot, the animals avoid him, and he can no longer run to keep up with them. The harlot says to him: "You are wise, Enkidu, and now you have become like a god. Why do you want to run wild with the beasts in the hills?"[30] The harlot persuades Enkidu to come with her to the city and become the companion of Gilgamesh. There Enkidu imbibes all the pleasures of civilization: fine clothes, scent, wine, and the companionship of a great king. He is hooked. Later, on his deathbed, he starts to curse the harlot as the agent of his destruction, but then thinks better of it and expresses gratitude for the gifts she brought him.

There are several lessons in the tale. First, as with Adam in the second creation story in Genesis, men are supposed to have women as their companions, not animals. In neither story is it implied that a man might have sex with a female animal, or that a male human is required to make a choice between a female animal and a female human. No, the choice is simply between women and all animals, and men should choose women. The categories, then, are male humans, female humans, and animals (male and female), as in Genesis. Women are intermediate between men and animals: lower than the first, higher than the second. They are superior to animals because they are farther removed from nature. In the second Genesis creation story and the *Epic of Gilgamesh* the acceptance of a woman (and the rejection of animals) brings wisdom and an advance towards divinity—note the role of Eve in bringing Adam to the tree of the knowledge of good and evil.

The second lesson is that all male humans are required to move out of the natural state and integrate themselves into civilized life—no exceptions allowed! The penalty for refusal is destruction. Once it has been recognized that men have become wise and godlike (i.e., civilized), then all men (i.e., males) must accept this condition. Refusal to do so constitutes a threat—others might be tempted to run with the animals, or even mate with them, and eventually undermine the progress that has been achieved in trapping, husbandry, land cultivation, and all the human arts—arts which Adam also had to acquire when he was forced out of the garden. The "Coming of Enkidu" is a moral tale about the necessity of universal acquiescence to civilization. Its subject Enkidu posed a visible threat. In modern parlance, we would say that he was "proactive" or "in your face"—an ecological protowarrior out to fight the system, a Greenpeace activist before Greenpeace. He had only himself to blame if he encountered problems.

The next two tales exemplify wild men or anthropoid monsters to whom the phrase "proactive" does not apply, creatures who might be identified with the state of nature, but were removed from the purview of civilization. The monsters in these tales neither threatened civilized life, nor expected to be threatened by it. The first of these tales is another episode in the *Epic of Gilgamesh*. It concerns the adventure of Gilgamesh and Enkidu into a cedar forest, with the object of clearing the forest and making a name for themselves. The forest, however, is guarded by a ferocious giant named Humbaba, who is referred to by Gilgamesh as "evil". Enkidu describes him to Gilgamesh:

> When I went with the wild beasts ranging through the wilderness I discovered the forest; its length is ten thousand leagues in every direction. Enlil has appointed Humbaba to guard it and armed him in sevenfold terrors; terrible to all flesh is Humbaba. When he roars it is like the torrent of the storm, his breath is like fire, and his jaws are death itself.[31]

Despite his power and tremendous size, Gilgamesh and Enkidu, with the aid of the god Shamash, succeed in overpowering him. Before he is killed, Humbaba pleads for his life, explaining that he was not born of a mother and father, but "of the mountain", and was divinely appointed as guardian of the forest.[32] His plea did not save him. Humbaba perished along with the entire forest he was appointed to protect.

The second tale is well known from Homer's *Odyssey*. It is the episode of Odysseus's encounter with a Cyclops, an anthropoid monster with a single eye in the center of the forehead. Odysseus describes the species as follows:

> In the next land we found were Kyklopes,
> giants, louts, without a law to bless them.
> In ignorance leaving the fruitage of the earth in mystery
> to the immortals gods, they neither plow
> nor sow by hand, nor till the ground, though grain—
> wild wheat and barley—grows untended, and

wine-grapes, in clusters, ripen in heaven's rain.
Kyklopes have no muster and no meeting,
no consultation or old tribal ways,
but each one dwells in his own mountain cave
dealing out rough justice to wife and child,
indifferent to what the others do[33]

Homer then elaborates on the lack of art and technology among the species, noting that there was a nearby island with good arable land. However, the Cyclopes practiced no agriculture, and even if they did, they could not have reached the island because they did not build ships. There follows a description of Polyphemus, the particular Cyclops whom Odysseus and his men encounter:

A prodigious man slept in this cave alone, and took his flocks
to graze afield—remote from all companions,
knowing none but savage ways, a brute
so huge, he seemd no man at all of those
who eat good wheaten bread; but he seemed rather
a shaggy mountain reared in solitude.[34]

We learn from these lines that the Cyclopes practised husbandry, and a later passage tells us that they lived on the milk and cheeses which they made.

Odysseus had no business to negotiate with the Cyclopes, nor did he pitch up in their territory as the result of a storm or veering off course. On the contrary, like a modern anthropologist, Odysseus was driven by the desire to discover the character of these alien creatures. The result of his curiosity is well known. Most of the companions whom Odysseus took with him were devoured alive, and Odysseus himself and two companions barely escaped the Cyclops's grip after Odysseus had managed to blind him. Odysseus, to be sure, had foreseen danger, and took with him a skin of wine, which he used to intoxicate the unwary and uncultured Polyphemus. Culture triumphed over nature, at least temporarily.

The two exempla are, by no means, a perfect match. Humbaba belongs wholly to nature, while Polyphemus and the other Cyclopes have been exposed to husbandry and understand the fermentation of milk, although the fact that they are not "bread-eaters" (cultivator of grain) is a mark of lower status.[35] Humbaba lives completely alone, whereas the Cyclopes live in small nuclear families, though these lack contact with each other. Humbaba is a devotee of Enlil, but Polyphemus and his relatives have no care for any god. More trivially, Humbaba is utterly destroyed, whereas Polyphemus is "merely" irreparably mutilated. However, in what are arguably more important matters, the two tales are in agreement. Both myths contain disapproval of solitude and removal from society. Both myths condemn savage monsters and exalt civilized heroes, and both validate the destruction of savage creatures by the civilized. More precisely, both myths justify an unprovoked invasion of the natural world by the representatives of civilization. Neither Humbaba nor Polyphemus had harmed anyone outside his own sphere (in contrast to other natural monsters such as Enkidu before his conversion). They were known only by repute, but this repute had been exaggerated, in the case of Humbaba, to a condition of absolute evil, whereas the Cyclopes were "merely" savage and lawless.

The immutable law of progress, however, tolerates no exceptions. It is not good enough *not* to oppose progress, all living creatures are required to aid it actively. Humbaba's cedar forest left to its natural state was an example of "mismanagement", as it served no civilized purpose, just like the arable island which the Cyclopes were unable to cultivate on account of their ignorance of human arts. The ignorance and indolence of savage creatures, which in their deadly combination inhibits the exploitation of nature, creates an entitlement for civilized men to invade and exploit that which was meant to be exploited in the plan of the far-seeing gods. As with the Indians of the New World, there were only two options for dealing with the likes of Humbaba and Polyphemus: civilize them, or destroy them. One way or the other, the civilized man is both entitled and destined to exploit their natural resources for the good of progress. After all, this was the gods' decree. The race of men, abetted by rebel angels or archons, abandoned their life with animals, and seeking to be wise like gods and live like gods, learned to mate with the race of women, drink wine, eat bread, and live in cities. However, the gods, being gods, had another trick up their sleeves. They kept immortality to themselves. By doing this they ensured that men would become both rapacious and eager for fame, for fame is the only form of immortality available to men. The desire for "fame that goes up to heaven"[36] and the need to make an enduring name would ensure the unlimited advance of civilization and the retreat of nature.

We began this essay with a reference to structuralism, and return to this method in search of a conclusion. If one understands "mediation" not as a more or less exact compromise between polar opposites, but as the resolution of a problem, then we see it at work here. By consorting with women rather than with animals, men align themselves more closely with the divine element (culture) than with the animal (nature). Men are not midway between gods and animals, but much closer to gods, and are expected to behave as such. Matters are brought into a semblance of balance by the acceptance of a partner that is higher than the animals but lower than men, and by the loss of immortality, which establishes a point of commonality with the animals. These factors mitigate the culture aspect of men and permit a modicum of human identification with nature; but the factors are only mitigating, not truly mediating. In a longer discussion, we might have pointed to episodes in the *Epic of Gilgamesh* and the *Odyssey* in which the heroes are punished for their intrusions into the natural world and the injury done to its protectors. But the punishments are not perpetrated by the supreme gods, and both heroes come out rather well in the end: *finem lauda*. Male heroes, who are frequently portrayed as "godlike" in the texts do what they are programmed to do, and cannot be held accountable for the way they are wired. In effect, the conflict between nature and culture in Mesopotamian and Greek myths is resolved with most of the points going to culture. This is "the great code" that has been accepted, without an excessive amount of critical thought, by western civilization.

Notes

1. Richard M. Dorson, "The Eclipse of Solar Mythology," in Thomas A. Sebeok, ed., *Myth: A Symposium* (Bloomington: Indiana University Press, 1955), 25-63. There is a remarkable record of the debate between Müller's "philological school" and the anthropological interpretation of myth contained in Andrew Lang's article "Mythology" in vol. 18 of the ninth edition of the *The Encyclopedia Britannica* (Edinburgh, U.K.: Adam and Charles Black, 1884), 135-58.

2. Claude Levi-Strauss, *The Raw and the Cooked*, trans. John and Doreen Wightman (New York: Harper & Row, 1969). See the detailed discussion of Levi-Strauss's main hypotheses by G. S. Kirk in *Myth: Its Meanings and Functions in Ancient and Other Cultures* (Cambridge: Cambridge University Press, 1970), 42-83.

3. The notion that male sky gods are exclusive to Indo-European society and that feminine chthonic deities derive from non-Indo-European societies has few adherents today. See the effective critique by Jean-Pierre Vernant, *Mythe et société en Grèce ancienne* (Paris: François Maspero, 1974), 104-20. Vernant identifies the limitations of etymology in explaining the functions of the gods. His unnamed opponents are the neo-comparativists and their attempt to revive philology-based exegesis of myth and religion. The controversy is practically a replay of the nineteenth-century debate between Müller and Lang. Relevant to the discussion in this chapter is the fact that both Mesopotamian and Greek mythologies have patriarchal sky gods, and both have powerful chthonic female deities.

4. For the idea of "codifying myths" see Bronislaw Malinowski, "Myth as Primitive Psychology," in Malinowski ed., *Magic, Science and Religion* (Garden City, N.Y: Doubleday, 1948), 93-148.

5. For a survey of these influences on Greek mythology see Charles Penglase, *Greek Myths and Mesopotamia: Parallels and Influences in the Homeric Hymns and Hesiod* (London: Routledge, 1994).

6. N. K. Sandars, *Poems of Heaven and Hell from Ancient Mesopotamia* (London: Penguin Books, 1971), 33, 55.

7. *Enuma Elish* (*The Babylonian Creation*), trans. N. K. Sandars, *Poems of Heaven and Hell*, 98.

8. Sandars, *Enuma Elish*, 92.

9. Hesiod, *Theogony*, line 127, trans. H. G. Evelyn-White, in *Hesiod. The Homeric Hymns and Homerica* (London: William Heinemann, 1967), 87.

10. Hesiod, *Theogony*, lines 521-616.

11. Hesiod, *Theogony*, lines 120-22.

12. The sources for Prometheus's role in the creation of man as well as the traditions recording his part in bringing various arts to mankind are assembled in *Der kleine Pauly: Lexikon der Antike in fünf Bänden*, vol. 4 (Munich: Artemis Verlag, 1975), col. 1173.

13. Sandars, *Enuma Elish*, 97-98. It should be noted that, in some of the accounts of Prometheus's creation of man, Prometheus accomplished this at the behest of Zeus, just as Ea acted at the behest of Marduk. See note 11.

14. This is clearly shown in "The Secret Book of John," ed. and trans. Willis Barnstone, *The Other Bible* (San Francisco: Harper & Row, 1984), 58-59.

15. The Roman grammarian Servius (ca. 400 C.E.) preserves a tradition that Prometheus climbed up to heaven to steal fire from the sun. See his commentary on Vergil's *Eclogues* 6.72: *Servii grammatici qui feruntur in Vergilii carmina commentarii*, Georg Thilo and Hermann Hagen, eds., vol. 3 (Leipzig: Teubner, 1887), 72.

16. See the interesting exegesis on the two trees of paradise in Barnstone, "The Secret Book of John," 58-59. The exegesis reverses the significance given them in the canonical Bible.

17. Genesis 1:27.

18. Indeed, it was Epimetheus who accepted the treacherous gift of woman (Pandora) from the hands of Hermes: Hesiod, *Works and Days*, lines 83-89.

19. Genesis 1:20.

20. Hesiod, *Theogony*, 90-93.

21. The phrase "men who eat grain" occurs in the same context in *Theogony*, lines 510-14 and *Works and Days*, lines 80-82. For the demonstration that Hesiod's two accounts of the Prometheus tale and the origin of women derive from a single myth, see Vernant, *Mythe et société*, 178-94.

22. Genesis 1:27.

23. Genesis 1:26.

24. Genesis 1:28.

25. "Adapa: The Man," trans. Sandars, *Poems of Heaven and Hell*, 169.

26. However, see references in *Der kleine Pauly* (note 11) pointing to a variant of the Prometheus myth, in which Prometheus created men from the matter of excess animals.

27. Hesiod, *Works and Days*, lines 110-120.

28. See Lewis Hanke, *Aristotle and the American Indians: A Study in Race Prejudice in the Modern World* (London: Hollis and Carter, 1959), 12-27.

29. *The Epic of Gilgamesh*, trans. Sandars, 63.

30. Sandars, *Gilgamesh*, 65.

31. Sandars, *Gilgamesh*, 71.

32. Sandars, *Gilgamesh*, 82.

33. Homer, *The Odyssey*, Book IX, lines 105-15, trans. Robert Fitzgerald, *The Odyssey of Homer* (Garden City, N.Y.: Doubleday, 1961), 148.

34. Homer, *The Odyssey*, lines 187-91.

35. If one ignores the moralizing element of the Genesis redactor, the murder of Abel by Cain legitimizes the superiority of agriculture to husbandry and marks "progress" in civilization, as Cain goes on to build a city (Gen. 4:17).

36. Homer, *The Odyssey*, Book IX, line 20 (my translation).

2

ORDER, HARMONY, AND JUSTICE: THE GREEK CONCEPTION OF THE ENVIRONMENT

Hideya Yamakawa

I

Referring to "*Die Ehrfurcht zum Leben*" (the reverence for life), Albert Schweitzer once asked what 'morality' is, and answered as follows: "it means *the infinitely expanded responsibility to all living things*." What dignity, it might be asked, distinguishes the "responsibility" of his utterance from that of the hungry ghost who greedily devours the lives of other living things? What makes it possible to raise our egoistic and anthropocentric sense of responsibility to a level of *minimum dignity,* in virtue of which we might narrowly retain our humanity?

The question reminds me of the Four Noble Truths preached by the Buddha in his first teaching after gaining enlightenment.[1]

1. All is suffering.
2. There is a cause of this suffering.
3. There is a release from suffering.
4. The path to that release is the path of the right view.

The cardinal point of Buddha's teaching lies in its emphasis on the suffering of all sentient beings (*samsara*)[2] and relief from it. The matter at issue is not merely the suffering of human beings proper.

Thus, if we are going to come to grips with the above-mentioned question, we should confront the present states of ecological crisis globally and look the suffering of all sentient beings in the face. And we must discern the root causes of this crisis. Then, we should attempt to grasp the conceptual framework within which measures for the relief of sentient beings in pain can be precisely delineated and defined. Finally, we must develop a wisdom which functions on a global scale and which can overcome the environmental crisis.

However, these four requirements are so inseparably interconnected with one another that it is not easy to attain even one of them. Nevertheless, it is beyond doubt that the main origins of the present state of ecological crisis can be attributed to the quality of our civilization which has so far been firmly based on a mismatched confrontation between the mind and the outer world. This mismatching came from the inherent properties of the modern worldview which E. Husserl in his *Die Krisis der europäischen Wissenschaften und die transzendentale Phänomenologie* (1935-36) radically criticized .

Considering such a state of affairs, it is preferable that the fundamental conceptual framework on which an ecological philosophy is to be based be a holistic one, in virtue of which solidarity, togetherness, and symbiosis between sentient beings can be facilitated and guaranteed. By reason of this, ecological justice too has to be defined as a principle of symbiosis, so that injustice will be defined as the encroachment and destruction of the interdependent relationship among all living things. So ecological wisdom must also be defined as an intuition which discerns the essence of the interrelationship among all sentient beings and also as an emergent faculty which draws up a plan aiming at their peaceful coexistence. The inherent property of this wisdom is its insight into beauty. According to Parmenides, such wisdom is a faculty which can gaze upon absent things as though present, and bring them into a harmonious unity.[3] As such it is a much needed faculty for approaching environmental problems.

II

Greek philosophy may be regarded as an exceptional case which can cope with the above mentioned requirements. Since Anaximander of Miletus, Presocratic philosophers had been preoccupied with investigating Life and Justice in the *kosmos* (world order). Gazing on the downfall of Ionia, they bequeathed to us the very best legacy of speculation about the destiny of man and cosmos. Should we not therefore follow them and bring their thinking to bear on our time with as much clarity as we can?

In view of ongoing destruction of the environment, many scholars have realized that the natural world is an organic whole wherein all living things, including human beings, reside in a *symbiotic* relationship, and that the root cause of environmental destruction consists in the human *encroachment* upon and *destruction* of the *symbiotic* order of the natural world. Such a conception of the natural world reminds us at once of the cosmological thinking of the Greeks. It seems that we are now unwitingly returning to the Greek conception of *kosmos* (world order).

The *Gaia Hypothesis* presented by J. Lovelock is a good example of the recurrence of thecosmological thinking of the Greeks. The hypothesis draws a clear line of demarcation against the mechanistic view of nature that has been dominant since the age of the scientific revolution. In Lovelock's words, "the air, the ocean, and the soil are much more than a mere environment for life; they are a part of life itself."[4] It is a statement which cannot fail to remind us of the words of Anaximenes:[5] "As our soul being air holds us together and controls us, so does wind and air enclose the whole world."

Here, I would like to summarize the minimum essentials of the conception of environment that may be regarded as a revival of Greek thought:[6]

(1) Nature is a great living thing in which all other living things reside. In other words, it is in itself a huge living *oikoumene* (habitat) where all other living things have their own habitats.

(2) In this respect, the natural world may be regarded as a cosmic ecosytem which encloses the global ecosystem as its part.

(3) The global ecosystem itself is also a living habitat composed of many dynamically interacting ecosystems as its parts.

(4) Each and every ecosystem maintains its autonomy, and maintains a symbiotic relationship with other ecosystems.

(5) Thus, there are some hierarchic and isomorphic structures that run vertically through each level of ecosystems, and at each level there are also many horizontal and coexistent interactions between members.

Each ecosystem exhibits a remarkable condition which may be called an "equifinal" "steady state" of life, a state which appears to exhibit an optimum condition forindividual living things.

III

Greek philosophers from Thales to the Stoics uniformly regarded the natural world as a *kosmos* (world order), as a place of life, and as an inviolable *oikoumene* (habitat) of all living things. The Greek way of thinking about the cosmos was *ab initio* conspicuously ecological. The Greek concept of *kosmos* is a beautiful crystal constituted of three cardinal concepts: Order, Harmony, and Justice, which can be regarded as the key concepts of ecological philosophy and are usefully translated into our own terminology as System, Interdependent Relationship, and Symbiosis.

Let us begin to verify the case with Anaximander's way of viewing natural order. Fragment 1 (DK) runs as follows:

> And into those things from which coming-into-being for existing things takes its rise, their destruction (*phthoran*) too comes about, "in accordance with necessity (*kata to chreon*); for they render justice (*didonai diken*) and reparation to one another for their injustice (*adikia*) in accordance with the ordinance of time (*kata ten tou chronou taxin*)." (Anaximander's own words in quotation marks.)

The words "those things" may be regarded as a reference to the opposite powers represented as the *hot*, the *cold*, the *dry*, and the *wet*. Every cosmic process seen in our universe, according to Anaximander, is a result of their dynamic interactions. The opposites qua opposites are equal to one another in a horizontal order. However, when one of them is powerful enough to encroach upon another, injustice will be the result; then, *in accordance with the ordinance of time* Justice will be rendered, and will be compensated for by reparation, as we see in the cycle of the seasons.[7] Thus, the dynamic equilibrium or the steady state of opposites will be restored *in accordance with necessity,* which is a divine ordinance of *to apeiron* (the Boundless) that guarantees that cosmic order will be maintained.

The equilibrium in question, it should be added, should not be taken to be a precise (physical) one. Where there is precise equilibrium, there can be no symptom of life. It should be regarded rather as one which is maintained in a dynamic process. In order to distinguish clearly the latter from the former, it may be better to define the latter as a steady state which operates independently of time, or one of equifinality in the dynamic interaction of its constituent powers.

Thus, whereas *injustice* or *reparation* for it arises according to *time*, they are always regulated by a time-independent factor, i.e., Justice (*dike*); hence the "overshooting" by one power will approach, asymptotically, a steady state, with the result that cosmic order will be maintained.[8]

IV

Anaximander's thoughts on "justice" (=the principle of symbiosis) had an immense influence on succeeding generations. So, Alcmaeon, Empedocles and some Hippocratic writers were happy to accept his bold conception of the natural order.[9] However, there were also some philosophers who envisioned the same problem from soewhat different viewpoints: Heraclitus and Parmenides.[10] However, here I will only mention Heraclitus.[11]

Heraclitus's approach was motivated by an anthropological interest: to get over "the egocentric world-view." This approach turns out to be significant when we reflect upon a simple fact: the environmental problem is, after all, the direct result of our own selfish desires.

Heraclitus went in search of himself *(edizesamen emeauton*; fr.101). The word *emeauton* (myself) implies that Heraclitus's real self was once lost and had to be found again. Anyone who loses his sight of himself does so by falling into his own *idios kosmos* (private world; fr.89) and by merging into *polloi*. The word *polloi* means a gathering of the "they" who may be said to be simply *pareontas apeinai* (absent while present; fr.34). Each member of them (*hekaston*; fr.89) represents himself as an *ego* to be sure, but the *ego* in question is no other than one who is absolutely equivalent to anybody. Thus, the *idios kosmos* is a closed world where people cover their ears to the message of *logos*.[12] From their own individual, egocentric viewpoints the Common Logos will always appear "strange" (*xena*; fr.72), thanks to their differing *perspectives.* Thus, the world of *polloi* is a mere arithmetical total of such distorted projections. No genuine freedom could exist in such a world. Genuine feedom is possible when and only when each one awakes from his dreaming and begins to be attentive to the Common Logos.

If the above mentioned account is correct, we are also justified in saying that in making his self-search, Heraclitus aimed at getting over a purely *perspectival* viewpoint; or, to put it differently, Heraclitus's insight into the "unity of opposites" was attained by him through a process of getting over the *perspectival* worldview.

It is notable that the Anaximandrian level of the horizontal interactions between opposite powers corresponds exactly to the above-mentioned *perspectival* worldview. But if this is the case, where and how, in a Heraclitean context, can the symbiotic ideal (i.e., that of a steady state) be discovered? I believe there are a number of ways in which this question can be approached.[13] Let us start with fragment B67:

> The god: day and night, winter and summer, war and peace, satiety and hunger. It alters, as when, mingled with perfumes, it gets named according to the pleasure of each one. (trans. C. H. Kahn)

In the first paragraph, the eight nouns succeeding "the god" are arranged so as to be polarized into two groups, and these themselves are again divided into two further groups. First, two representative patterns which dominate the natural world (N) and the human world (H) are distinguished, and then, on the one hand the natural world (N) is divided into day (D) and year (Y) disjunctively, each of these being then further subdivided into two groups: {day (α) *or* night (α')} and {winter (β) *or* summer (β')}; on the other hand, the human world (H) is divided into two important sets of human affairs which symbolize state (S) and individual (I), each of these being then furthersubdivided into two groups: {war (γ) *or* peace (γ')} and {satiety (δ) *or* hunger (δ')} respectively.

Each pair of the disjunctive opposites forms a whole of which parts consist of a pair of complementary extremes; and they themselves are expressions of the subject "god." Here we should take note of the remarkable fact that there is no conjunctive relationimmediately connecting each pair.

This fact does not, however, permit us to introduce "conjunction" in order to connect each pair. What factor, then, does connect them? The most plausible answer lies in the reading of the second paragraph; it is the "the ever-living fire" (fr.30).

The Heraclitean god does not appear in multifaceted fashion according to each person's egocentric wish. Persons miss an important facet of reality when guided merely by their own *egocentric* and *perspectivistal* viewpoints. For what is truly the case is as follows: "One, the only wise, is unwilling and willing to be called by the name Zeus" (fr. B32). The Heraclitean god cannot be expressed fully even by the name of "Zeus," although all things are steered through all things (fr. 41) and could be brought to *syllapsies* (conjunction, fr.10) by the medium of his wisdom.

Taking the above into consideration, we can now recapitulate the contents of the fragment B67. If Ω is taken to be "the god," the total structure of fragment B67 can be formulated as follows: Fragment B67 expresses a peculiarity of Heraclitean thought in a remarkable way.

$\Omega=\{\alpha\alpha'\}\{\beta\beta'\}\{\gamma\gamma'\}\{\delta\delta'\}$.

(1) It proves eloquently that the Heraclitean doctrine that "all things are one" was born of his struggle against a purely perspectival worldview; and

(2) it makes clear that Heraclitean reality has a hierarchic and isomorphic structure which runs vertically through the whole of reality from the cosmic elements[14] to the whole cosmos itself, and that at each level in the vertical hierarchy a number of the unified opposites act horizontally; and finally

(3) it indicates the Heraclitean god's way of working: transcending all perspectival approaches, he steers all things through all things like Anaximander's *to apeiron.*

What I have said about the Heraclitean way of disposing of perspectivism may also be formulated as follows: it is a creative and emergent manner of thinking which grasps all fragmentary items as a whole and brings them into unity.[15] And as such it is a great reversion of the ordinary way of thinking. The case is analogous to using a concept of "conic sections" in order to grasp different plane figures like circle, ellipse, parabola, and hyperbola. These different plane figures, called conic sections, are produced when our point of sight is shifted to different projective planes. But all figures are products of one and the same original circle, and a source of light. The case thus corresponds to the above mentioned requirement (4): that is, wisdom is inseparably connected with the creative sense of beauty.

V

In Heracleitean contexts, the wisdom in question appears in different figures, such as beam, gleam, bright light (*auge,* fr.118) and thunderbolt (*keraunos*), all of which are symbolic expressions ofwisdom. When this wisdom is active, all things are brought into a harmonious unity, so that they are seen *sub specie pulchritudinis.* Thus, Heraclitus said: "A heap of random sweepings is the most beautiful order (fr.l24)." One who can penetrate into the depth of reality discerns the beauty even in a heap of abominable things such as "shit and piss."[16]

When Plato in the *Symposium* said through the mouth of Diotima that "suddenly (*exaiphnes*) he shall see . . . a wondrous vision, beautiful in its nature" (210E), he was pointing to that extreme point where the deepest penetration into reality will be attained. The case corresponds entirely to Plato's other utterance in *Letter* VII (341C-D): "it does not at all admit of verbal expression like other studies, but, as a result of continued application to the subject itself and communion therewith, it is brought to birth in the soul on a sudden (*exaphthen*), as light that is kindled by a leaping spark, and thereafter it nourishes itself. (Bury's translation)

Although Plato's utterance in this passage may appear to be a statement of the impossibility of any verbal expression of the deepest tenets of philosophy, his emphasis is not placed on the philosophical tenet itself, but on the verbal transmission of it. The matter concerns how communication between a master and his disciple can be realized. The master's creative thought could be transmitted to his disciple's mind when and only when they were completely connected by means of something like "a leaping spark," namely a mean that is proportional between them.[17]

What Plato says about the communication between a master and a disciple is applicable also to a situation in which a person is lost in contemplating a beautiful thing. In such a situation there is no distinction between the contemplating subject and the contemplated object. This extreme situation may be called "pure experience," which in itself leaves no room for Cartesian dualism.[18] On the contrary, it must be recognized as a primal field wherein the consciousness of differentiation between two poles of subject and object originates.

Of course, there is no mysticism here. It is simply a facet of our daily experience. So what Plato said in *Letter* VII (341C-D) simply addresses the familiar factwe witness when looking at a genius' creative power. It has relevance to so-called "knowing how" as a kind of "tacit knowing". However, it should not, without further ado, be simply identified with Ryle's "knowing how" or Polanyi's "tacit knowing."[19] Whereas they are characterized as a "tacit-embodied knowledge," the faculty in question here is rather a kind of "not-yet-embodied act of knowledge."[20]

About seventy-five years ago, the Japanese philosopher Kitaro Nishida (1870-1945) noticed the faculty in question and defined this as *Koi-teki-chokkwan* (intuition in action or intellectual intuition) which had its root in *Zettai-mu-no-basho* (the Field of Absolute Nothingness). The fact is noteworthy, since Nishida's thought on this matter was a result of his long deliberation on the concept of *chora* which made its appearance in Plato's dialogue *Timaeus.* Inspired by Plato's thought, Nishida elaborated his own thoughts on the Field of Absolute Nothingness, publishing his monumental article "Badho" (Field) in 1926. The publication antedates Heidegger's *Sein und Zeit* (1927).

Nishida's thought[21] has favorably influenced many scholars. Some of them have utilized his thought to overcome the preconceptions of certain modern European worldviews. Recently Nishida's philosophy has been reevaluated by ecological thinkers who based themselves on New Science (including approaches based on the concept of Autopoiesis), and who also took their orientation from various system theories like General System Theory or Non-equilibrium Thermodynamics, which relies on the concepts of fluctuation and dissipation. However, I cannot here undertake to explicate the details of Nishida's thought.

Considering the origin of the concept of "the Field of Absolute Nothingness," it is not surprising that Nishida's thought has proved so stimulating and productive forposterity. For it was born of Plato's rich concept *chora*, which was in its origin nothing other than a revision of Anaximander's *to apeiron*.

Notes

1. My ideas concerning the significance of Buddha's teaching on the four noble truths for the modern ecological crisis owe much in their origin to Hiroshi Tanaka, although my approach to the Four Noble Truths is different from his own. See Hiroshi Tanaka, *A. N. Whitehead* (Tokyo: Kodansha, 1998), 189.

2. I use the phrase *sentient beings* (Sanskrit: samsara) to denote all living things, including human beings.

3. Parmenides, fr.4; see also fr.8, 42-44 and Proclus *in Tim.* II, 69. 8-24 (Diehl).

4. See Lynn Margulus and James E. Lovelock, "Biological Modulation of the Earth's Atmosphere," *Icarus* 21, 471-489.

5. Anaximenes, fragment 2. See also Cicero, *De natura deorum* 1,10,26: "post Anaximenes aera deum statuit eumque gigni esseque immensum et infinitum et semper in motu, quasi aut aer sine ulla forma deus esse possit . . . aut non omne quod ortum sit mortalitas consequatur."

6. What I intend here is to abstract some features of intersection between Greek cosmological thinking and some modern holistic or organicistic approaches to the natural order. As representatives of various modern approaches, I have in my mind such theories as General System Theory, advocated by L. von Bertalanfly, and Erich Jantsch's theory of the self-organizing system (see, for example, his book *The Self-Organizing Universe, Scientific and Human implications of the Emerging Paradigm of Evolution* [New York: Pergamon, 1980]).

7. Cf. G. Vlastos, "Equality and Justice in Early Greek Cosmologies," in D. J. Furley and R. E. Allen, eds., *Studies in Presocratic Philosophy*, vol. I, *The Beginning of Philosophy* (London: Routledge, 1970), 76-82.

8. Cf. L.von Bertalanfly, *General System Theory* (New York: George Braziller, 1968), 142.7.

9. See G. E. R. Lloyd, "Hot and Cold, Dry and Wet in early Greek Thought," in D. J. Furley and R. E. Allen, eds., 255 ff.

10. See my paper "Heraclitus and Chan-tzu, A Dialogue on the Unity of the Opposites between East and West" in Hideya Yamakawa, *Greek Philosophy and the Modern World*, Studies in Greek Philosophy Series (Athens: The International Center for Greek Philosophy and Culture, 1998), 27-51.

11. Heraclitus's utterance concerning the *idios kosmos* sheds light on the problems of "otherness." Historically, the problem of otherness made its appearance as an index which exposed the limitations of modern thought: the problems of unconsciousness, death, woman, child, stranger, etc. And, at the central point, there was the figure of silent nature. For modern European thought, nature was "the other" which must be conquered and fully exploited. Modern thought sought to make sure of its propriety through the suppressing and eliminating of the other; "privacy" and "liberty" were the trophies obtained by the conquest of nature. However, there was a pitfall. The word "privacy" is originally derived from the Latin verb "privare," which means "to deprive." Therefore, the word "privacy" does not express something positive, but something negative. Here, it is noteworthy that the "private life" or "private domain" was conceived by Heraclitus as

an autistic world where one covers his ears to the message from the "common world" (fr. 89).

12. For example, the approach from the Heraclitean view of "psyche" is an attractive one; Heraclitus investigated his own psyche (fr. 101), and realized finally a great connection between his own psyche and the Logos of all things: "the soul has a logos which increases itself" (fr. 15). In this respect it is interesting that a late source reports the Heraclitean view of the relevance between the soul and the body as follows: "As a spider," he says, "standing in the middle of its web is aware the instant a fly breaks any one of its threads and runs there swiftly as though lamenting the breaking of the thread; so a man's soul when any part of his body is hurt hastily goes there as though intolerant of the hurt to a body to which it is strongly and harmoniously conjoined" (67a). The authenticity of this fragment is doubted. Marcovich says: "there is nothing from Heraclitus in this fragment" (M. Marcovich, *Heraclitus*, Editio major [Merida, 1967], 577) and Kahn accepted this: "both doctrine and imagery come from Chrysippus," *The Art and Thought of Heraclitus* (Cambridge: Cambridge University Press, 1979), 399; however, see also Marcel Conche, *Heraclite. Fragments, texte etabli, traduit, commenté* (Paris: Presses Universitaires de France, 1986), 323-326. Whatever the case, it is very attractive to imagine a situation where the simile is enlarged so as to include "kosmon" in fragment 30; then, the following proportion will hold true: Spider: Web=Human soul: Human body=The god: Cosmos.

13. At the bottom level of hierarchic structure in the Heraclitean natural order there is a dynamism of pyros tropai ("fire's turning"; see frs. 3la and b; see also 36).

14. See fr. 10: "syllapsies hola kai ouch hola, sympheromenon diapheromenon, synaidon diaidon kai ek panton hen kai ex henos panta."

15. This is a reference to the words of Chuang-tzu. See my paper "Heraclitus and Chuang-tzu, a Dialogue on the Unity of Opposites between East and West." in Hideya Yamakawa, *Greek Philosophy and the Modern World*, International Association for Greek Philosophy, Studies in Greek Philosophy Series No. 26, 1998.

16. Yamakawa, "Heraclitus and Chan-tzu."

17. It is the extreme situation wherein Chuang-chou didn't know if it was Chuang-chou who had dreamt he was a butterfly or a butterfly dreaming he was Chuang-chou.

18. Nishida, K., Zen no Kenkyu, Nishida Kitaro Zensyu, Iwanami-shoten, vol. 1, 4-17.

19. See G, Ryle, *The Concept of Mind* (London: Hutchison, 1949); Michael Polanyi, *The Tacit Dimension* (London: Routledge, 1966).

20. C. O. Schamer calls this "Self-Transcending Knowledge." See his paper "Self-Transcending Knowledge: Organizing around Emerging Realities," *Organizational Science* 33.3 (March 2000), 14-29.

21. Nishida differentiated among three fields:
(1) the field of universals (or "the field of being")
(2) the field of relative nothingness, and
(3) the field of absolute nothingness.

First, the field of universals covers the entire domain of Aristotelian ontology and epistemology in a broad sense. The relationship of entities in this field is expressed in the form of judgment "SP". According to G. Ryle's terminology the knowledge of which this field consists corresponds to "knowledge that." Second, the field of relative nothingness covers the entire domain of consciousness wherein the field of universals obtains; in other words this is the field wherein the judgment "SP" obtains. According to G. Ryle's terminology the knowledge of which this field consists corresponds roughly to "knowledge how" or M. Polanyi's "tacit knowing." And finally, the field of absolute nothingness consists of that deepest dimension that subsumes each of the other two fields. The reason why the knowledge obtained in the field of absolute nothingness is called "intuition in action" or "intellectual intuition" becomes clear when Nishida's thinking about self-knowledge is contrasted with Plato's way of thinking about *chora*.

3

UNA VOLTA FUI ARBUSTO E MUTO PESCE DEL MARE

[Once I was a Tree and a Silent Fish of the Sea]

Giovanni Casertano

[Summary]

[Once upon a time, there lived a man who had been tree, bird, fish, wild animal and god. That man lived in Sicily, in the golden city of Acragas. He was a magician, a philosopher, and a healer of body and soul. His name was Empedocles. In Acragas, it is easy to discern the four roots of all things: the clean air, the luminous water, the golden earth, the fire that rises powerful from the volcanic mountains.

In his verses Empedocles captured all of these things, claiming that they could be understood as well as simply seen. But humans are too shortsighted to fully understand, and thus to respect the harmony of the cosmos. They mistakenly believe that they can dominate life, while ignoring the existence of death. They even dream of molding and perhaps even creating life itself.

But the truth is that "life" and "death" are merely words. The sum of things has always existed, immortal and ungenerated. When one only sees what is immediately present, one ignores the eternal mixture of the four roots, and the flowing of all things according to the harmony of Love and Strife.

Superficial mortal thought does not see the cosmic flow of time and eternity, nor does it comprehend the emergence of change from the unchangeable, or of movement from that which is immovable.

The same shortsighted humans believed that they could understand enough to construct not only a science of life, but also one of death. The latter they cleverly disguised as progress, as peace, as democracy. But their misguided efforts produced a colorless similarity that eliminated the endless variety of sounds, tastes and colors that nature herself has created.

They forgot that only true knowledge frees us and heals us. Their blind ignorance allowed strife to fill the minds and hearts of mortals, while it also filled the world with its poisonous products.

Only turning to Aphrodite and Love will bring back the harmony, because she is the dispenser of life and the restorer of beauty, joy, and love. Aphrodite will lead mortals to friendship, benevolence, and peace, and away from war and the quest for profit and other forms of egotistical self-regard that will, eventually, kill the cosmos itself.]

a Graça

C'era una volta un uomo che non era stato sempre un uomo, ma albero, uccello, pesce, fiera, dio. C'era un dio che era anche un uomo venerato, amato, benedetto. Le creature infelici si recavano da lui, bisognose di una parola che le guarisse da affanni, tormenti, paure; di una parola che sapesse far sognare un domani di pace e di tranquillità. Perché quell'uomo, che era anche un dio, ed era stato fanciullo e fanciulla, albero, pesce, e che sarebbe stato ancora un dio, un albero, un fanciullo, una fanciulla, un pesce, era capace di vedere là dove non riuscivano a vedere dieci e venti generazioni di uomini, vedeva nel passato e vedeva nel futuro. Perché la sua mente, che era il suo corpo, che era tutte le menti e tutti i corpi che erano vissuti, che vivevano e che sarebbero vissuti, rimaneva saldamente ancorata al suo senno, forte nella sua mobilità, agile nella sua fermezza.

Quell'uomo viveva in Sicilia, nella bionda città di Akràgas, che a febbraio era circondata dalla neve dei mandorli in fiore (e bianche erano le bende che gli cingevano il capo), che a giugno era circondata dall'oro delle spighe mature (e dorate erano le vesti che gli avvolgevano il corpo). Quell'uomo era un mago: sapeva calmare i venti; era un fisico: sapeva come e di quali radici sono costituite tutte le cose del mondo; era un filosofo: sapeva l'essere e il non essere del pensiero; era un medico: sapeva guarire i mali del corpo e quelli dell'anima. Una volta il suo nome era Empedokles.

Ad Akràgas le quattro radici di tutte le cose erana visibili a tutti: nell'aria limpida che forma la cupola del cielo in cui volano gli uccelli, nell'acqua luminosa e azzurra del mare in cui guizzano i pesci, nella terra bionda che nutre i dolci frutti, nel fuoco che s'innalza potente dalle bocche della montagna. Ma Empedakles le catturò nei suoi versi e le rese docili al pensiero: tutti gli uomini potranno allora non solo vedere, ma anche capire. Ad Akràgas l'odio e l'amore erano visibili a tutti: nelle guerre che opponevano padri a figli, fratelli a fratelli, nelle dolci unioni che legavano la femmina al maschio, in tutti gli esseri viventi. Ma Empedakles li catturò nei suoi versi e li rese docili al pensiero: tutti gli uomini potevano allora non solo vedere, ma anche capire.

Gli uomini dalla vita di un giorno scorgono solo una misera parte della vita, nella loro vita di breve destino, eppure si vantano di scoprire il tutto; per i deboli poteri che sono diffusi nelle lora membra, e per i molti mali che li affliggono, hanno pensieri ottusi; con le loro parole e con le loro opere costruiscono follie, credendo di superare tutti i limiti ed immaginandosi un potere che consenta loro di farlo. Credono di plasmare se stessi e le cose, credono di plasmare il mondo, e non sono più capaci di penetrare nell'intimo di se stessi, di sentire le case con gli occhi, con gli orecchi e con tutte le loro membra, in cui invece sono le vie per conoscere; non sono più capaci di capire e rispettare l'armonia del mondo.

Fanciulli, questi uomini dai pensieri corti, credono di dominare la vita e fingono di ignorare la morte, sognano di plasmare e addirittura di creare la vita sperando di dominare la morte. E non sanno che vita e morte non sono che nomi, che puri nomi, perché non c'è né c'è mai stata né mai ci sarà nascita di nessuna delle cose che muoiono, non c'è e non c'è mai stata né mai ci sarà morte funesta di nessuna delle cose che vivono. Ma tutto è stato, è e sarà sempre, mes-colanza e separaziane di ciò che è immortale, ingenerato, ed eterno: le radici di tutte le case: l'aria che non è il cielo, l'acqua che non è il mare, la terra che non è quella che calpestiamo, il fuoco che non è quello che distrugge le nostre città. Non può nascere ciò che prima non è, non può distruggersi ciò che è.

Ma gli uomini dal corto pensiero pensano di essere i signori della vita e della morte, non vedono di là dell'immediato, del loro breve destino, e non si curano di ciò che era e di ciò che sarà. Se il nome di nascita è il nome della mescolanza delle radici eterne, e il nome di morte è quello della separaziane delle eterne radici, essi non vedono come tutte le nascite e tutte le morti che si sono sempre susseguite e continueranno ad avvicendarsi per sempre non sono altro che le maniere sempre diverse, particolari ed irripetibili, di una vicenda eterna in cui le loro stesse vite e morti son solo una luce ed un'ombra effimere.

Persi dietro i loro sogni di potenza, e credendo che la loro presenza nel mondo sia come quella di un potere dominante in una terra occupata, gli uomini dal corto pensiero e dai sensi offuscati hanno perso la capacità di vedere negli uomini, nelle donne, negli alberi, negli uccelli, nelle fiere, nelle acque, nei monti, nelle divinità, quell'unica legge eterna che rende manifesti e poi fa scomparire gli infiniti esseri che nascono e che muoiono. Sono diventati incapaci di slanciarsi con pensieri veloci per tutto il cosmo, di vedere il cosmo intero come un tutto che eternamente vive e muore nelle infinite nascite e morti che formano la sua immortalità e la sua eternità.

Gli uomini dal corto pensiero non sanno vedere il respiro cosmico di questo intrecciarsi di tempo ed eternità, scandito nei ritmi dell'Amicizia e della Contesa. *Philotes* e *Neikos* sono appunto i nomi che segnano queste due forze cosmiche che sempre erano e saranno, giacché mai di loro sarà vuoto l'infinito tempo. Amicizia e Contesa connettono e separano le radici dando luogo alla vita e alla morte di tutte le cose. Ed ogni cosa è "uno," la singolarità irripetibile ed originale delle radici sempre uguali.

Ma gli uomini dal corto pensiero non sanno vedere come dall'uguale nasca il diverso, dall'immobile il mutevole, dall'eterno il temporale. Duplice infatti è l'uno, duplice la sua nascita, duplice la sua morte: "uno" è il singolo ente, quest'uomo, quell'albero, quel fiume; ma "uno" è pure il cosmo, il tutto. Amicizia aggrega gli elementi a comporre la forma del singolo ente e Contesa li disgrega per passare alla composizione di nuove forme e di nuovi enti; Amicizia aggrega gli elementi a comporre la forma dell'universo nel suo regno, e Contesa li disgrega dando luogo ad un nuovo ciclo. Questa è la tensione, il respiro dell'universo intero, in cui generazione e dissoluzione sono strettamente unite. Dove la vita delle cose mortali passa attraverso la morte di altre cose mortali, ma anche la vita del cosmo si riforma dalla sua morte; così la morte delle radici nella loro forma propria è la nascita dei composti nelle loro diverse forme. La nascita degli uomini, degli animali, delle piante, è la morte degli elementi che entrano nella loro composizione; la nascita del cosmo uno è la morte della molteplicità degli elementi che lo compongono; ma anche la nascita del molteplice è la morte dell'uno, ed il mutamento del cosmo non può esserci senza il permanere di ciò che rimane immobile nel mutamento stesso.

Gli uomini dal corto pensiero hanno creduto di costruire una scienza della vita ed una scienza della morte, ma mentre nel costruire la loro scienza della morte sono stati bravissimi a camuffarla sotto i nomi del progresso, della pace, dell'equilibrio, della democrazia, nel costruire la loro scienza della vita non hanno saputo fare altro che clonare l'identico, il malato, l'uguale. Uccidendo così i colori e i suoni e i sapori sempre diversi che la natura pittrice disponeva sulla tavolozza del mondo, le hanno impedito di mescolarli armonicamente nelle loro varie misure, hanno mortificato la sua sapiente composizione degli uomini, delle donne, degli dèi, degli uccelli, dei pesci, che in numero infinito ella si preparava a render manifesti, meravigliosi a vedersi, agli occhi dei mortali.

Gli uomini dal corto pensiero, infatti, non solo vanno perdendo la capacità di vedere con occhi infaticabili cìo che la divina Afrodite aveva preparato loro, e rendono sempre più piccola la parte destinata alla lieta luce, ma perdono anche la capacità di congiungere le une alle altre le vette dei loro discorsi. Che diventano sempre più piccoli, cancellano sempre di più le loro vette per strisciare, per comodo, per indifferenza, per opportunismo, entro l'orizzonte della piccolezza. Vanno perdendo sempre più la via dei canti che, derivando discorso da discorso, convergevano nell'unità dell'Amicizia. I loro discorsi spezzettati, di parte, che tracciano confini dappertutto, che inventano artificiosamente sempre nuovi confini, che separano tutto ciò che dovrebbe essere unito, riescono a costruire con grande facilità i tortuosi sentieri di Contesa.

Gli uomini dal corto pensiero hanno commesso la loro colpa più grave separando la morte dalla vita. Hanno riempito la vita di contese e gemiti mentre proclamavano di volerne alleviare i dolori; hanno abbassato la Contesa da forza cosmica, necessaria al manifestarsi della terra e dell'acqua, e dell'etere e del sole, alla volgare e furente causa delle discordie umane, che quotidianamente agitano e contrappongono gli uomini gli uni agli altri: alla volgare e furente contesa che li spinge ad uccidersi tra di loro, a prestare falsi giuramenti, ad errare nel corso del tempo mutando i penosi sentieri della vita, che li getta in un vortice di odio che abbraccia mare e terra ed etere e che va al di là dello stesso ciclo della vita di un uomo, fino a diventare forza distruttrice dello stesso mondo.

Hanno abbassato la morte, ipocritamente nascondendola in un velo di scientificità, al bruto contrario della vita, facile da raggiungere ma ancor più facile da dare, nel corpo e nell'anima. Hanno abbassato la morte a mancanza di memoria, a sonno, ad oscurità, alla massima delle sventure, ad eco funesta di una vita funesta. Hanno distrutto l'unica forma di immortalità concessa all'uomo, quella di riuscire a conquistarsi un grande sapere, di riuscire a tendere la sua intelligenza, di riuscire soprattutto ad essere d'ausilio agli altri in opere sagge d'ogni specie.

Gli uomini dal corto pensiero hanno tolto ai loro fratelli l'unica maniera di poter essere felici, cioè di acquistarsi ricchezza non di oro ma di intelligenza divina, nel mentre che gli prospettano, imbandendogliela in tutte le religioni possibili ed impossibili, una immortalità di sopravvivenza individuale, che rimedi in un orizzonte di non essere alle miserie e ai dolori che hanno seminato nell'orizzonte concreto del loro essere. Hanno nascosto che l'anima dell'uomo non è che l'espressione di quella specifica mescolanza che costituisce quel singolo uomo, è quella proporzione e connessione determinata che esprime quel singolo individuo, è quella misura della mescolanza irripetibile e fragile che dura lo spazio di un sol giorno, e che andrebbe perciò allevata e nutrita con cura. Hanno separato la vita dalla morte proprio mentre pretendevano e promettevano una vita eterna nel chiuso di un'individualità sempre chiusa in se stessa, egoisticamente uguale a se stessa ed inutile agli altri esseri. Hanno separato la vita dalla morte cospargendo di morte la vita e progettandosi una vita etema che non è che morte.

Gli uomini dal corto pensiero hanno riempito la loro vita delle cose solite fra gli uomini, della sete di guadagno, di dominio, di onori, hanno chiuso tutti gli uomini nella piccola monade della loro individualità, di singoli o di classi o di popoli, ed hanno dimenticato il faticoso cammino della conoscenza, che è l'unico rimedio ai mali ed alle sofferenze proprio perché apre tutte le porte e tutte le finestre di tutte le monadi additando la via di Amicizia. Solo lo stare saldamente appoggiato ad una forte intelligenza e ad una forte sensibilità, il contemplare le cose con esercizio e sollecitudine puri, autentici, per tutta la vita, consente di elevarsi sulle monadi, di evitare le molte sofferenze, di aiutare chi da lungo tempo è trafitto da aspri dolori e non sa alleggerire l'animo dalle tristi angosce. La conoscenza è ciò che consente ad Empedokles di incantare, di incantarci a vicenda con la parola, il principale strumento di liberazione: *baxis euekés* è la parola che bisogna imparare a pronunciare per guarire i dolori degli uomini: *baxis* è la voce, la parola, il discorso, ma dev'essere *euekés,* cioè capace anche di ascoltare l'altro ed esaudire volentieri alle sue richieste: è l'unico strumento, rimedio *(akos),* per guarire *(akeomai),* portarci soccorso vicendevolmente.

Gli uomini dal corto pensiero nelle loro notti invernali accendono la luce di strumenti che li illudono di comunicare con il mondo, al quale confidano in segni muti e sempre uguali i loro bisogni sempre più piccoli nell'apparente vastità degli orizzonti, rinchiudendosi sempre più nella loro piccolezza nell'illusione di aprirsi alla conoscenza di tutte le cose; hanno dimenticato come si accende il lume, splendore di fuoco ardente, che consentiva di proteggersi dal vento dell'ignoranza, hanno dimenticato come quel lume voleva protezione e amore e fatica e lunga consuetudine con le parole dette e ascoltate; hanno istituito la molteplicità infinita dei soliloqui facendola passare per un dialogo; hanno scambiato il sembrare per l'essere; hanno ben imparato l'arte di mascherare i loro piccoli discorsi di potere, di ricchezze, di dominio, con parole menzognere, aggiungendo sempre più contesa a Contesa.

Gli uomini dal corto pensiero hanno costruito un'infinità di monadi piccole o grandi, e le hanno contrapposte le une alle altre, dimenticando che nelle loro contese non solo si danneggiavano a vicenda, ma andavano inquinando e danneggiando sempre più irrimediabilmente l'orizzonte fisico e mentale nel quale essi stessi vivevano ed operavano.

Il canto doloroso di Empedokles aveva visto come Amicizia, egualmente prima tutt'intorno librata, si fosse ritirata agli estremi confini del cielo di fronte all'avanzare di Contesa funesta. Contesa non tratteneva più in alto la legge del disgiungersi di tutte le cose, ma calata al centro del turbine aveva riempito del più profondo abisso la mente e il cuore dei mortali, e i sentieri del mondo si riempivano dei suoi velenosi prodotti: dappertutto la cecità degli uomini spargeva ricchezze e miserie, non mescolate. Le mani delle dolci fanciulle non giocavano più con clessidre di rame ben lavorato, mescendo e misurando le gioie e le ansie degli uomini, ma le mani di uomini servi di altri servi, dal pensiero offuscato e pieno di invidia, mescolavano solo il sangue e l'oro degli uomini mortali, con l'unico pensiero di trarre l'oro dal sangue. E tutte le cose che gli uomini servi di un altro servo producono nello spirito di Contesa vanno errando per diecimila stagioni: l'impeto dell'etere le rigetta nel mare, il mare le rigetta sul suolo terrestre, la terra nei raggi del sole splendente, che a sua volta le getta nei vortici dell'etere: ogni elemento le accoglie da un altro, ma tutti le odiano, ed esse non trovano nè danno ai mortali mai pace.

Ma il canto gioioso di Empedokles aveva visto anche come Amicizia sarebbe tornata dal profondo abisso in cui era stata ricacciata a spandere sul mondo pensieri ed opere di pace. Perciò Amicizia doveva chiamarsi anche Afrodite Citerea e Ciprogenea, per poter abbracciare e congiungere l'Oriente e l'Occidente; e poi Amicizia sarebbe diventata Armonia, la bella e giusta e necessaria proporzione dell'eterna aggregazione e dell'eterna disgregazione.

Cipride è infatti colei che imprime le infinite forme agli elementi, consegnandole al fuoco perché le consolidi, ciascuna con le proprie specifiche caratteristiche; per la sua comparsa provvidenziale succede che i principi di tutte le cose, che erano non mescolati, solitari, siano presi dallo spirito d'amore dovuto ad Amicizia, ed Afrodite era la forza vitale, dinamicizzante, che scuote dall'immobilità e spinge alla mescolanza, dei sessi delle opere dei pensieri. Afrodite dovrà essere ancora la forza dell'amore, non solo tra gli elementi, ma tra gli uomini, tra gli esseri animati in generale, perché è essa che spinge all'unione dei sessi e quindi dà vita al ciclo delle nascite. Perciò essa viene chiamata *zéidoros,* dispensatrice di vita. Con la sua opera essa già una volta pose fine ai maldestri tentativi di aggregazione di elementi e delle parti in esseri strani e mostruosi, esseri con due volti o con due petti, stirpi bovine con volti umani, o, viceversa, stirpi umane con volti bovini, sessi e forme maschili e femminili mescolati insieme: mostri che nascevano e morivano senza nessuna condizione di stabilità, e che però riempivano l'ampia terra delle loro mostruosità. Finché Afrodite non produsse composti armonici di esseri mortali, l'armonizzazione dei corpi e delle opere tanti quanti erano e dovrann'essere resi armoniosi.

E con Afrodite venne già una volta nel mondo e dovrà tornare la bellezza, e la gioia e l'amore che essa fa nascere, la bellezza che si vede e che attrae e che si gode. La bellezza che si vede: gli occhi infaticabili sono il prodotto più specifico di Afrodite: nelle mani di Cipride per la prima volta essi nacquero insieme. Agli occhi, ed alla memoria che grazie ad essi nasce in noi, si deve appunto il desiderio d'amore. Ad Afrodite si deve dunque questo legame inscindibile che connette insieme vista, bellezza e amore. Afrodite è dunque ciò che rende amici, che spinge all'amore reciproco, è il bisogno/desiderio ineludibile che dà piacere e gioia.

Questo cantò con bellissima voce Empedokles, invitando i mortali di sessanta e dieci e cinque generazioni ad essere amici di tutte le parti, lo splendore del sole, la terra e il cielo e il mare, affinché, armonicamente disponendole nella mescolanza, reciprocamente si amassero resi simili ad opera di Afrodite, solo così pensando cose amiche e compiendo opere di pace.

Perciò Empedokles cantò con voce alta il suo sdegno per gli uomini che commettono ingiustizie ed empietà, che si divorano reciprocamente, il suo sdegno per i padri che strappano la vita ai figli, per i figli che uccidono i padri: il suo sdegno per l'assurda cecità della mente dei padri e dei figli che uccide il mondo.

Perciò Empedokles sognò can voce dolce una *koinonia* tra gli uomini, tra tutti gli esseri animati, tra gli esseri animati ed il mondo, un mondo in cui predomina Amore, in cui non ci sia né Ares, né Tumulto, né Zeus sovrano, né Crono, né Poseidone, ma in cui sola regni la Cipride regina, in cui uomini che vivono in pace le offrano, invece di nobili tori, uccisi e mangiati sugli altari degli dèi della guerra, del profitto, dell'avidità, dell'egoismo, della sopraffazione, splendidi dipinti, e profumi dall'odore sottile, e biondo miele; un mondo di concordia e di comunanza tra tutti gli esseri animati, illuminato da sentimenti e pensieri di *philophrosyne,* di benevolenza e di amicizia.

4

ENVIRONMENTAL ISSUES IN HELLENISTIC PHILOSOPHY

Helen Karabatzaki

As the ecological crisis has deepened during the past decade, advocates of different ecological theories have attempted to study the origins of modern ecological approaches in the works of ancient Greek philosophers. Most of them, however, have tended to focus their interest on Plato's and Aristotle's views, which were more easily accessible for consideration.[1] Some of them, such as J. B. Calicott, have located the origins of modern "antinaturalism" in the materialist and mechanistic theories of the Atomists and Pythagoras,[2] and in so doing have misread important aspects of Greek thought. The founder of social ecology, M. Bookchin, realizes the necessity of emphasizing the Greek roots of recent inquiry into the human biosphere, observing that the Greek world combines the necessary elements of a disciplined rationalism, technological diversity, social action, and a personal morality, while the advocate of ecophilosophy, H. Skolimowski, generally acknowledges that the core problem of the contemporary ecological crisis is the separation of cosmology and ethics, which were inseparately linked in ancient Greek philosophy.[3]

As far as Hellenistic philosophy is concerned, the interest of modern environmentalists and scholars of the history of philosophy has, as far as I know, been exclusively concentrated on Stoic philosophy, ignoring the very important Cynical movement of the late classical period, with its strong ecological implications and impact on Stoic philosophy, and the Epicurean and Sceptic philosophies. Thus, J. Cheney sees the Stoics as forerunners of deep ecology, a view, rightly in my opinion, refuted by W. O. Stephens on theoretical and historical grounds.[4] According to Stephens, a proper examination of the central ideas of Stoic ethics reveals the coherence and insightfulness of Stoic naturalistic rationalism. Although Stoicism does not provide the basis for a "deep ecology" environmental ethics, it does contain some very fruitful concepts, which are much more closely parallel to the social ecology of M. Bookchin. In a similar spirit Alan J. Holland argues that the supposed anthropocentrism of the Stoics has been overstated, and that their fortitude could well be put to use in our thinking about the environment.[5]

In this chapter, I shall attempt to give a short comprehensive presentation of ecological elements in the thinking of the three main Hellenistic philosophies, Epicureanism, Scepticism, and Ancient and Middle Stoicism. The reason for my concern is twofold: first, the realization that Epicureanism and Scepticism have been totally ignored as contributors to the understanding of modern ecological approaches; and second, the aforementioned articles on the Stoic contribution have mostly utilised texts belonging to the New Stoa of Graeco-Roman times, which laid emphasis almost exclusively on ethics, unlike the Old and Middle Stoa, which studied ethics on the basis of a logically grounded physical theory. Overlooking, however, the physical philosophy of the Stoics is a hazardoius procedure, since Stoic physical and ethical naturalism are intrinsically interwoven. In developing my arguments, I will concentrate on certain questions asked by modern theorists, such as whether there is a recognition of subsistence rights for all species, and of the inherent worth, intrinsic value and external value of Nature and other beings. Given the long lifespan of the three schools I will focus on their ancient period, while keeping in mind, when developing my theme, the warnings of Professor Rist concerning the dangers of transferring current debates about environmental issues to the world of the ancient Greeks, to whom they were irrelevant.[6]

Epicureanism

Epicurean philosophy, thanks to its mechanistic, materialist perspective in cosmology and its anthropocentric hedonism in ethics, seems to be the one least able to provide any serious ecologically relevant arguments. However, even though Epicurean ontology is purely mechanistic, with all beings seen as the product of the random movement of atoms, and living beings and men as the products of an evolutionary process, Epicurus does express a high respect for Nature as a *vis artifex* and as creative. Indeed Epicurus is the only ancient Greek philosopher who has clearly suggested that life is not an exclusive privilege of Earth, because the principle of life is an inherent element of Nature Herself: "we must believe that in all worlds there are living creatures and plants and other things we see in this world."[7] In fact Epicurus views Nature from two points of view: (a) a *mechanistic* one, which connects the formation of material beings with the movement of atoms, and b) a *vitalistic* one, which sees in Nature the source of what is necessary and expedient for human and animal species alike. Though Epicurus rejects any teleological involvement of Gods in natural processes, he claims that Nature is the only supplier of what is expedient and pleasurable to man and all other creatures. Nature is actually characterized as "blessed" "because She has made what is necessary easy to supply, and what is not easy unnecessary."[8] Epicurus's views on Nature as procreative power are, however, better illustrated if we consider what a later Epicurean has to say. Lucretius, in his famous poem *De rerum natura,* considers Earth as actually a

Gaia-mother, because she is characterised as the mother of all previously and currently existing living beings.[9] Though an empiricist, Epicurus in his ethics argues for a quality of life that satisfies "necessary" limited desires, and denies satisfaction to secondary "unnecessary" ones, which are responsible for the deterioration of man's moral life. Among Epicurus's extant fragments there is an imperative of the utmost ecological gravity: "We must not violate nature, but obey her; and we shall obey her if we fulfil the necessarydesires and also the physical, if they bring no harm to us, but sternly reject the harmful."[10] It is plain from this text that Epicurus, though a hedonist, rejects the pursuit at any costs of the satisfaction of luxurious needs, which lies behind modern technological exploitation of nature motivated by a profit-based economic system. So, although Epicurus denies to other animals intrinsic value as such, Nature is clearly given an inherent worth. At this point he agrees with the Stoics and argues in favour of a scarce-economy dictated by Nature, attacking luxury pursued by men's vanity and false ideas about Nature and their place within Her: "The wealth demanded by nature is both limited and easily procured; that demanded by idle imaginings stretches to infinity."[11]

Biocentrism of the Sceptics?

Within the framework of a generally rationalistic Greek philosophy there is one philosophical school which defended an antirationalist perspective, and in so doing comes close to modern biocentric views. The Ancient Sceptics, in their effort to challenge the doctrine of the certain knowledge of the essence of things maintained by Dogmatists, like Stoics, challenged the validity of human sense-impressions in terms of the differential sensual multiplicity which exists among different animal species. Sextus Empiricus, our main Greek source about Scepticism, in introducing the first mode of suspension of judgement, presents cases from the animal kingdom, each one of which refutes the other in terms of the validity of sense-impressions. The conclusion drawn from these *isosthenic* arguments is that, since man's defective sense-impressions are a part of the problem, man is not in a position to judge the sense-impressions either of other animals or of other humans; hence man is forced to suspend judgment about the real essence of things grasped by the senses.[12] Sceptical antianthropocentrism extends to a point of where it challenges the supposed superiority of human sense-impressions to those of other animals, and in this it offers a counterargument to the Stoics, who claimed that any rightful comparison between men and animals is unequal because of human rationality. Sextus utilizes arguments from the Stoics (particularly Chrysippus) to show that animals, such as dogs, are better equipped than man, because they have stronger senses, and exhibit signs of internal reasoning.[13] Although the Sceptic-Stoic dispute was mostly epistemological, with some strong moral implications, the Sceptics, following the Cynics, were the only Greek philosophers who challenged the prevailing rationalistic anthropocentrism, arguing that this alleged superiority has no natural foundations. Of course because of their ethical goals their "biocentrism" is of a negative type, since their aim was not to defend any animal rights but to achieve the desired tranquility of mind and soul. Ancient Scepticism, more than its modern counterpart, challenged human cognitive arrogance, and proposed a critical attitude towards scientific knowledge. Its basic argument was that man with his imperfect "sense-perceptions" is a part of the cognitive problem, which means that he cannot speak or decide in the name of other beings, which are not inferior because they are different.

Stoicism

Stoic philosophy, in its ancient and middle phase, seems to have produced the most fruitful ecological insights both ontologically and ethically, thanks to the influence the Cynic attitude to Nature had exercised upon the founder of the Stoa, Zeno, who was a pupil of the Cynic Crates. Their cosmic view, with its accompanying concepts of *Pneuma, Sympathy, Oikeiosis, Heimarmene,* and *Providence,* is quite close to modern theories concerning the interdependence and interconnection of ecosystems, and specifically concerning the relationship of Earth itself to the whole Universe. In fact the Stoic definition of the Universe has two complementary aspects, one *systemic* and *holistic*, which includes all material beings, inanimate, and animate alike, and a second *ratiocentric*, in terms of which the universe is defined as the place of accommodation of gods and men with all other beings existing for the sake of men: "The Universe is a system consisting of the sky and earth and all natural beings in them."[14] More than any other philosophical school in antiquity the Stoics defended the interdependence and unity of one Universe, in which everything depends on something else through the operation of a series of inexorable moving causes, which they called *Heimarmene.*[15] Modern environmentalists have rediscovered the view the Stoics shared with Heraclitus, according to whom there is an interdependence of physics and ethics, and happiness is confined to the maintenance ofthe natural order governed by a causal nexus of laws established by a provisional Natural Reason. In this causally structured Universe the interaction of the four basic elements (fire, earth, water, air) through the influence of an all-pervading power called *pneumatic tension*, is the material substratum of the natural *sympathy* existing among the different parts of the world, among men and other beings in terms ofshared common material elements, and between men themselves and the divine Natural Reason in terms of shared rationality. A text of Philo thoroughly expresses the whole sequence of the relevant Stoic argument: "Nous has many capacities, binding, physical, psychical, rational, intellectual. Hexis is commonly shared with inanimate beings, stones and wood, because our stone akin bones participate in it. Physis runs through plants, too. In our body some parts, such as nails and hair, partake of plant-nature. Physis is defined as hexis which is already moving. Soul is a physis which has presentation and drives, and it is common in irrational animals … intellectual capacity belongs to nous, and reason is commonly shared by the most divine beings, but individually among mortal beings it belongs to men."[16] The Stoics, Ancient and Middle, and particularly Posidonius, seem to have established their views of natural sympathy by citing cases of interdependence among what we today call ecosystems. So, Athenaeus reports that Chrysippus, in the fifth book of his work *On Good and Pleasure,* tells how he had observed the case of a crustacean (pinna) and its accompanier crub (pinnoteres), which cooperate for their survival. From Philo we receive the information that Chrysippus attributed a kind of symbiotic sociality to plants, as the case of a tree and ivy shows. A text of Nemesius attributed by Theiler to Posidonius clearly shows the awareness of a human nature participating in inanimate and animate life through its bodily operations and in divine life through its reason. In the same text there is an interesting view of the interdependence of different ecosystems, in which animal and plant species are all working harmoniously for the preservation of the whole and of the parts alike.[17]

As far as the animal kingdom is concerned, there is a hierarchical *scala naturae* for the Stoics, who, unlike Plato and Aristotle, do not recognize any quality of life in plants, on the ground that they lack movement, which means that they are not ensouled: "Stoics and Epicureans (say) that plants have no soul. For some things possess an impulsive and desiring soul, others possess a rational, too; but plants move in an automatic way."[18] Themistius states that, by characterising plants as ensouled but not animals proper, Aristotle stands at the mid point between Plato and the Stoics. Galen clarifies one aspect of the Stoic view of *physis*, claiming that the Stoics called the governing part of plants not soul but *physis* in the proper meaning of the Greek term, as something growing. This apparent undermining of the nature of plants is contradicted by the fact that one of the basic concepts of Stoic ontology, that of *spermatikoi logoi* (seminal reasons), is drawn from plant-life.[19] Galen clearly reports that both the *physis* of plants and *animal-pneuma* are aspects of the same *world-pneuma*, which differ in their qualities. These two kinds of *pneuma* (*physical* and *psychical*), together with the third kind *hecticon* (the one that connects inanimate things) simply denote the different levels of natures structure, inorganic, organic and sentient. But if we consider that according to the Stoics qualities are not secondary, *per accidens* attributes, but essentially structural elements of matter formed by the action of the energetic principle on the passive material substratum, a firm respect and consideration for Nature as *vis artifex* emerges, that rationally and providentially controls all her parts: "The deity (i.e., Nature), say they, is a living being, immortal, rational, perfect or intelligent in happiness, admitting nothing evil, taking providential care of the world and all that therein is."[20]

As far as the relation of man with animals is concerned, the Stoics, following Aristotle, accept sensation and movement as the common biological element, which in the form of psychical *pneuma* ensouls animals and men alike.[21] But by placing a special value on humans' rationality the Stoics are seem to defend an anthropocentrism incompatible with any ecocentrism. It is true that animals seem to be considered by the Stoics as being inferior to men only on purely moral grounds. They are thought of as not sharing a conception of justice, because they do not form societies in the conscious way men do: "It is their doctrine that there can be no question of right as between man and the lower animals, because of their unlikeness."[22] Animals are thought to be incapable of proper moral action, because they cannot distinguish between virtue and vice, but this reservation does not exclude the fact that men can recognise animal rights, if they rationally discover that Nature dictates this. Cicero makes this argument more explicit, stating that Chrysippus recognized the right of humans to make use of other animals for their own purposes without injustice.[23] In my opinion this apparent anthropocentrism is limited if we consider their central doctrine of "living according to nature" in combination with their views on *oikeiosis*. As Gunderson rightly states, this argument has three aspects: living in accord with the nature of the cosmos, living in accord with human nature, and living in accord with one's own individual nature.[24] The hierarchical ranking of these aspects and the Stoic views of *oikeiosis* address the problem in an ecological manner. It is well known that for the Stoics every organic being has its own instinct for preservation, i.e., the inherent drive to pursue what is beneficial and to avoid what is harmful. They seem to believe, like modern biologists, that *oikeiosis* belongs to each individual, not the species. In this framework the Stoics asserted that irrational animals, when fulfilling their *oikeiosis*, attain happiness. Diogenes Laertius states that the Stoics attributed appropriate acts to animals and plants alike.[25] In this spirit Chrysippus was led to the point of attributing a sense of justice to cooperating animals, even of a lower rank, such as pina and its satellite crab, between trochilus and pompilus, and according to one of our sources the same Stoic had considered the case that certain animals, like dogs, show evidence of understanding through signs and advanced syllogisms that they make.[26] Man's *oikeiosis* consists in the development of his inherent rationality, which enables him (a) to understand Nature's laws, and (b) to realize his common bonds with all animals, fellow men, and gods. This view of morally binding rationality is the answer to the question whether Stoic philosophy has environmental relevance. Given their basic distinction between the true judgement of the wise and the false judgement of fools, the Stoics would characterise our modern ecological crisis as the product of a false ideology, which runs contrary to natural laws in their totality. Technology, based on the instrumental utilization of scientific knowledge, destroys the environment, because it serves man's partial and superfluous goals. A wisely used rationality should always subordinate partial interests to the economy of the whole. This means that human rationality, as the vital part of human *oikeiosis*, is a mechanism for the survival not the destruction of human and other animal species, upon which indeed such survival depends.

The Stoics in fact maintain that everything coming fron Nature has an intrinsic value in relation to the economy of the whole, and an instrumental value in the hierarchy of beings. But since the whole has an ontological and deontological priority, any instrumental value is subordinate to the inherent value of the whole. Within this spirit the Stoics saw all living beings as teleological centers of life, which are ordained by Nature to unfold the potentialities inherent in their seminal reasons. Modern moral philosophers seem to agree with the Stoics that all organisms, whether rational or irrational, are teleological centers of life in the sense that each is a unified, coherently ordered system of goal-oriented activities that has a constant tendency to protect and maintain the organism's existence.[27] The first and most important *kathekon* of each being is to preserve its own constitution by keeping all things in accordance with nature, which means that any violation of Nature is excluded *in principio*. We must not forget that the Stoics even state that animals share with humans the element of sociability expressed in their affection for their offspring.[28] In the light of these arguments I do not agree with Stephens that natural objects have no intrinsic value in themselves for the Stoics. Nature herself has an inherent value as the source of all expedience and beauty, all her creatures have an inherent value in the economy of the whole, and man has moral superiority because he is in a position to make right or wrong arguments. At this point they seem to foreshadow the ecophilosophy of Skolimowski, according to whom moral and cognitive alienation are interrelated.[29]

The Stoics more clearly than any other Hellenistic philosophy defended the Platonic emphasis on the relation between truth, morality and beauty, a perspective totally foreign to the till recently dominant Cartesian spirit, underpinned by the mechanistism of Newtonian thermodynamics and Darwinian evolutionism. The newly emerging shift towards another paradigm, onevery close tothe synthetic, naturalistic holism of the Stoics, is described by Paul Davies as follows: "For three centuries science has been dominated by Newtonian . . . thermodynamic paradigms, which present the universe either as a sterile machine, or in a state of degeneration and decay. Now there is the new paradigm of the creative universe, which recognises the progressive, innovative character of physical processes. The new paradigm emphasises the collective, cooperative and organizational aspects of nature; its perspective is synthetic and holistic rather than analytic and reductionist."[30] It seems that the old Greek, and specifically Stoic hylozoism has reemerged to remind us that man was created by a life-producing universe. Modern vitalists, unknowingly following Epicurus and the Stoics, claim that life, far from being an accident, is the consequence of an incarnate "biotectonic" principle.[31] Furthermore, it seems to me that the Stoic principle of "living according to Nature" is the long sought-for basis for a sound environmental ethics, in the sense that it expresses the ultimate ethical attitude out of which moral actions can be judged on a universal scale.

Conclusion

From what we have discussed, it emerges with clarity that all three main Hellenistic philosophies had a positive attitude towards Nature, which is given an inherent worth, while all other beings, inanimate and animate, are given an intrinsic value as interrelated parts of a holistic and integrated whole. Unlike our modern scientific materialism, Epicurean materialism does not exclude the conception of a providential Nature, avoiding in this way the pitfall of searching for moral wisdom in a Universe without purpose, while the Sceptics advocated a form of biocentrism based on the assumption that there exists an egalitarian unity of all species with no special place for humans. From this point of view the Sceptics can be seen as the forerunners of cognitive ethology, i.e. the science which studies animal awareness.[31] What modern environmental moralists consider to be a new claim the Stoics had maintained long ago. In fact the consideration of the existence of teleology in the Universe is currently discussed and supported by modern theorists, like S. Sterling and John Haught. The first calls for an "ecological-holistic" worldview to replace the old "mechanistic Cartesian" perspective by reactivating a vitalistic view of the Universe as a living and progenitive reality. And Haught discusses the issue of whether there is a question of cosmic purpose, which reactivates the old isue of universal and natural teleology.[32] The Stoics, in fact, were among the first to realize that if a larger reality is found to have its own integral and constant properties, then these should be applicable on a social scale. Nature's integrative synergy and sympa thy provides the standards for human societies, so that it becomes the source of a *jus universalis*, which applies for all men and all societies.[33] More and more of humankind should realize the moral implications of the imperative dominant in Hellenistic philosophy, which pays great respect to Nature as a truthful source of the useful and the morally good.

Notes

1. See Timothy A. Mahoney, "Platonic Ecology, Deep Ecology," in Laura Westra and Thomas M. Robinson, eds, *The Greeks and the Environment* (Lanham, Md.: Rowman and Littlefield, 1997), 45-54, along with, from the same volume, Madonna R. Adams, "Environmental Ethics in Plato's *Timaeus*", 55-72; Owen Goldin, "The Ecology of the *Critias* and Platonic Metaphysics," 73-82; Laura Westra, "Aristotelian Roots of Ecology: Causality, Complex Systems Theory, and Integrity," 83-98; C. W. DeMarco, "The Greening of Aristotle," 99-120; Richard Shearman, "Self-Love and the Virtue of Species Preservation in Aristotle," 121-132; and Mohan Mathen, "The Organic Unity of Aristotle's World," 133-150; G. R. Carone, "Plato and the Environment," *Environmental Ethics* 20 (1998): 115-123; John P. Anton, "Aristotle and Theophrastus on Ecology," in K. Boudouris and K. Kalimtzis, eds, *Philosophy and Ecology*: *Greek Philosophy and the Environment* (Athens 2000), vol. 1, 112-121, along with, from the same volume, Toshio

Kuwako, "The Possibility of Environmental Discourse in Aristotle," 112-121; Keekok Lee, "Aristotle: Towards an Environmental Philosophy," 121-128; and Thomas M. Robinson, "The Cosmic Environment: Some Implications of Plato's *Timaeus*," 155-162.

2. J. B. Callicot, "Traditional American Indian and Western European Attitudes towards Nature: An Overview," in *Defence of the Land Ethic* (Albany, N. Y.: State University of New York Press, 1989), 177-201; cf. Westra-Robinson, introduction, 4. For a similar argument see Freya Mathews, *The Ecological Self* (Savage, Md.: Barnes & Noble, 1991).

3. M. Μπούκτσιν, *Κοινωνική Οικολογία*, μτφ. Μ. Κοριακιανίτης, Αθήνα, 1992, σ. 110, H. Skolimowski, *Οικοφιλοσοφία, Καινούργια τακτική για τη ζωή*, μτφ. Δ. Κούρτοβικ, Αθήνα, 1984, Πρόλογος στην ελληνική έκδοση.

4. J. Cheney, "The Neo-Stoicism of Radical Environmentalism," *Environmental Ethics* 11 (1989): 293-325, W. O. Stephens, "Stoic Naturalism, Rationalism, and Ecology," *Env. Ethics* 16 (1994): 275-286. M. Gunderson has reconsidered the issue of Stoicism and deep ecology, arguing that it provides certain principles that can resolve issues raised by this radical environmental theory. Gunderson particularly defends the view that the Stoics did not overlook the intrinsic value of nonhuman living beings, counter to the dominant view of Stoic anthropocentrism.

5. Alan J. Holland, "Fortitude and Tragedy: The Prospect for a Stoic Environmentalism," in Westra-Robinson, *Environment*, 151-168.

6. J. M. Rist, "Why Greek Philosophers Might Have been Concerned about the Environment," in Westra-Robinson, *Environment*, 19-21.

7. *Letter to Herodotus* I, 74, in *Epicurus, The Extant Remains*, with short critical apparatus, translation and notes by C. Bailey (New York: Hildesheim, 1975).

8. *Fragmenta Epicurea* 67 (Bailey)

9. 5, 795-810 (Loeb).

10. Fr. xxi.

11. *Principal Doctrines* 15 (Bailey).

12. Sextus Empiricus, *Outlines of Pyrronhism* I, 59 (Loeb).

13. Sextus Empiricus 1, 65 (Loeb). See Luciano Floridi, "Scepticism and Animal Rationality. The Fortune of Chrysippus's Dog in the History of Western Thought," *Archiv fuer Geschichte der Philosophie* 79, 1 (1997): 37-57.

14. Stobaeus *Eclogae* I. P. 184, 8 W (SVF II 527); see also SVF II 529 (a definition belonging to the Middle Stoic Posidonius).

15. Diogenes Laertius VII 14 (SVF II 915). See also SVF II 912-914, 916-920.

16. Philo, *Leg. Alleg.* II and 22, I. 95,8 Wendl (SVF II 458); see also SVF II 439-457. For an excellent discussion of the concept of *Sympathy* in the Ancient Stoics and Posidonius see Karl Reinhardt, *Kosmos und Sympathie* (New York: Hildesheim, 1976 [1926]).

17. Athenaeus, *Deipn.* III 89d (SVF II 729a, b); Philo, *De animalibus adv. Alexandrum* 1 69 (SVF II 730). For the Posidonian argument see Nemesios 1 38-43, 43-45, 48-52 Matth., Willy Theiler (hrsg.), *Poseidonios, V. I Die Fragmente* (Berlin: Walter de Gruyter, 1982), fr. 309a.

18. Aetius, *Plac.* V 26, 3 (SVF II 708).

19. Themistius, *Paraphr. in Arist. De anima* II 2, 83 Sp. (SVF II 709), Galen, *De Hipp. et Plat. Plac.* VI (509 M. 561K.) (SVF II 710).

20. Diogenes Laertius VII 147 (SVF II 1021); see also SVF II 1133-1139.

21. SVF II 715, 716, 718.

22. Diogenes Laertius VII 129 (SVF III 367).

23. Philo, *De Opif. Mundi* 73, I 24, 21 Wendl (SVF III 372), Cicero: *De finibus* III 20, 67 (SVF III 371).

24. "Stoic Principles and Deep Ecology," in Boudouris and Kalimtzis, 93.

25. Diogenes Laertius 7, 107; see also SVF III 368, 375.

26. Sextus Empiricus, *Adv. Math.* VIII 270 (SVF II 727).

27. See Paul W. Taylor: *Respect for Nature: A Theory of Environmental Ethics* (Princeton, N.J.: Princeton University Press, 1986), 112.

28. SVF II 724.

29. Skolimowski, 28.

30. Paul Davies: *The Cosmic Blueprint* (New York: Simon & Shuster, 1988), 2, quoted by Arthur J. Fabel, "Environmental Ethics and the Question of Cosmic Purpose," *Env. Ethics* 16 (1994): 307.

31. See Carolyn Ristau, ed., *Cognitive Ethology* (Hillsdale, N.J.: Erlbaum, 1991).

32. S. Sterling, "Towards an Ecological World View," in J. Ronald Engel and Joan Gibb Engel, eds, *Ethics of Environment and Development* (Tucson: University of Arizona Press, 1989), J. Haught, "The Emergent Environment and the Problem of Cosmic Purpose," *Environmental Ethics* 8 (1986): 139-150. Cf. Arthur J. Fabel, "Environmental Ethics and the Question of Cosmic Purpose," *Environmental Ethics* 16 (1994): 309.

33. For a short discussion of ecological connotations in Stoic and Posidonian philosophy see H.Karabatzaki-Perdiki, *Ο Ποσειδώνιος και η αρχαία Στοά, Συμβολή στη μελέτη της Στωικής φιλοσοφίας* (Posidonius and the Ancient Stoa) (Ioannina: University of Ioannina Press, 1998), 370-371.

5

IL PIÙ ANTICO DECRETO ECOLOGICO A NOI NOTO E IL SUO CONTESTO

[The Oldest Known Ecological Law in Context]

Livio Rossetti

[Summary]

[I shall discuss a decree promulgated in Athens around 430 B.C.E. This decree is interesting in two ways: on the one hand, as we shall see, this is the earliest example of an enactment intended to eliminate polluting activities deemed to be hazardous; on the other hand, this decree provides an unexpected proof for what appears in Plato's *Phaedrus* to be an indication that an entire area was restored to health in the space of about twenty years.

First, the facts. In 430 B.C.E. a decree in Athens forbade certain serious forms of pollution. It is apparently unprecedented to find such a document so early. The provisions of this document can be compared to the provisions of Roman public works with regard to the *cloaca maxima* in the matter of human waste. Rome had decided to compel a certain number of well-to-do citizens to cover the costs of directly polluting the area within the city limits.

It is a discovery of some importance to find that classical Athens too was able to design this sort of regulation. (a) It was aware of the kind of environmental degradation in question; (b) it was equally aware of the causal connection between environmental degradation and certain routine activities; (c) it acknowledged that practices more respectful of the environment were consequently called for; and (d) it believed that activities that were disrespectful of the environment could no longer be left to individual discretion and viewed as lying outside the purview of the law. Hence the decree clearly treats degradation of the environment as an illegal activity.

The Decree

The decree was discovered on the east side of the Acropolis around 1920, and reported in *Inscriptiones Graecae* in 1923. The text is as follows:

> (the present decree) be inscribed on a stone and let it be placed on both sides. (It is not allowed) to put skins (in the river), and thus to pollute the Ilissus by the mount of Heracles' temple, or to practice tannery and dispose of the waste in the river.

The inscription expressly refers to the river Ilissus and the temple of Heracles by the city gates. Hence we can locate with some precision the location of the environmental problem. However, given the fact that the first lines of the inscription are missing, we have no information about who promulgated the decree, or about who would have been responsible for overseeing its implementation.

Neither a Holy Law nor a Local Norm

Although, as noted, the inscription is incomplete, we can see that the intent of the decree was not simply to protect a single specific area. Tanneries have long range environmental effects that cannot be easily contained. The decree does not, however, forbid the activity altogether; it merely provides regulations to ensure that such activities take place at a location far from the river, the temple, and the city.

Reasons for the Decree: Ecological, Religious, Sanitary and Economic

The decree is explicitly intended to protect a holy site, yet its effects are also economic, and the protection of public health also appears to be a primary concern. The removal of hazardous and noxious materials from the vicinity of the temple will achieve two related results: public attendance at the religious site will increase, and so will donations.

Consequences Indicating Some of the Reasons for the Decree

The historical conditions at the time indicate some of the reasons for the decree. These conditions include an unexpected concentration of commercial enterprises in the affected areas, with health consequences hazardous enough to convince political leaders and legislators in Athens to put at risk the entire leather production industry, an important craft at that time.

The possible emergence of an outbreak of the plague in 430 BC may well have influenced the decision, especially if environmental degradation was believed to be a cause of this disease. Such a belief would have been sufficient to generate urgent recommendations to legislate a cleanup.

The Evidence of Plato's *Phaedrus*

In 1987, Hermann Lind discovered some unexpected evidence: as early as 370 B.C.E. Plato had noted the incompatibility between pollution and the respect and admiration all felt for pure water and the beauty of nature. Hence, if the incompatibility was already perceived at that time, it is plausible that legislators would have initiated regulations for the protection of those values, even if it would take decades to effect a restoration of the natural environment (a restoration attested by the *Phaedrus*).

Further evidence in Solon, Plato (*Laws*) and Aristotle (*Politics*) also suggests a strong commitment on the part of all three of them to the importance of clean water for a healthy city. Which leads us to think that it is to Greek civilization that we must look for the origin of views of surprising modernity in the matter of dealing with what may well be one of the most dangerous of all forms of pollution.]

1. Preliminari

Il mio intervento verterà, per l'essenziale, su un decreto emanato ad Atene intorno al 430 a.C. e rinvenuto sulle pendici dell'Acropoli.

Il suo più immediato motivo d'interesse è duplice: da un lato per il fatto di costituire, *ut videtur,* il più antico esempio a noi noto di norme che pretendono e ottengono di far cessare particolari comportamenti allo scopo di arrestare un processo di inquinamento ambientale ritenuto fin troppo pericoloso; dall'altro per l'impensata prova, che sembra emergere dal *Fedro* platonico, dell'efficacia di questo decreto, cioè dell'avvenuto disinquinamento della zona a distanza di circa due decenni.

Occupiamoci, per cominciare, del fatto: un decreto emanato a Atene intorno al 430 a.C. che istituisce divieti allo scopo di contenere alcune forme gravi di inquinamento. Che in epoca così "alta" si sia potuto pensare a introdurre dei vincoli di legge per questo scopo è una circostanza significativa in primo luogo dal punto di vista epigrafico, cioè *quoad nos,* in quanto è del tutto eccezionale avere accesso al testo di una norma anti-inquinamento e precisamente al testo che all'epoca venne reso pubblico. In effetti sembra che nessun altro documento comparabile d'area greca o latina sia pervenuto fino a noi. In ogni caso non fa parte delle conoscenze correnti l'individuazione di atti di govemo espressamente dedicati alla tutela dell'ambiente.

Ma c'è poi una eccezionalità oggettiva del decreto in esame, eccezionalità che emerge dal confronto con i dati relativi alla realizzazione di opere pubbliche sul tipo della *cloaca maxima* a Roma. Mentre in questo ed altri casi consimili si parla di spese che le città fanno per prevenire forme diffuse di inquinamento addirittura all'interno delle mura urbane, il decreto in oggetto attesta che la città prese la decisione di obbligare i privati—probabilmente un certo numero di facoltosi industriali—a trasferire i propri laboratori lontano da una certa zona perchè in quella zona il tasso di inquinamento era diventato insopportabile. In questo secondo caso non è dunque la città a sostenere delle spese, ma sono i privati a doverlo fare su imposizione delle autorità locali, e non per realizzare un'opera di pubblica utilità né sotto la pressione di eventi bellici bensì, molto più semplicemente, perché viene loro imposto di trasferirsi altrove. Si ammetterà che il fatto è davvero eccezionale, anche alla luce di ciò che accade ai nostri giorni in materia di misure anti-inquinamento.

Costituisce dunque un evento scoprire che l'Atene classica seppe darsi anche questo tipo di norme a tutela dell'ambiente, e il fatto prova che all'epoca l'opinione pubblica era già pervenuta a riconoscere la pericolosità sociale di alcuni comportamenti abituali e l'opportunità di imporre limiti ed espliciti divieti anche a costo di obbligare qualcuno a sostenere per questo delle spese importanti. Il fatto ci parla perciò di una comunità civile che in una certa epoca (a) prese coscienza di un caso o tipo di degrado ambientale, del danno che ne deriva un po' per tutti e del pericolo che esso rappresenta, (b) prese coscienza di un preciso nesso di causa ed effetto tra il degrado ambientale constatato e determinati comportamenti abituali; (c) prese coscienza della possibilità di imporre comportamenti più rispettosi dell'ambiente naturale, e (d) ritenne appropriato dichiarare illegali anche certi comportamenti che in passato erano stati lasciati al libero gioco delle consuetudini e dell'iniziativa individuale, che erano stati cioè trattati come legittimi o almeno estranei alla sfera d'influenza del *nomos.*

La delibera di cui ora tratteremo, oltre a lasciar intravedere un ragionamento complesso e innovativo, documenta perciò l'affermarsi non semplicemente della propensione a pensare che, a tutela dell'ambiente naturale e quindi della sanità pubblica, sarebbe corretto intervenire anche con atti ufficiali, ma di una precisa volontà politica: la decisione di contrastare fattivamente il degrado ambientale e di dichiararlo, per così dire, fuori legge.

2. Il reperto epigrafico

Ciò premesso, vediamo questo documento, che è stato reperito sulle pendici orientali dell'Acropoli intomo al 1920 e pubblicato per la prima volta nel 1923. Si tratta dell'iscrizione classificata come *IG*^{3} 257.

Come si legge nel *corpus* delle iscrizioni greche (*IG*^{3} I, p. 230), la stele, *rudi opere confecta,* propone una serie di *litterae Atticae vulgares* disposte a scacchiera (*stoichedon,* ivi). In base alle caratteristiche del manufatto le proposte di datazione del decreto oscillano tra il 440 e il 420 a.C. con netta prevalenza per il decennio 440-430, cioè per l'ultimo periodo dell'età di Pericle.

Il testo[1] può così essere tradotto:

> dracme e sia il basileus a provvedere. (Il presente decreto) sia trascritto su un blocco di pietra e sia collocato dai due lati. (Non é consentito) nè mettere i pellami a imputidire nell'Ilisso a monte del tempio di Eracle nè praticare la concia (di pelli) nè gettare gli scarti (della lavorazione del cuoio) nel fiume

L'iscrizione nomina espressamente il fiume Ilisso e un tempio di Eracle, effettivamente localizzato in prossimità del fiume, alle porte della città. Sorprende un poco, perciò, che la stele sia stata ritrovata piuttosto lontano da questi luoghi e precisamente sulle pendici dell'acropoli, come se un terzo esemplare dell'iscrizione fosse stato collocato in città allo scopo di conferire un supplemento di notorietà al divieto.

L'iscrizione è priva delle prime righe di testo, in particolare del prescritto contenente, secondo l'uso, l'indicazione dell'organismo che approvò la decisione e delle persone che all'epoca ricoprirono i ruoli canonici di pritano, di *epistates,* di arconte eponimo, di segretario e di proponente. A questo riguardo si deve peraltro considerare che, siccome il decreto risale ad epoca relativamente alta, il prescritto avrebbe potuto essere privo di alcuni elementi del successivo standard.

Nella parte sopravvissuta dell'iscrizione si parla dapprima della somma da stanziare allo scopo di predisporre due *stelai* di uguale tenore, quindi si dà mandato all'arconte *basileus* di provvedere (*scil.* alla realizzazione dei manufatti ed all'impiego delle somme stanziate per questa operazione).

Il documento non ci permette di capire a chi spetta di occuparsi invece dell'effettiva osservanza del divieto. Una ipotesi ragionevole consiste nel supporre che a far rispettare il decreto debbano provvedere gli *agronomoi* o altri organi di polizia, forse con la collaborazione degli stessi gestori del tempio.

3. Non si tratta di una "loi sacrée" né di una norma di interesse locale

Il documento è stato talora interpretato come norma che delimita l'area nella quale si deve mantenere maggiore pulizia (Sokolowski) o addirittura come *hieros nomos* in considerazione dell'esplicita menzione dell'arconte *basileus,* cioè proprio l'arconte che ha competenza in materia religiosa, e di un'area protetta corrispondente ai dintorni di un luogo sacro ben identificato. Si è del pari supposto che la delibera sia stata adottata su proposta e dietro le insistenze delle persone più direttamente interessate al futuro di quel particolare luogo di culto (sacerdoti e amministratori del tempio di Eracle).

Particolarmente tenace è stata l'idea che il decreto avesse un interesse solo locale, e proprio per questo motivo nella terza edizione delle *Inscriptiones Atticae* (1981) il decreto è stato collocato tra i *Documenta phratriarum, gentium, pagorum, tribuum, trittyum.* Questa almeno fu l'opinione dell'editore del volume, David Lewis; scopriamo però che l'editore del decreto, Jameson, appare propenso a supporre che esso sia stato emanato non da qualcuno degli enti territoriali minori (o da altre entità istituzionalizzate) ma dalla *boule* e dal *demos* cittadini. Scrive infatti che *Decretum populi totius fortasse est.*

Il Jameson ha senza dubbio ragione,[2] perchè la delibera è esplicita nell'affidare compiti esecutivi all'arconte *basileus,* cosa che nessuna tribù, demo o fratria avrebbe potuto decretare. Del resto il demo o i demi più direttamente interessati a questa delibera—in ipotesi il demo *Diomeia,* o il demo *Alopeke*— non vengono menzionati nemmeno allo scopo di identificare con precisione i luoghi.

Abbiamo dunque la virtuale certezza che il decreto in esame venne portato all'esame preventivo della *boule* e fu successivamente votato *dall'ekklesia* e ciò equivale ad affermare che il documento in esame avrebbe ben meritato di essere di considerato un normale *psephisma* (che, dato il carattere permanente del divieto, viene comunque ad assumere tratti prossimi al *nomos*)[3] e di essere quindi inserito nella serie principale dei *Decreta et leges* anteriori all'arcontato di Euclide.

Sembra d'altronde fuor di luogo pensare che il decreto potesse pretendere unicamente di creare una zona di rispetto e quasi delimitare degli spazi attorno al tempio (Sokolowski): se così fosse, la delibera non sarebbe stata assunta dalla *polis* in quanto tale ma da un demo; la lavorazione dei pellami produce, del resto, effetti a largo raggio (inquinamento delle acque, emanazione di cattivi odori ecc.), per cui non avrebbe senso vietarla in un punto e autorizzarla cento metri più in là, e per l'appunto il decreto non dice che questa particolare attività economica è vietata in prossimità del tempio mentre è autorizzata un po' più lontano.

4. La ratio della delibera: preoccupazioni di carattere religioso ed igienico-sanitario, effetti di rilevanza economica, oltre che ecologica

Il decreto, sia pure con l'obiettivo dichiarato di tutelare un luogo sacro, introduce dei divieti che riguardano unicamente un'attività economica, i suoi effetti negativi sull'ambiente e la conseguente necessità di porre fine a questa attività in una certa zona (laddove la sua presenza ha suscitato un particolare allarme) ed imporre quindi il suo trasferimento in altre sedi.

Probabilmente furono i responsabili del tempio di Eracle a mobilitarsi per proporre e far approvare questo decreto. Se è così, dobbiamo supporre che essi abbiano vissuto con speciale fastidio la presenza in zona di laboratori dediti alla lavorazione dei pellami, con conseguente inquinamento dell'acqua ed eventuale moria di animali (se non anche di bambini), diffusione di cattivi odori,[4] proliferazione degli insetti aerei *et sim.* ravvisando in ciò la causa della progressiva decadenza del tempio e di una parallela diminuzione dell'afflusso di donativi. Essi avrebbero cioè ricondotto le loro inquietudini sul futuro del tempio al degrado ambientale e avrebbero chiesto (con successo) l'intervento del legislatore allo scopo di rimuovere tale causa ponendo fine alla lavorazione dei pellami nella zona.

È in ogni caso evidente che il divieto persegue *anche* un obiettivo di carattere religioso, ma solo indirettamente, e che gli effetti propriamente voluti dal legislatore non sono di tipo religioso ma *in primis* di tipo economico—divieto di continuare a svolgere una particolare attività economica nella zona a causa dell'inquinamento prodotto, inquinamento giudicato eccessivo—e, di riflesso, di tipo igienico—sanitario. La promozione del culto entra in gioco solo come ulteriore e più indiretto *cui prodest.* Il documento è infatti esplicito nel deliberare che sia posto fine all'uso di tenere i pellami (verosimilmente grandi quantità di pellami) immersi nel piccolo corso d'acqua, e così pure fine all'uso di gettare lì i materiali di scarto della lavorazione.

Ciò significa aver individuato una vera e propria catena causale: lavorazione dei pellami—inquinamento ambientale—danni gravi per la salute—ridotto appeal del tempio di Eracle. Anche in concreto, però, è verosimile che l'adozione di questo decreto abbia significato *prima di tutto* imporre la fine di ogni lavorazione dei pellami nell'intera zona; *in secondo luogo* attendersi che, per effetto di tali misure, si determini, sia pure con la necessaria gradualità, un sostanziale risanamento sia delle acque dell'Ilisso sia delle rive, sia dell'atmosfera; *in terzo luogo* attendersi, sia pure soltanto nel medio periodo, un netto miglioramento della qualità della vita per chi viveva nella zona; e solo *in quarto luogo* attendersi anche un progressivo incremento dell'afflusso di fedeli (e donativi) al tempio di Eracle.

È dunque facile immaginare che i responsabili del tempio di Eracle si siano mobilitati per proporre e far approvare questo decreto, ma nel presupposto della sempre più manifesta incompatibilità fra il luogo di culto e gli effetti che, particolarmente in quella zona, la lavorazione dei pellami aveva sull'ambiente.

5. Dalle conseguenze al verosimile movente del decreto

Una volta giunti a tale conclusione, si delinea una intera serie di inferenze ulteriori che propongo di considerare importanti.

(I) Se la decisione ha riguardato solo una particolare area è probabile che il livello dell'inquinamento avesse raggiunto livelli particolarmente gravi in quella zona più che altrove, al punto da determinare un circoscritto ma inequivocabile disastro ambientale. È probabile perciò che nella zona ci fosse non semplicemente una forte concentrazione di aziende ed artigiani del settore ma la maggiore concentrazione in Attica (altrimenti il decreto avrebbe riguardato un intero gruppo di zone) e che il decreto emanato dalle autorità ateniesi abbia avuto la pretesa di sradicare da lì un intero settore produttivo.

(II) È dunque verosimile che la richiesta si sia scontrata con gli interessi corporativi di un numero considerevole di artigiani del cuoio, tra i quali anche alcuni imprenditori ricchi e potenti. All'epoca, infatti, la lavorazione dei pellami rappresentò un settore produttivo molto importante e un'attività economica di grandi proporzioni che, non a caso, proprio nel corso degli ultimi decenni del quinto secolo fece la fortuna di uomini pubblici come Cleone e Anito.

(III) Di conseguenza solo un'autorità politica importante avrebbe potuto contrastare, in nome di interessi "generali," gli interessi di un gruppo imprenditoriale importante. Se invece fosse stato un semplice demo a dover prendere una simile decisione, il tessuto di interessi legato alla presenza in zona di molte aziende e di molti lavoratori del cuoio, nonché di molto denaro, sarebbe probabilmente riuscito a bloccarla. Comprendiamo, sulla base di tali considerazioni, per quale motivo furono la *boule* e il *demos* dell'intera Atene a prendere una decisione così traumatica.

(IV) Eppure, se gli industriali del settore avessero ingaggiato un buon retore per tentar di prevenire l'approvazione del decreto, questi avrebbe potuto verosimilmente produrre argomenti pressoché irresistibili. Per esempio avrebbe potuto sostenere che la decisione di diminuire il tasso di inquinamento nella zona dell'Ilisso avrebbe necessariamente comportato la generazione un maggiore inquinamento in altre zone (senza contare poi l'inutilità delle enormi spese connesse al trasferimento dei laboratori), dunque che gli effetti derivanti da un simile divieto sarebbero stati transitori, non risolutivi e quindi pressochè illusori. Avrebbero potuto sostenere, del pari, che sussiste una grave sproporzione tra l'enormità del danno economico, immediato e certo, e il carattere tutt'altro che immediato dei benefici attesi, benefici che possono anche essere considerati solo probabili (solo sperati).[5] In effetti è difficilmente immaginabile che i legislatori non abbiano previsto l'inevitabile riprodursi, in un futuro non lontano, di forme analoghe di inquinamento in altre zone fluviali dei dintorni. Analogamente l'aspettativa di un rinnovato afflusso di fedeli al tempio una volta eliminata la principale causa di inquinamento nella zona poteva ben dirsi molto, troppo teorica per giustificare divieti capaci di produrre effetti economici così importanti.

A ben vedere queste sono considerazioni molto intuitive, anche se discutibili, e probabilmente sarebbe stato possibile farle valere anche senza l'apporto di un retore di professione. Al confronto, infatti, le contro—obiezioni che vengono subito in mente—argomentare che, mentre l'inquinamento derivante dalla lavorazione dei pellami ha bisogno di anni per cominciare a nuocere in maniera grave all'ambiente, il disinquinamento potrebbe assicurare benefici tangibili alla salute in tempi molto più brevi—sono molto meno intuitive perché si fondano su stime intorno al tempo necessario per il prodursi di effetti che, in ogni caso, potrebbero divenire vistosi solo nel corso di alcuni anni.

(V) Da qui la domanda: come mai i politici e i legislatori di Atene non esitarono a mettere in seria difficoltà un intero settore produttivo? Non si impone il trasferimento di un intero comprensorio industriale solo perché la sua concentrazione in una certa zona nuoce al benessere dei residenti. Infatti l'abbondanza delle opportunità di lavoro e la molta ricchezza prodotta hanno sempre costituito un più che efficace antidoto contro le iniziative di bonifica del territorio per le esigenze di chi vi abita, e difficilmente Atene può aver fatto eccezione a una simile regola. Possibile dunque che una simile decisione sia stata presa solo per accontentare i sacerdoti e gli amministratori del tempietto di Eracle, ovvero gli allevatori di animali della zona? Dietro a una simile decisione dovrebbe esserci stata, io credo, una ragione proporzionata, un'emergenza così grave da prevalere sull'attesa di conseguenze drammatiche per l'economia dell'intera zona e dunque più forte delle stesse esigenze fatte valere, come si suppone, dai sacerdoti del tempio di Eracle.

Quale avrebbe potuto mai essere questo grave o gravissimo motivo?

(VI) La stele è concordemente ritenuta databile intomo al 430 a.C., con circa dieci anni di tolleranza massima, e quello è stato il periodo in cui ad Atene scoppiò una terribile quanto famosa pestilenza. Orbene, la pestilenza potrebbe ben aver offerto quel movente più grave di cui abbiamo cominciato a intuire l'esigenza. La decisione pottebbe cioè essere stata presa *a causa* della pestilenza e del conseguente desiderio di intervenire su alcune possibili cause o concause di quella tremenda strage di viventi con una determinazione motivata dalle proporzionata alle drammatiche dimensioni assunte dal contagio. In tal caso il carattere solo transitorio e locale dei benefici che ne sarebbero derivati per l'ambiente naturale e quindi per le persone, sia pure con danni cospicui e immediati a carico di un settore produttivo importante, pottebbe essere stato ammesso senza per questo ravvisare in ciò un buon motivo per non agire.

L'incombere della pestilenza, infatti, fu senza dubbio tale da comportare anche un certo numero di misure urgenti.

Da qui l'eventualità che i legislatori abbiano sperato, con un simile decreto, di incidere in maniera credibile su un pericolo evidente per la salute pubblica senza per questo provocare immediatamente analoghe situazioni di rischio in altre zone. Pottebbero aver pensato cioè—e non senza motivo—che l'urgenza di fare comunque qualcosa fosse un buon motivo per eliminare subito un evidente focolaio di malattie (magari provvedendo anche, *una tantum,* a raccogliere e bruciare i residui della lavorazione dei pellami sparsi lungo le rive dell'Ilisso) e nel frattempo confidare che la produzione di inquinamento ad opera dei nuovi insediamenti della lavorazione dei pellami fosse accettabilmente diluita nel tempo (tanto da rappresentare un pericolo di gran lunga minore al confronto con il livello di degrado già osservabile sulle rive dell'Ilisso) e venisse efficacemente contenuta (grazie all'accresciuta sensibilità per il problema della salute che la peste verosimilmente ottenne di inculcare nella popolazione).

Tutto ciò con riferimento a una situazione di grave ed evidente emergenza sanitaria.

(VII) Se invece rimuoviamo questo riferimento, diventa difficile resistere alla tesi, già accennata, della prevedibile inefficacia e inopportunità di un simile provvedimento: qualunque retore avrebbe potuto perorare il rigetto del *probouleuma* argomentando, per cominciare, che la sola misura veramente efficace sarebbe stata, semmai, la soppressione di tutti gli insediamenti dell'industria dei pellami, e che dunque si trattava di decidere non su un problema circoscritto—il degrado ambientale di una piccola zona, l'eventuale declino di un tempio—ma sull'opportunità o meno di sopprimere una volta per tutte la lavorazione del cuoio in Attica. Sulla base di una simile premessa sarebbe stato addirittura facile argomentare l'irragionevolezza di ogni decisione volta a comportare la distruzione volontaria di una fondamentale fonte di ricchezza, l'assoluta necessità di calzature ed altri oggetti in pelle almeno in guerra, gli enormi costi di una eventuale importazione su larga scala di simili articoli, perfino l'imbarbarimento collettivo che sarebbe derivato dall'ipotetica rinuncia a usare calzari. La cultura sofistica dell'epoca avrebbe sicuramente consentito di costruire, sull'argomento, un *logos* molto convincente.

6. Un decreto efficace?La testimonianza del Fedro di Platone

Su tali premesse acquista valore l'aspirazione a sapere se il decreto—il più antico decreto ecologico a noi noto—fu o non fu efficace, ed è merito di Hermann Lind aver scoperto una evidenza molto pertinente ed eloquente, oltre che inattesa.

In un articolo del 1987 egli istituì un geniale collegamento fra questa descrizione e la descrizione delle rive dell'Ilisso che figura quasi all'inizio di un dialogo platonico, il *Fedro* (230bc), rilevando prima di tutto la totale incompatibilità dei due dati: da un lato una situazione di intollerabile degrado ambientale e dall'altro un senso di franca ammirazione per la limpidezza delle acque e l'estrema gradevolezza dell'ambiente naturale. Con l'occasione Lind osserva inoltre che, almeno intorno alla metà del quarto secolo nella zona erano localizzati, come si evince da un'altra iscrizione, dei servizi di tutt'altra natura: dei servizi di lavanderia che evidentemente presupponevano la buona qualità delle acque e delle stesse rive. Ne deduce, correttamente, che il passo del *Fedro* costituisce un buon indizio per pensare che il decreto emanato intorno al 430 ebbe concreta e tangibile attuazione e che, di conseguenza, la zona un tempo inquinata subì un efficace processo di disinquinamento, fino a trasformarsi, nell'arco di alcuni anni, in una zona pulita e addirittura esteticamente gradevole (con bei prati e aria profumata, come scrive Platone). Per arrivare a una simile trasformazione saranno probabilmente occorsi alcuni anni (ad es. cinque o dieci anni), ma ciò significa che le tracce dell'inquinamento erano verosimilmente scomparse non solo all'epoca in cui fu composto il *Fedro* (intorno al 370 a.C.), ma anche all'epoca della vecchiaia di Socrate, quando anche Platone cominciò a frequentare il filosofo.

Pertanto è perfettamente possibile che la rappresentazione in positivo della zona dell'Ilisso non abbia nulla di intenzionale ma si limiti a rispecchiare un dato di fatto. Anche da questo punto di vista, perciò, posso solo sottoscrivere appieno alle osservazioni del Lind.

7. Una iniziativa episodica? La testimonianza di Plutarco, Platone ed Aristotele

Per l'interpretazione di *IG*³ 257 è, come sempre, necessario richiamare un contesto più generale, e cioè l'insieme delle normative prodotte ad Atene in materia di inquinamento, degrado ambientale e tutela della salute. In questa sede mi sembra appropriato segnalare alcune evidenze concernenti Solone e, soprattutto, Platone ed Aristotele.[6]

Plutarco (*Sol.* 23) riferisce che Solone dettò norme riguardanti la distanza minima tra i pozzi d'acqua, non sappiamo se prendendo in considerazione anche l'eventualità dell'inquinamento,

Platone dedica due intere sezioni delle sue *Leggi* al tema della tutela delle acque dall'inquinamento. Queste preziose micro-trattazioni figurano nell'ambito delle norme concernenti l'agricoltura e trovano posto nel corso del libro VI e verso la fine del libro VIII.

In VI 760b-761a Platone si sofferma, per cominciare, sull'esigenza di costituire un corpo di *agronomoi* e su come organizzare questi gruppi di pubblici funzionari; in 761a-c egli parla con una certa ampiezza della necessità di tenere sotto controllo il flusso dell'acqua con argini, piccoli corsi d'acqua e sorgenti, soffermandosi inoltre sull'opportunità di abbellire le sorgenti con prati e muretti, di far affluire sufficienti quantità d'acqua nei boschi sacri e nei ginnasi. Il discorso prosegue con considerazioni sugli *agronomoi,* le mense a loro riservate, l'eventualità che essi si comportino talora ingiustamente, l'esigenza che vivano insieme, all'incirca come un reparto militare, e su altri problemi connessi al buon funzionamento della loro attività (761d-763c).

Quando poi, nel corso del libro VIII, Platone affronta di nuovo temi connessi all'agricoltura, egli introduce prima di tutto, un embrione di normativa riguardante la realizzazione di pozzi e canalizzazioni, il diritto per chi non trova acqua nel suo campo ad attingere a certe condizioni all'acqua ed altri casi di conflittualità nella gestione delle acque destinate a qualche forma di irrigazione dei campi (844a-d).

Significativamente, nello svolgere questa seconda micro-trattazione egli fa esplicito riferimento ai *palatoi kai kaloi nomoi* relativi alle acque dei campi e precisa che è superfluo riproporre in dettaglio le stesse notme.

Il confronto con il poco che sappiamo sul conto delle norme dettate da Solone ci dà la virtuale certezza che Platone intenda riferirsi proprio a quelle antiche normative.

Poco più avanti (VIII 845de) l'autore si sofferma infine sulla precarietà dell'acqua, che può essere facilmente inquinata, e che «pertanto ha bisogno di una tutela legale». Seguono sanzioni a carico di chi inquina l'acqua degli altri. Può così prendere forma qualcosa come un vero e proprio "reato ecologico" consistente nel *diaphtherein hudor.*

Anche a questo riguardo è ben poco verosimile che Platone abbia potuto ideare una norma specifica *ex novo.* Più probabilmente egli avrà avuto notizia di specifiche norme finalizzate alla gestione delle vertenze in materia di inquinamento idrico e si sarà limitato a riformularle senza troppo modificare.

Anche Aristotele ha modo di accennare all'argomento nel corso del libro VIII della *Politica* e precisamente alla pagina 1330^b4-18. Egli esordisce con una considerazione perfino banale, e cioè che le città devono essere collocate laddove ci sia abbondanza d'acqua. Prosegue poi affermando che bisogna pensare alla salute degli abitanti e questo dipende non soltanto dalla posizione ed esposizione della zona ma anche dalla disponibilità di acque sane cioè pulite, e aggiunge (cito) che «di ciò bisogna darsi pensiero e non alla leggera». Proprio per questo, prosegue Aristotele (cito), «in tutte le città sagge, se le fonti non sono tutte ugualmente pure e non ce n'è abbondanza, si deve tener separata l'acqua potabile da quella adibita ad altri usi». Quest'ultima frase è manifestamente mal concepita, ma il suo significato è trasparente. Aristotele intende affermare che non è saggia quella città che non predispone opportune misure allo scopo di proteggere le risorse d'acqua potabile e prevenire il loro inquinamento. La salute pubblica è un bene importante, chi governa la città deve preoccuparsi di garantirla, e dunque fra l'altro deve aver cura di assicurare che le fonti di acqua potabile siano adeguatamente sorvegliate e protette.

Anche Aristotele si limita dunque a richiamare, sia pure in modo più sfumato, le norme di cui ci ha parlato più in dettaglio Platone (e che, almeno in parte, dovrebbero risalire addirittura a Solone).

8. Atene ha conosciuto il reato di "diaphtora hudatos"?

Questa convergenza dei tre autori è significativa, perché ci informa nel modo più convincente sul conto di una ben stabilita attenzione delle autorità statali (quindi anche del legislatore) per la tutela delle acque e la prevenzione o repressione di specifiche forme di inquinamento. Le fonti giuridiche non ci parlano anche del reato di **diaphtora hudatos,* ma è significativo che Platone abbia usato l'espressione tecnica *an tis diaphtheirei hudor allotrion,* «qualora venga inquinata l'acqua altrui». Ciò è buon indizio dell'avvenuta definizione, appunto, di un reato che forse era denominato, come suggerivo un momento fa, *diaphtora hudatos.*

Si tratta, del resto, di norme che, non a caso, ritroviamo in forme comparabili anche nel codice di Gortina e nella giurisprudenza romana.

Orbene, se il diritto attico ha conosciuto sin dai tempi di Solone, o comunque sin da tempi molto antichi, il reato di *diaphtora hudatos,* allora comprendiamo meglio il senso del decreto concernente la lavorazione dei pellami sulle rive del fiume Ilisso. Tra la norma di carattere generale e questa norma particolare sussiste una intuitiva connessione in quanto, almeno in teoria, gli abitanti del luogo avrebbero potuto argomentare che la lavorazione dei pellami comportava precisamente una forma grave di *diaphtora hudatos.* Ma trattandosi di un' attività economica concentrata in quella zona da tempo immemorabile, di un'attività molto redditizia e, per di più di un'attività che produceva beni di uso quotidiano ritenuti indispensabili dall'intera popolazione, per poter incidere in modo efficace sull'inquinamento di quella particolare zona non poteva essere sufficiente appellarsi a una singola norma che, oltretutto, era riferita ai rapporti tra singoli agricoltori. C'era dunque bisogno di un intervento legislativo più specifico e di motivazioni molto speciali: anche questa circostanza induce a pensare che ad imporre misure eccezionalmente drastiche—la cessazione forzosa di un'intera produzione industriale nella zona e il suo trasferimento forzoso in altre zone—fu una vera e propria emergenza, la peste che imperversò ad Atene all'inizio della guerra Peloponnesiaca. Su queste premesse è verosimile che il riferimento al tempio di Eracle sia servito più per indicare con precisione la zona e per rafforzare la norma che non per introdurre motivazioni religiose non necessarie e non determinanti.

9. L'acqua potabile è una eredità greca?

È impressionante constatare che, a distanza di millenni, la disponibilità di acqua potabile è assicurata pressoché soltanto laddove la civiltà nata in Grecia si è affermata e sviluppata, mentre quasi tutto il resto del mondo è alle prese con il drammatico problema di un inquinamento delle riserve d'acqua apparentemente irrimediabile, tanto da dover ricorrere quasi ovunque a sistematiche procedure di potabilizzazione che sono lente, faticose e tali da produrre solo acqua potabile bollita, dunque un'acqua di infima qualità, che non produce malattie intestinali ma non presenta certo i benefici dell'acqua naturalmente non inquinata.

Dire che noi "occidentali" siamo greci da molti fondamentali punti di vista è quasi un luogo comune. Notiamo con una certa sorpresa—e con un senso di gratitudine—che ai greci va ascritto anche il merito di aver elaborato una "cultura" della tutela della potabilità dell'acqua che non ha solo preparato il terreno per l'*aquaeductus* romano ma tuttora marca, a distanza di millenni, la differenza fra i popoli che hanno elementi ellenici nel loro DNA e i popoli che non hanno avuto un simile privilegio.

Note

1. L'iscrizione, che non pone alcun serio problema di decodifica, é stata pubblicata per la prima volta in *Karousos* 1923, poi i.a. in Sokolowski 1962, nelle *Inscriptiones Graecae* (1981) e in Lind 1987.

2. Lo rileva anche Lind (1987, nota 3).

3. La circostanza non può sorprendere, dato che la distinzione tra nomos e psephisma si è irrigidita e precisata, come è noto, solo dopo la guerra del Peloponneso.

4. È significativo che già in Esopo, favola 309 Chambry, compaia il tentativo di imporre a un conciatore di pelli di trasferirsi altrove proprio a causa dei cattivi odori prodotti nell'esercizio della sua attività.

5. Dobbiamo infatti immaginare che, all'epoca, non si avesse notizia di misure comparabili a queste e che, di conseguenza, non fossero disponibili conoscenze di sorta sul conto degli effetti che potevano derivare dall'avvenuta adozione di simili misure.

6. Ricordo inoltre che un nutrito elenco di evidenze epigrafiche è disponibile in Sokolowski 1962, 19.

Bibliografia di base

I. Karousos, "Apo to Hiraklion tou Kunosargous," *Archaiologikon Deltion* 8 (1923): 96-98.

H. Lind, "Neues aus Kydathen. Beobachtungen zum Hintergrund der 'Daitales' und der 'Ritter' des Aristophanes," *Museum Helveticum* 42 (1985): 249-261 [257 s.].

———. "Sokrates am Ilissos. *IG* I3 1 257 und die Eingangsszene des platonischen 'Phaidros'," *Zeitschrift fur Papyrologie und Epigraphik* 69 (1987): 15-19.

F. Sokolowski, *Lois sacrées des cités grecques. Supplément* (Paris 1962): [19] Alcuni testi di inquadramento.

P. Fedeli, *La natura violata. Ecologia e mondo Romano* (Palermo 1990). E. Klingenberg, "La legge platonica sulle fontane pubbliche," in A. Biscardi, H. J. Wolff, J. Modrzejewski, e P. Dimakis (ed.), *Symposion* 1974 (Köln-Wien 1979): 283-305.

S. Lilya, *The Treatment of Odours in the Poetry of Antiquity* (Helsinki 1972).
O. Longo, "Ecologia antica. Il rapporto uomo/ambiente in Grecia," *Aufidus* 5 (1988): 3-30.
———. "Conciapelli e cultura in Grecia antica", *Lares* 57 (1991): 5-24.

6

ROMAN FORESTS, VERGILIAN TREES: OUR AMBIGUOUS RELATIONSHIP WITH NATURE

Lorina Quartarone

In *Aeneid 8*, when Aeneas marvels at the site of ancient Arcadia, King Evander states "haec nemora indigenae Fauni Nymphaeque tenebant" [The Fauns and the native Nymphs once possessed these groves] (8.314). His remark illustrates the Roman belief that nature was divine, that *numina* or "spirits" resided in such natural settings as trees, forests, groves, lakes, streams, and rivers. This ancient concept of nature as "animate" illustrates Harvey Cox's assessment of ancient man's understanding of the world: "Presecular man lives in an enchanted forest. Its glens and groves swarm with spirits. Its rocks and streams are alive with friendly or fiendish demons. Reality is charged with a magical power that erupts here and there to threaten or benefit man."[1] This view of nature as animate is the predominant view of nature in the *Aeneid.* Vergil primarily portrays trees and groves as sacred or divine, and often associates them with holy rites or awe-inspiring events: Aeneas's initial encounter with his goddess mother occurs in a "silua" [forest] (1.314), and the site of Juno's temple is the "lucus" [sacred grove], around which Dido had built her city (1.44). The Trojans find Andromache making offerings to the memory of Hector "in luco" (3.302), and a "lucus . . . sacer" [holy grove] houses the tomb of Aeneas's father Anchises (5.761). Like Juno's temple, Latinus' palace was constructed around a "laurus . . . / sacra" [sacred laurel] (7.59-60). An ominous voice addresses Latinus "ex alto . . . luco" [from deep in a grove] (7.95). Father Tiber tells the dreaming Aeneas that he will find the white sow, the portent which signals the location of the future city, "sub ilicibus," [under the holm-oaks] (8.43), Aeneas finds Evander and Pallas offering rites to Hercules "in luco" (8.104), and Venus gives Aeneas his new, divinely-wrought arm "sub . . . quercu" [under an oak] (8.616). Trees possess a spiritual presence and offer a protective aura.

Vergil also suggests that there is a compelling, tangible link between trees and human beings in Evander's full description of Arcadia's ancient groves: "haec nemora indigenae Fauni Nymphaeque tenebant / gensque uirum truncis et duro robore nata," [The Fauns and the native Nymphs once possessed these groves, and a race of men born from the tree-trunks and hardy oak] (8.314-15). Elsewhere, Vergil elicits the connection between human beings and trees by employing either personification to invest trees with human traits or similes to compare human beings to trees. In a striking passage, Vergil compares the hero Aeneas to an oak tree:

> ac uelut annoso ualidam cum robore quercum
> Alpini Boreae nunc hinc nunc flatibus illinc
> eruere inter se certant; it stridor, et altae
> consternunt terram concusso stipite frondes;
> ipsa haeret scopulis et quantum uertice ad auras
> aetherias, tantum radice in Tartara tendit:
> haud secus adsiduis hinc atque hinc uocibus heros
> tunditur, et magno persentit pectore curas;
> mens immota manet, lacrimae uoluuntur inanes
> (4.441-49)

> [And just as the Alpine north winds strive between themselves, with blasts from now this side, now that, to uproot an oak tree, sturdy in its aged strength; a whistling noise goes up, and the high leafy branches strew the ground when the trunk has been violently shaken; the tree itself clings to the rocks and, by so much as it reaches with its head toward the upper air, it stretches with its root into the Underworld: in this manner the hero is beaten with relentless voices from this side and that and feels a deep anxiety in his great breast; but his spirit remains unmoved, tears fall in vain.]

Vergil employs the simile to emphasize Aeneas's resolve: like a tree with roots that reach down to Tartarus, Aeneas remains fixed. The tree, which reaches deeply into the earth and upward toward heaven, displays its link not only to the earth but also to the nether and upper worlds: it is earthly, yet grows toward both immortality (Rome, the future) and is rooted in its past (Troy)—two apparently contradictory goals. These goals reflect Aeneas's circumstances as he advances toward Italy and the future Empire: he is both deeply entrenched in the past and reaching toward the future. Vergil enhances this tension through an implicit contrast between the human and nonhuman. By virtue of its similarity to Aeneas, the tree becomes ennobled, sympathetic, possibly even heroic. Conversely, Aeneas is naturally strong and resilient, but sometimes lacks sensitivity. Sadly, both Aeneas and the tree must rely on strength during critical times, such as the turbulent transition from Troy to Rome, when either being must suffer dramatic changes in order to survive.

Just as living trees symbolize living beings, whether human or divine, so too does the tree trunk connote a human corpse. In Book 11, Vergil describes the trunk, representing the fallen Mezentius, upon which Aeneas hangs his dead foe's armor and weaponry, and calls attention to the trunk's "human" form:

ingentem quercum decisis undique ramis
constituit tumulo fulgentiaque induit arma,
Mezenti ducis exuuias, tibi, magne, tropaeum,
bellipotens: aptat rorantis sanguine cristas
telaque trunca uiri, et bis sex thoraca petitum
perfossumque locis, clipeumque ex aere sinistrae
subligat atque ensem collo suspendit eburnum.
(11.5-11)

[On a mound he placed a huge oak with its branches cut away from all sides, and dressed it in the shining weapons, the spoils of the leader Mezentius, a trophy for you, great war-wager (Mars); he fastens the helmet crests wet with blood, the mutilated weapons of the man, and the breastplate attacked and pierced in twelve places; and he binds the shield made of bronze to the left hand and he hangs the ivory sword from the neck.]

Aeneas's actions recall the Roman generals' practice of erecting the *spolia opima*, the arms taken from a defeated enemy leader, on a tree trunk which represents the body of the fallen foe. Vergil's allusion to this practice demonstrates that the assimilation of tree to human body is not his peculiar poetic trope, but a notion integral to Roman thought and ritual. At the same time, the equation of the dead tree to the dead foe establishes the tree as "the other." On the one hand, the association of the dead tree to the dead human is a corollary to the association of the living tree to the living human, or even to *numina*; on the other, the use of the tree trunk as trophy exemplifies reification, a necessary aspect of a utilitarian attitude toward nature.

In his book *Pan's Travail*, Donald Hughes identifies the opposing views of animism and utilitarianism. He observes, "Traditionally, the Greeks and Romans regarded the world as a sacred place where the gods of nature, who shared some human qualities, were present. Thus it would be expected that they would treat the environment with awe and care, and this was true to a considerable extent."[2] But Hughes also confirms "The actions of a people, after all, did reflect their perceptions and values, even if many of these were confused or contradictory. Ancient attitudes varied from worship of nature to curiosity, desire for prudent use, and greed leading to wasteful exploitation."[3] In contrast to the several moments in the text (noted above) where Vergil portrays nature as sacred or mysterious, he also demonstrates that human beings can and do approach nature from a utilitarian perspective. Two such passages describe the funeral preparations and pyre for Misenus. "itur in antiquam siluam, stabula alta ferarum, / procumbunt piceae, sonat icta securibus ilex / fraxineaeque trabes cuneis et fissile robur / scinditur, aduoluunt ingentis montibus ornos," [They go into an ancient forest, the deep abodes of wild beasts; the pitch pines fall, the holm-oak, struck by axes, resounds, and the ash-wood trunks and the fissile oak-tree are split with wedges, and they roll the huge mountain-ash trees from the mountains] (6.179-82). Vergil's deployment of the passive verbs *itur* (literally: there is a going) and *scinditur* (is broken apart) and the absence of a subject for *aduoluunt* (they roll) diminish individual responsibility; this removal of personal agency suggests a "mob mentality" or irresponsible behavior. At the same time, his description of the forest as *antiquam* (ancient) evokes the thought of huge trees (as they are described in the final line), and the cutting of such trees amidst " the deep abodes of wild beasts" suggests danger and intrusion.[4] Vergil's language thus suggests human irresponsibility, or at least a lack of prudence, for being in such a place and performing such an action. Since, as Richard Thomas observes, "Tree spirits are obviously hard to detect, and any tree is therefore potentially numinous, any tree felling potentially hazardous,"[5] Vergil may be subtly condemning this action despite the absence of any overt criticism. Thomas examines this episode with two others in which he claims that Vergil "fail[s] to allude in any way to the necessary retribution"[6] expected; yet, the suggestion of improper behavior and the lack of personal responsibility are clear even if the Trojans do not appear to pay an immediate cost. Furthermore, Vergil later suggests that the use to which these trees are put is wasteful: "principio pinguem taedis et robore secto / ingentem struxere pyram, cui frondibus atris / intexunt latera, et feralis ante cupressos / constituunt, decorantque super fulgentibus armis," [At first they construct a pyre, heavy with pines and huge with cleaved oak, whose sides they intertwine with dark branches, and they erect funereal cypresses in front and adorn it above with the gleaming weapons] (6.214-17).[7] Although Aeneas deeply revered Misenus, he is a minor character in the poem, and the felling and burning of so many large, ancient trees seems excessive.[8] Vergil employs the same word to describe the pyre—*ingens*—that he uses earlier to describe the ancient trees. A survey of Vergil's uses of *ingens* reveals that this adjective often indicates an inherent or natural greatness of either power or size; Vergil frequently applies the adjective to warriors, omens, and supernatural beings.[9] His application of *ingens*, then, to the pyre indicates that the mass is more than is needed to cremate a single man. His use of *pinguem*, "rich," "fat," or "fertile," further suggests waste. Although Williams claims that the adjective means "that the huge pyre is amply provided with pine and oak,"[10] Vergil again subtly criticizes by employing an adjective which suggests life and fertility (of animals it means "well-fed") and brings out the impropriety of the scene through irony: these violated trees will never be living or fertile again. These passages thus indicate a significant step toward what Cox calls the "disenchantment" of nature: the Trojans consider the trees something available for their use, something they do not think twice about killing or injuring. This behavior echoes Cox' understanding of the death of the "magical" view of nature in the Book of *Genesis*, where "the Hebrew view of Creation . . . separates nature from God and distinguishes man from nature."[11] Cox argues that this "disenchantment" "allows man to perceive nature itself in a matter-of-fact way" and "makes nature itself available for man's use."[12] These opposing views of nature as "enchanted" and "disenchanted" lie at the heart of our modern, tortured relationship with nature, which comprises "our need for some external absolute to which we can look for authorization . . . [and] the requirement of a fundamental separation of "human" and "nature" for a modern world-view."[13] Our "modern" western view of nature has deep and dichotomous cultural roots.

In an arresting tree simile, Vergil employs personification to evoke compassion and a sense of regret concerning utilitarianism. As Aeneas narrates the fall of Troy, he compares the city to a falling ash tree:

> tum uero omne mihi uisum considere in ignis
> Ilium et ex imo uerti Neptunia Troia:
> ac ueluti summis antiquam in montibus ornum
> cum ferro accisam crebrisque bipennibus instant
> eruere agricolae certatim; illa usque minatur
> et tremefacta comam concusso uertice nutat,
> uulneribus donec paulatim euicta supremum
> congemuit traxitque iugis auulsa ruinam.
> (2.624-31)

> [Then indeed it seemed to me that the whole of Ilium was sinking into flames and Neptunian Troy being upturned from her foundation; just as when farmers, on the tops of mountains, attempt emulously to overturn an ancient ash tree, which has been cut with iron and by frequent axe-blows; and it continually wavers and, trembling, its top violently shaken, it nods its head until, conquered little by little with wounds, it groans one last time and, torn from the ridges, violently falls down.]

Vergil's personification of the tree, which "nods" and "groans" like a human being, evokes sympathy for it, just as the narrating Aeneas encourages his audience's sympathy for Troy. That no good reason for felling the tree is stated further reflects Aeneas's attitude: in his eyes, there was no good reason that Troy should fall. But through the violence of the language (conveyed by *accisam*, *eruere*, *uulneribus*, and *auulsa*), Vergil suggests that humans use technology to harm nature rather than cultivate it, and the protraction of the falling (which reflects the length of time it took to conquer Troy) calls attention to the simile and evokes sympathy, sadness, and a sense of loss or waste.

If, as Hughes has suggested, "animism entailed an "enchantment" of nature that made people think twice before harming it,"[14] then we should expect not to find human beings attempting to manipulate nature. But manipulation is certainly characteristic of our relationship with nature. What has to occur for humans to employ nature, as Cox argues, is its disenchantment; once humans objectify nature and no longer think of it as animate, they can subject it to utility.Vergil, as if portraying disenchantment, depicts humans harming enchanted trees, and thus subtly criticizes human behavior. In four poignant episodes, the poet presents a collision between the attitudes of utilitarianism, or the matter-of-fact employment of nature, and enchantment, or the view that nature is inhabited by spiritual essences. In each of these episodes, Vergil suggests that human beings injure nature by neglecting its enchantment and focusing instead on utilizing it for their own purposes. In every instance, the consequences of human actions are in some way destructive. In the first two episodes, Aeneas is the central figure, whose behavior Vergil marks as questionable. In the latter two, Vergil maintains his criticism of human attitudes toward nature through his focus on Turnus.

In Book 3, the exiled Trojans attempt to establish a city in Thrace. As Aeneas prepares to offer sacrifice, he tries to gather boughs with which to adorn the altars:

> forte fuit iuxta tumulus, quo cornea summo
> uirgulta et densis hastilibus horrida myrtus.
> accessi uiridemque ab humo conuellere siluam
> conatus, ramis tegerem ut frondentibus aras,
> horrendum et dictu uideo mirabile monstrum.
> nam quae prima solo ruptis radicibus arbos
> uellitur, huic atro liquuntur sanguine guttae
> et terram tabo maculant.
> (3.22-29)

> [By chance there was a mound nearby, on top of which was a cornel thicket and a myrtle, dread-inspiring with its crowded spear shafts. I approached, and having tried to tear away the green shrubbery from the ground so that I might cover the altars with the leafy boughs, I witnessed an omen awful and amazing to describe. For on the tree which is first plucked from the ground, its roots broken, drops of dark blood appear, and they stain the earth with their putrid gore.]

Aeneas, although terrified at this omen, inexplicably plucks branches a second time; the blood drips again. When he tries, undeterred, a third time, "*maiore . . . nisu*" [with greater effort] (3.37), a groan and a voice emerge from deep in the mound. The voice is that of Polydorus, who had been treacherously slain on the site. Even though Polydorus is not a nymph or quasi-divine power, the presence of his spirit in the thicket is similar to that of a *numen*;[15] Vergil again adapts traditional Roman thought to reflect his poetic purpose, which is to provide an omen indicating that the Trojans are not in the proper place to establish their new city. But the elements he chooses to include—Aeneas's mindless persistence, bleeding branches, and Polydorus' question *quid miserum, Aenea, laceras?* "why do you tear/ruin poor me, Aeneas?" (3.41)—are significant.[16] In portraying Aeneas as heedlessly injuring the thicket, Vergil illustrates the human tendency to harm nature without thinking. Despite signs that the thicket is enchanted, Aeneas proceeds not once, but twice, to harm it again. His irreverent behavior directly opposes his awareness of nature as enchanted. Although Aeneas later performs funeral rites for Polydorus once he learns of the circumstances, his initial behavior is insensitive and improper.

Aeneas's actions are again questionable when he plucks the Golden Bough:

quale solet siluis brumali frigore uiscum
fronde uirere noua, quod non sua seminat arbos,
et croceo fetu teretis circumdare truncos,
talis erat species auri frondentis opaca
ilice, sic leni crepitabat brattea uento.
corripit Aeneas exemplo auidusque refringit
cunctantem, et uatis portat sub tecta Sibyllae.
(6.205-211)

[Just as in the woods during the winter cold the mistletoe[17], which an unrelated tree fosters, is accustomed to grow green with new leaf, and to embrace the graceful stems with yellow fruit: so was the appearance of gold as it took leaf in the dark ilex, and thus the gold-leaf rustled in the soft breeze. Immediately Aeneas snatches it away and greedily breaks off the hesitating bough, and carries it to the dwelling of the prophet, the Sibyl.]

The bough is the "ticket," as it were, which will allow Aeneas passage to the Underworld. As such, it functions as a symbol. The branch is recognized not for its intrinsic arboreal essence but for what this particular branch represents, divine sanction:—the Olympian gods (excepting Juno) favor Aeneas's mission and the emergence of the coming Empire. Clearly, the golden bough is a unit of exchange, like a coin, which Aeneas uses to obtain his passage to the Underworld. The fact that it is golden may simply represent its magical, unusual nature; gold, however, was precious and tended to corrupt, and this reference recalls its power to inspire greed and improper behavior. In Book 3, Aeneas himself narrates the tale of Polydorus, who had been sent to Thrace "*auri . . . cum pondere magno*" [with a great weight of gold] (3.49), and the king of Thrace, who "fas omne abrumpit: Polydorum obtruncat, et auro / ui potitur," [broke every sacred law: he killed Polydorus, and took the gold by force] (3.55-56). Vergil's description of Aeneas as *auidus* when he breaks off the bough thus recalls the greed of the Thracian King who slew Polydorus and suggests improper behavior.[18] The hesitation of the bough further suggests violation, as it counters the Sibyl's earlier advice: "ergo alte uestiga oculis et rite repertum / carpe manu; namque ipse uolens facilisque sequetur, / si te fata uocant; aliter non uiribus *ullis* / uincere nec duro poteris conuellere ferro," [And so search out with your eyes lifted and properly pluck the bough, once discovered, with your hand; for it will follow easily and willingly, if the fates are calling you; otherwise, you will not be able to win it with any strength nor tear it away, even with a cruel sword] (6.145-48). But the bough does not come away easily and willingly; it "hesitates" (*cunctantem*) before it yields. Through words such as *uolens*, *sequetur*, and *cunctantem*, Vergil attributes a will to the bough, portraying it as animate.[19] Furthermore, Vergil's repetition of the verb *conuellere*, which he had used at 3.24 and 31 to describe Aeneas' breaking of Polydorus's branches, encourages a connection between the two scenes through Aeneas's forceful behavior.[20]

When Aeneas captures the bough, he ensures the future for himself and his people, the proto-Romans. Its capture suggests that the future is both golden, like the bough, and divinely sanctioned, like its capture. The bough hesitates as if to delay the future, but cannot effectively resist because that future is fated. Its will has been overpowered. And as Aeneas's ticket to the Underworld, it is reified. The bough thus symbolizes the reification of nature: an animate tree has become a stagnant, disenchanted tool. Segal states "The plucking of the bough, then, may be viewed as a symbolical anticipation of the rude loss of innocence which awaits the peaceful forests of Italy."[21] By describing Aeneas as *auidus* or "greedy" when he breaks the bough, Vergil represents the attitude necessary to reify nature. Aeneas, demonstrating neither reverence nor awe, does not marvel at the magical nature of the bough but seeks only what it affords him. He quickly snaps off the bough, taking something marvelous in nature and converting it to a unit of exchange.[22] The trees in Italy will lose their innocence because Aeneas has lost his.

In the Polydorus and Golden Bough episodes, Aeneas is the central figure. In the first scene, he injures nature but subsequently appears to understand his error and behave properly by offering rites to Polydorus. In the second, he seems not to appreciate the magical nature of the Golden Bough and proceeds to employ it to secure his future. Thus, in the first half of the poem, Vergil suggests that human beings, represented by the hero Aeneas, behave with an insensitivity to nature's animism and consequently calls the actions of Aeneas, the founding father of Rome, into question.[23] While Aeneas reacts properly after he learned that Polydorus' spirit resided in the thicket, his behavior with the Golden Bough is clearly less reverent and more selfish. In these two important encounters, Vergil suggests that a utilitarian attitude toward nature is necessary for the progress which the Empire represents.

In the second half of the poem, the central figure in the significant encounters between humans and trees is not Aeneas but Turnus, the Rutulian warrior destined to become Aeneas' fallen opponent. By shifting the focus from Aeneas to Turnus, Vergil contrasts the attitudes of two different cultures—Trojan and native Italian. As Aeneas and his destiny become victorious in the final duel, so do the attitudes represented by Aeneas: an abandonment of the view of nature as enchanted and the adoption of a utilitarian perspective. Turnus, who persists in a view of nature as animate, becomes the victim of Aeneas just as the rustic Italians, with their earthy native deities (who are subordinated to the Olympian pantheon), become subjected to the coming Empire.

During the metamorphosis of the ships (9.77-122), when Turnus threatens to burn the Trojan fleet, Vergil portrays the Earth or Great Mother as grieving for the intended ignominious fate of her trees (which she had earlier readily given for a better purpose):

> Quis deus, o Musae, tam saeua incendia Teucris
> auertit? tantos ratibus quis depulit ignis? . . .
> ipsa deum fertur genetrix Berecyntia magnum

uocibus his adfata Iouem: "da, nate, petenti,
quod tua cara parens domito te poscit Olympo.
[pinea silua mihi, multos dilecta per annos,][24]
lucus in arce fuit summa, quo sacra ferebant,
nigranti picea trabibusque obscurus acernis.
has ego Dardanio iuueni, cum classis egeret,
laeta dedi; nunc sollicitam timor anxius angit.
solue metus atque hoc precibus sine posse parentem
ne cursu quassatae ullo neu turbine uenti
uincantur: prosit nostris in montibus ortas."
(9.76-77, 82-92)

[Which god, Muses, turned away those torches, so cruel, from the Trojans? Who turned away such great fire from the ships? The mother of the gods herself, the Berecynthian, is said to have addressed Jupiter with these words: "Son, grant to me, a suppliant, what your dear mother asks of you, now that you have tamed Olympus. There was a grove on a mountain summit, my pine forest, beloved for many years, a place where humans used to bring me offerings, dark with the black pitch-pine and trunks of maple. These I happily gave to the Trojan youth when he was in need of a fleet; but now a troubling fear torments me, and I am uneasy. Bring an end to these fears, and allow a parent to have influence with prayers to this effect; that they not be overcome, shaken neither by any journey or blast of wind. Let it be a benefit that they were born on our mountains."]

Jupiter responds by allowing the Great Mother to keep Turnus and his firebrands away from the ships: she turns them into nymphs. Interestingly, at 9.120, Vergil applies the same phrase, *mirabile monstrum*, which he used of the bleeding bush in Book 3 to this awe-inspiring event.[25] Vergil's choice to represent the trees as first made into ships, then nymphs, is also telling: the trees are clearly enchanted, and humans once again act improperly as Turnus threatens to destroy the ships with fire.

Despite modern commentators' claims that this scene is "the most incongruous episode in the whole Aeneid" (Williams), "somewhat ludicrous" (Page), and "absurd and unworthy of epic stature" (Heyne),[26] this unusual episode emphasizes two important matters.[27] First, Vergil portrays nature as offering her trees for human use, but not allowing them to be destroyed wantonly; the metamorphosis demands respect for reified nature. Secondly, Vergil demonstrates that even reified nature retains its spirituality; the enchanted trees were made into ships, but can still become nymphs. This portrayal evokes a cyclical view of nature and illustrates that "dead" matter remains part of the life cycle. Turnus misinterprets the *mirabile monstrum* as signifying a divine removal of the Trojan fleet, which would prevent the Trojans' escape, and mistakenly thinks that his intention—to prevent Aeneas's escape—coincides with divine will. Turnus fails to comprehend that the escape allowed is that of the ships, not the Trojans, since they, having arrived at their destined land, no longer need the ships.[28]

Through Turnus's misinterpretation, Vergil demonstrates a human lack of understanding of nature and natural forces. Yet, Turnus does not persist in trying to harm the ships-become-Nymphs, and does not appear surprised to witness their transformation. Unlike Aeneas, who did not initially recognize the enchantment of Polydorus's thicket and never acknowledged the animism in the Golden Bough, Turnus fully comprehends animism.

In Book 12, the Trojans cut down a tree sacred to Faunus when they clear the field for battle: "Forte sacer Fauno foliis oleaster amaris / hic steterat, nautis olim uenerabile lignum, / seruati ex undis ubi figere dona solebant / Laurenti diuo et uotas suspendere uestis; / sed stirpem Teucri nullo discrimine sacrum / sustulerant, puro ut possent concurrere campo," [By chance, a bitter-leaved wild-olive tree, sacred to Faunus, had stood here, a tree once reverend to the sailors, where they, saved from the waves, were accustomed to affix offerings to the divine Laurentian and to hang up their promised garments; but the Trojans–with no sense of distinction—had removed the sacred tree, so that they might be able to engage in battle in a clear field] (12.766-71). Vergil portrays the Trojans, who act *nullo discrimine*, as irreverent, either ignorant of or insensitive to the rustic Italian god.[29] His description of the native Italian ritual emphasizes the contrast between the Italians' appreciation for divine powers and the Trojans' earlier dressing of the tree representing the dead Mezentius. More importantly, in this scene Vergil depicts Turnus, who evokes Faunus in prayer, as pious: "Faune, precor, Miserere," *inquit*, "tuque, optima ferrum / Terra tene, colui uestros si semper honores, / quos contra Aeneadae bello fecere profanos," [Faunus, I pray you, he said, and you, most excellent Earth, have pity, hold fast that sword, if I have ever protected your glory, which, in contrast, the followers of Aeneas have made profane with war] (12.777-79). His words both emphasize the impiety of the Trojans and echo Aeneas's words to the Sibyl (*alma, precor, miserere*, 6.117), thus marking Turnus with a sense of piety normally characteristic of Aeneas.[30] His inclusion of *Terra*, "Earth," in his prayer reveals that he recognizes the important, life-giving connection between the earth and the tree. Faunus and Terra grant his plea as Aeneas's spear, which had become entrenched in the trunk, remains immovable. Juturna then assists Turnus by restoring his sword, which gives him the advantage, and Venus becomes enraged. In turn, she releases Aeneas's spear from the tree trunk, overturning Faunus's and Terra's fulfillment of Turnus's plea.[31]

Throughout the poem, Vergil portrays Venus, the patron goddess of the Romans and mother of Aeneas, as a primary proponent of the coming Empire. Her action in this scene, which overpowers a native Italian god, illustrates that the emerging Empire—not the rustic Italians—will dominate the culture on the Italian peninsula. Her support of the Trojans, the proto-Romans, who have desecrated the worship of Faunus and Terra, heralds divine support for the disenchantment of nature: the Trojans suffer no consequences for cutting down the tree sacred to Faunus.[32] Although Thomas interprets this lack of consequence as Vergilian ambivalence,[33] Vergil's sadness and subtle criticism are certainly clear. Vergil demonstrates that the utilitarian approach to nature will take precedence over animism or enchantment as the specter of Empire looms in the distance.

In all four of the passages examined above, Vergil maintains nature's enchantment and represents human beings (and usually Aeneas) as either ignorant or irreverent. It is impossible to know whether his verses reflect a shift which he witnessed in the world around him, whether he clearly perceived a change in attitude toward nature which we might call its disenchantment, but it is possible to observe in his poetry a distinct potrayal of human ignorance and insensitivity toward nature. In both Vergil's text and in Western culture, the concept of nature as enchanted does not completely disappear, but becomes subjugated to its disenchantment, which enables human beings to utilize it for their own purposes. In fact, Vergil announces this attitude when the Trojans first arrive in Italy: "iuuenum manus emicat ardens / litus in Hesperium; quaerit pars semina flammae / abstrusa in uenis silicis, pars densa ferarum tecta rapit siluas inuentaque flumina monstrat," [the band of youths ardently leaps forth onto the Hesperian shore; some seek the seeds of fire concealed in veins of flint, some seize the forests, the thick houses of wild beasts, and point out discovered streams] (6.5-9). As Williams comments, "they are seeking timber for fuel, water and meat for food."[34] Immediately upon arrival in their "new world," they overlook the enchantment of nature and allow utilitarianism to determine their actions.[35] As Vergil presents it, in our struggle for survival and progress, we human beings lose respect for the divine powers of the natural world.

Notes

1. 1 Harvey Cox, *The Secular City* (New York: Macmillan, 1966), 21.

2. J. Donald Hughes, *Pan's Travail: Environmental Problems of the Ancient Greeks and Romans* (Baltimore, Md.: Johns Hopkins University Press, 1994), 45.

3. Hughes, *Pan's Travail*, 5.

4. Richard F. Thomas, "Tree Violation and Ambivalence in Virgil," *TAPA* 118 (1988): 268, likewise finds in antiquam "a note of empathy and animism....the words antiquam siluam imply that the woods could be numinous, and that we are dealing with the disruption of an old order."

5. Thomas, "Tree Violation," 263.

6. Thomas, "Tree Violation," 265.

7. For a survey of Vergil's use of the image of the cypress tree and its mythological underpinnings, including an association with both life and death, see Catherine Connors, "Seeing cypresses in Virgil," *CJ* 88.1 (1992): 1-17.

8. Thomas quotes Skutsch's assessment: "the enormous preparations for the funeral of one man, Misenus, are astonishing" ("Tree Violation," 267).

9. As K. W. Grandsen, *Virgil. Aeneid. Book VIII* (Cambridge: Cambridge University Press, 1976) ad 8.43, notes, Vergil often associates the adjective ingens with mysterious power or might. Cf. Denis Feeney, *The Gods in Epic: Poets and Critics of the Classical Tradition* (Oxford: Oxford University Press, 1991), 167, who observes an etymological

wordplay between ingens and ingenium ("nature" or "natural character") in the description of Amata as ingentibus excita monstris, "stirred up by huge other-worldly beings" (7.376).

10. R. D. Williams, *The Aeneid of Virgil* (London: St. Martin's, 1973), ad 6.214.

11. Cox, *Secular*, 22.

12. Cox, *Secular*, 23.

13. Neil Evernden, *The Social Creation of Nature* (Baltimore, Md.: Johns Hopkins University Press, 1992), 28.

14. Hughes, *Pan's Travail*, 70.

15. Williams, *ad* 3.19 ff., explains the connection: "it was Virgil's own invention, based upon such folklore as the spear thrown by Romulus onto the Palatine, which took root and grew into a tree, or the stories of Dryads or Hamadryads, the nymphs who lived in trees and were sometimes physically identified with them, so that injury to the tree caused them injury."

16. Williams *ad* 3.19 notes that "The grim and weird story of Polydorus and the drops of blood trickling from the myrtle shoots is not found before Virgil" and thus questions why Vergil chooses to portray this episode as he does. His solution: "It is intended to make us feel that the long voyage which ends in the foundation of Rome begins in tragedy, horror, and despair. It is an episode of primitive folklore, and in it Aeneas receives his first omen of the voyage, a grim and unhappy one." This explanation, however, does not account for Aeneas's persistent lack of awareness.

17. The fact that Vergil compares the bough to mistletoe is also significant, since mistletoe is an endophyte or parasitic plant which grows upon others. As a simile for the bough, which is itself a symbol for the future of Rome, mistletoe suggests a parasitic or utilitarian attitude. For a thoughtful discussion of the bough and mistletoe, see D. A. West, "The Bough and the Gate," in S. J. Harrison, *Oxford Readings in Vergil's Aeneid*, 224-238.

18. "The arguments of others, particularly D'Arms and Segal, are clearly correct, and now probably represent the communis opinio: the state of mind of Aeneas (auidus), the manner of his actions (corripit . . . refringit), and the resistant animism ascribed to the bough (cunctantem) create an uneasiness not dissimilar from that generated at the beginning of Book 3" (Thomas, "Tree Violation," 267). On *auidus*, Thomas notes "there can be little doubt that its affect is intended to disturb."

19. Charles Segal, "The Hesitation of the Golden Bough. A Reexamination," *Hermes* 96 (1968): 74-49, views the bough as animate, following John D'Arms, "Vergil's Cunctantem (Ramum), *Aeneid* 6.211," *CJ* 59 (1964): 265-68. Clifford Weber, "The Allegory of the Golden Bough," *Vergilius* 41 (1995): 3-34, argues that the animism of the bough is analogous to Aeneas' soul, further supporting the notion that Vergil draws a connection between human beings and trees.

20. Vergil employs forms of conuellere only eight times in all his poems. Of these, six occur in the Aeneid, two in the Polydorus episode. All instances convey a certain degree of violence.

21. Segal, "Hesitation," 79.

22. Cf. Aldo Leopold, "The Land Ethic," in *A Sand County Almanac* (Oxford: Oxford University Press, 1949), 201-226, where he maintains that we will not be able to develop a land ethic and live by it until we recognize the land as something valuable in itself, not something which is useful only in economic terms. Aeneas's behavior demonstrates this attitude.

23. Some readers will find this negative cast on Aeneas' character troubling; I maintain that such a characterization is consistent with Vergil's portrayal of Aeneas elsewhere in the poem, e.g., his abandonment of Dido or his killing of Turnus. Vergil presents Aeneas as a complex figure, both heroic and subject to human foibles.

24. Dittographia esse statuit Ribbeck [OCT]. Cf. Philip Hardie, *Virgil. Aeneid. Book IX* (Cambridge: Cambridge University Press, 1994), ad 9.85-87: "The awkwardness of the connection between lines 85 and 86 . . . may be indications that this passage lacks the summa manus or that 85 is to be deleted."

25. Interestingly, Williams also links this scene to the Polydorus episode ad 9.80: "This refers to the events at the beginning of Book 3." The phrase mirabile monstrum occurs only five times in the poem; the other three all distinguish remarkable, ominous events: the flame around Iulus's head (2.680), the white sow marking the future site of Rome (8.81), and the phantom Aeneas (10.637).

26. Williams, *ad* 10.77 ff.

27. Cf. Elaine Fantham, "Nymphas . . . e navibus esse: Decorum and poetic fiction in *Aeneid* 9.77-122 and 10.215-59," *CP* 85 (1990):102-119, who argues convincingly for the episode's propriety and integrity by examining literary precedent, allusion and criticism.

28. Hardie, *ad* 9.123-175, sums up the dominant scholarly perception of Turnus: "T's cohortatio, his first long speech in the poem, reveals a stubbornly misguided view of the divine and human worlds, based on a mistaken analogy with the past." But the situation is complex. Turnus is clearly wrong in his interpretation, but his speech, modeled on several of Hector's speeches in the Iliad, makes him sympathetic in humanity and fallibility.

29. Thomas, "Tree Violation," 269, also interprets this phrase as indicative of violation.

30. Whereas the discussion above on the Golden Bough focuses on Aeneas's questionable behavior, Book 6, in general, presents Aeneas as especially pious in his visit to the Sibyl, his sojourn to the Underworld, and his various encounters there, particularly with his father. He witnesses the pageant of Roman history and emerges "reborn," no longer hesitant but ready to assume the full burden of his mission. Thus, this echo of Aeneas's words in Book 6 points toward some of Aeneas's most pious behavior.

31. Thomas, "Tree violation," 270, interprets Faunus as being unable to protect his own. But he clearly is able to protect; rather, his effort is cruelly overpowered by the unscrupulous Venus.

32. In fact, Vergil conveys affinity to nature through the familial relationships of various leaders. Aeneas's mother is the Olympian Venus; in contrast, all the native Italians are closely related to rustic deities. Evander's mother is the nymph Carmenta (8.340-41), his father Mercury (8.138); Latinus's parents are Faunus and the Laurentian nymph Marica (7.45-9); Turnus's mother is Venilia, a sea nymph (10.76), his grandfather is Pilumnus, a Roman agricultural deity (9.4), and his sister is Juturna, whose territory includes "pools and resounding rivers" (12.139-40). Given the hierarchy of divine powers, it is predictable that Aeneas, child of an Olympian rather than some rustic Italian deity, should become victor.

33. Thomas, "Tree Violation," 270.

34. Williams, *ad* 6.7-8.

35. In fact, Vergil prefigures this adoption of utilitarianism as the Trojans assemble to depart from Troy. Aeneas recalls that they gathered near the temple of desertae Cereris, "abandoned Ceres" (2.714); it seems that the Trojans had already abandoned their worship of the principal earth goddess long before they left Troy.

7

AUGUSTINE AND LOVE OF THE ENVIRONMENT

Madonna R. Adams

In the *City of God*, Augustine notes the fundamental importance of the study of nature when he writes:

> Philosophers took their lead from this very truth when they decreed that the study of philosophy should be subsumed under three heads . . . physics [physica], the second logic [logica] and the third ethics [ethica]. . . . [For] it is certain that philosophers, though they may hold different views about nature, about method in the search for truth, and about the supremely good goal towards which we ought to direct all our actions, still agree in devoting all their study to these three important general fields of research. Thus, although there is a discordant variety of opinion on the question which sect each man should follow in any given field, no one doubts that there is some cause that explains nature [naturae causam], some formal system of knowledge [scientiae formam], and a highest motive in life [vitae summam].[1]

In order to identify Augustine's contribution in each of these three areas, I will (1) summarize the core principles of his philosophy that are relevant to thinking about the environment; and (2) emphasize the middle ground that he establishes between the two other major philosophies on nature that shaped his thought, namely Manichaeism and Neoplatonism, in order (3) to examine Augustine's views on our interdependence with, and proper relationship to, the rest of nature. Finally(4) I want to claim that the natural environment can only be fully understood, in a way that actually influences our way of dwelling within the world, if we perceive and embrace it within his major paradigm, that of the *ordo amoris,* or Order of Love.

Augustine's Metaphysics

In the *City of God,* Augustine speaks within the perspective of a Christian dispensation rooted in the notion of a transcendent Creator and a hierarchy of relationships and duties for human beings that derive from an order established by their transcendent Source. He also affirms the close correlation between his own faith perspective and Plato's hypothesis in the *Timaeus,* concerning (a) the formative work of the demiurge, (b) the development of complex beings from elementary particles, and (c) the principles and results of the activity of the demiurge, i.e., the harmony, intrinsic goodness, and integrity of the world of becoming.

Augustine maintains, much as Plato had, that in this metaphysical sense, nature, the universe, is essentially good. For him, as for Plato, *ontological evil* is an oxymoron. And so he concludes that:

> All natures, then, are good simply because they exist, and, therefore, have each its own measure of being, its own beauty, even, in a way, its own peace. And when each is in the place assigned by the order of nature, it best preserves the full measure of being that was given to it.[2]

Moreover, Augustine does not merely affirm the ontological goodness of nature, and the principles of order inherent in it, but details the particulars of this at length—thus complementing his metaphysical view with the careful observations of a scientific mind as well as those of an artist.

The Ontological Status of Nature: Augustine's Middle Ground

Augustine's philosophy of nature provides a middle ground between the contrasting metaphysical perspectives that influenced him the most: that of the Manichaeans, which he strongly rejects, and that of the Neoplatonists, which he transforms. For Augustine, as for Plato and Plotinus, Truth, Beauty, and Goodness are aspects of reality. And the importance of philosophy lies in the attainment of wisdom, an understanding based on love of the good.[3] Since truth provides the foundation for living, the importance of a metaphysical system or doctrine lies in its capacity to explain and support an integrated way of life in keeping with sound reason. An inadequate or self-contradictory philosophy lacks such capacity and results in a distortion in thought and practice. As such, metaphysics speaks to a historical context with political, ethical, and even theological implications.

Augustine and the Manichaeans

Throughout his writings, especially in such treatises as *On Free Choice of the Will* and *The Manichaean Way of Life*, Augustine argues vigorously against the metaphysical dualism of the Manichaeans who attribute substantiality to evil. "There is no nature contrary to God," he affirms.[4] In addition to arguing against their views, he stresses how the flaws in their doctrine lead to self-contradictions in their way of life, a key point for environmental ethics.

According to the Manichaeans, the life-force or souls of living beings are somehow entrapped or imprisoned in their bodily forms. Salvation demands freedom from this bondage, i.e., freedom from matter.[5] This doctrine requires them to justify such essentials of human life as eating and sexual activity by means of elaborate interpretations and rationalizations.[6] Thus they justify consumption of seed-bearing products of plants like grain and fruit by explaining it as an act that destroys the physical body of the plant, thereby releasing its life-force from material bondage.

Their dim view of human generation, inasmuch as it contributes to the imprisonment of the human soul in the body and increases the population of the kingdom of darkness, led them to attempt to justify sexual activity only outside of a woman's fertile period thus separating it from its natural fruitfulness. To put their doctrine into practice, the Manichaeans designed a framework of precepts and rituals ranging from essential prescriptions, to be observed by all the "hearers," or ordinary followers, to more detailed and stringent rules governing the lives of the "elect."[7]

Augustine inveighs against this doctrine by extensive arguments *ad absurdum* based on numerous examples taken from his own early experience as a Manichaean "hearer". His polemic exposes not only the weakness of their doctrine, but the hypocrisy concealed in their supposedly more perfect way of life. For example, meat and wine were forbidden to the elect. Yet Augustine pictures them as likely to despise the habits of a poor man who follows a subsistent diet consisting of a few plain vegetables, which he flavors with a little bacon fat and a bit of poor wine for his stomach. He contrasts the simple life of the latter with the hypocrisy of one of the elect who, while scrupulously avoiding meat and wine, feasts sumptuously on a great variety of fruits and vegetables, nutmeats and imported delicacies, all carefully prepared with exotic spices, and who takes care to drink only unfermented grape juice.[8]

He accuses them also of making legalistic distinctions based on human preferences: for example, in holding that it was less evil to kill a rat than some "higher animals," and in dispensing with the prohibition against killing living things in the case of "lice, fleas, or bugs"—all decided nuisances for humans.[9] In *City of God*, he makes a relevant point for environmental ethics when he remarks:

> Men, to be sure, are in most cases critical even of natural objects when they become a nuisance, for they do not view them disinterestedly but consider their own convenience.[10]

He also cites their cruelty such as refusing to pick a pear from a tree to feed a sick and hungry person, lest they deprive the tree of its life force.[11] And in another place he writes: "Rather than have harm come to a melon, you would see a man ruined by debt.[12]

But Augustine's chief criticism against the Manichaeans concerned their moral failure, especially among a great number of the so-called elect. Their attempt to abstract themselves from their own nature as embodied spirits led not only to pride and hypocrisy, but to behavior considered degenerate even by the public mores of the time. He cites his own experience of witnessing the elders, who had forsaken formal marriage, standing on open road crossings behaving shamelessly toward strange women in the very presence of other elders.[13]

> I personally saw, and I was not alone . . . at a busy crossroads in Carthage not only one but several of the Elect calling after some strange women with such lewd sounds and gestures as to surpass all ordinary shamelessness. This was quite evidently the customary behavior of these men, for none of them seemed the least perturbed by the presence of his companions, which indicates that all of them, or nearly all, were afflicted with the same disease. . . . We were greatly shocked by this incident and made a strong complaint. But did anyone think that the act even called for punishment . . . at least by a stern reprimand on account of the magnitude of the offense?[14]

On page after page of *De moribus Manichaeorum,* Augustine demonstrates his rhetorical command of the argument to the absurd with his analyses of a stream of shocking examples that expose the self-contradiction inherent in the Manichaean theory and the peril of attempting to base a coherent set of ethical practices upon such principles.

Augustine and Neoplatonism

On the positive side, Augustine also uses his polemic against the Manichaeans to affirm the goodness and beauty of nature in itself. When Plato names the Form of the Good as the source of being and knowledge (*Rep.* 6.509b), he explicitly acknowledges that one ultimately has to resort to hypothesis when speaking of the first cause of the world of becoming (6.510b). Likewise Augustine grounds his philosophy on a religious belief in a free and supremely good Creator. And just as Plato gives logical arguments to support his hypothesis concerning the goodness of the Maker (demiurge) of the cosmos (*Timaeus* 29e-30a), so Augustine provides sound philosophical arguments that lend support to his fundamental "hypothesis" or belief first, to show the impossibility of defining evil as a positive, substantial entity, and second, to affirm, as the logical and practical corollary of a supremely good first cause of the world of nature, that all creation has an essential participation in goodness by its very existence.[15]

Augustine praises Plotinus as the only one who fully understood Plato the master. And he embraces the well known features of neoplatonism, namely, that there is a transcendent source—the Form of the Good for Plato, *The One* for Plotinus; that all beings participate in the ontological goodness, truth, and beauty of this Source; that there is a hierarchy of natures; and that the human soul is destined to reach its final destiny by self-discipline and the development of understanding culminating in the contemplation of, and a return to, *The One*. But Augustine not only embraces the Neoplatonic vision of nature; he transforms it.

For Plotinus, the return of the soul to its unitary source admits of failure and regression along the way, but seems to be part of an irresistible movement of being toward the good from which it emanates, a movement that will ultimately achieve its goal. But to the Plotinian framework, Augustine brings a profound awareness of freedom, divine and human, and an awareness that has its roots in his personal experience. For Augustine, the human return to *The One* of Plotinus (or to God in Augustine's framework) is not inevitable. The outcome of the journey is fraught with an uncertainty that is inseparable from the vagaries of human freedom. It is this metaphysical claim that all of nature is essentially good, along with the claim that our right relationship to nature and our success in attaining our final destiny depends ultimately on our choices, that sets the stage for examining Augustine's views on nature and the environment in more detail.

Right Relationship with Nature

For Augustine, the right human relationship to the world of nature requires three things: (1) An understanding of the goodness in which all things exist participate in their own way—a point that I have discussed above; (2) a love and appreciation of these *other natures* for their own sake, because of their inherent goodness; and (3) the need for human beings to order their own nature—their desires and behavior—according to the classic virtues. The latter two requirements, love and virtue, have a reciprocal relationship. Let us look at what the second requirement, the love of other natures, means in practice.

Augustine's writings witness to an immediate, personal appreciation of life in every nature, one that is well articulated and deeply felt. His remarks go beyond drawing attention to these natures as *images* of a higher Being as did Plato. They express his deep wonder, delight, and joy in the differentiated beauty of many-faceted nature and witness to his native capacity for appreciating beauty. He relates to the world in an existential way and his principles require an existential response.

In *The City of God* 12.4, he emphasizes the harmony of the universe as a whole even in its transitory phenomena, and he notes that often we do not appreciate it because, "being ourselves by virtue of our mortal condition but threads in a part of the fabric (*intexti universum),* we are unable to perceive the whole, into which the details that displease us fit as neatly and prettily [becomingly] as need be.[16] "This shows," he continues, "that it is not nature as seen in the light of our own convenience or inconvenience, but nature seen in her own light that gives glory to her maker."[17]

Augustine would understand the entomologist who is fascinated by a species of insect life that she researches, and the microbiologist's amazement at discovering new and intricate aspects of the tiniest organisms.This is what Augustine would see as a disinterested love—rooted in an appreciation of the particular form or species as well as in its contribution to the ecological whole. When he remarks, according to a belief of the time, that "some animals enjoy a healthful existence" even in "burning heat," the modern reader might recall the recent scientific amazement at the discovery of bacteria that exist even in the molten furnace of earth's inner core.[18] Such appreciation does not negate other motives for the study of nature, such as researching the cause of a disease in order to prevent human suffering.It goes beyond it. And it is this appreciation of nature in itself that leads the scientist to respect the nature of things more deeply, thus contributing to a fuller insight into its right use.

Finally, Augustine speaks of the giftedness of nature and the consequences of its misuse by human beings when he writes that we are surrounded by blessings such as "air to breathe, water to drink," and he continues:

> These good gifts are granted, however, with the perfectly just understanding that whoever uses the goods which are meant for the mortal peace of mortal men, as these goods should be used, will receive more abundant and better goods . . . [i.e., the peace of immortality]; but that whoever misuses his gifts on earth will both lose what he has and never receive the better gifts of heaven.[19]

In other words, all that we share with other living beings should be used in a way that is subject to reason and in the spirit of pilgrims who are merely passing through—with moderation, order, and restraint.[20] Clearly, then, for Augustine, a genuine appreciation of nature, grounded in truth, requires a third factor, the development of virtue.

In affirming that each nature has its own proper goodness, Augustine, like Plato, argues that harmony and peace in human life depend not on an impossible abnegation of our embodied selves in a vain attempt to escape from matter, like the Manichaeans, but on the development of character, through the four classic virtues of moderation, courage, justice, and prudence. A peaceful life in human society is impossible without a modicum of these virtues. And for us human beings who live by choices, they are absolutely necessary for a right interaction with the environment and for its well-ordered use and care. Witness in our day the sufferings of human populations and the destruction of other species because of the despoiling of the environment because of individual and corporate excess and greed.

Some Controversial Points

Some views of Augustine touch on controversial views in environmental ethics today. He would argue against Peter Singer's view that in some extreme cases a deformed infant would have less value than a healthy animal. Contrary to any such conclusion, Augustine holds, supported by the example of Christ, that an absolute prohibition against "the killing of animals, and the destroying of plants is the height of superstition, for . . . there are no common rights between us and the beasts and trees" (*qui nullam nobis cum belluis et arboribus, societatem juris esse judicans).* Whereas "in the case of men . . . we are . . . joined in a community of rights" (*Nam et de hominibus, cum quibus utique sumus juris societate conjuncti*).[21]

Augustine clearly sees intelligent human life as superior to other animal life, though all within the framework of an ordered love. In his treatise, *Eighty-Three Different Questions*, he gives an interesting ad hoc argument for this position when he remarks that if this were not so, the animals would have domesticated us, rather than we them.[22]

Against the Manichaeans on the other hand, Augustine affirms that the use of plants and their produce, and of fish and meat for human consumption, is in keeping with our human condition. But he again distinguishes between their use to meet human needs and their use to satisfy human greed, mere luxury, and waste. The latter violates the well-ordered love that is his standard. Augustine would castigate an economic system, or the luxury of the few, that would create dire need while devastating the ecological whole.

Virtue, good character, is essential to replace a disordered self-love and the excesses that are as harmful for the physical and spiritual peace and happiness of the human community as they are for the integrity of the environment. It is also needed so that a well-ordered love may inform our behavior even as we enjoy the use of what the environment provides. In assuming this perspective, Augustine rejects the utilitarian approach of the Manichaeans and grounds his approach to nature in a contemplative attitude more akin to that of Plotinus that presupposes the development of a virtuous character as the precondition of a contemplative and holistic perspective.

The Order of Love

In *The City of God* 14. 28, Augustine distinguishes the two cities that are created by two kinds of love: the Earthly City by a selfish love of desire to the point of contempt for the Highest Good (*summum bonum*), and the City of God, generated by the unselfish love that is charity.[23] Citizens of the Earthly City use people and things as ends in themselves. They stop short of the true and highest good which, for Augustine, is God. Their desires are based on a false set of values. Consequently they view the goods of nature not as common goods to be valued in a manner that ensures their abundance and vitality, but as things merely to be possessed, an attitude that leads to conflict.[24] And, as we can clearly see, to environmental conflict.Citizens of the City of God, on the other hand, ground their relationship with nature on a true set of values and live according to a well-ordered love, seeing nature, even in its transient phenomena, as having its own measure of goodness. And only in this context is the proper relationship with nature established.

Like Plato, Augustine sees a gradation in nature from non-living, to living, from vegetative to sensate to intelligent life. This represents the fundamental order of being. For Augustine, an intelligent and moral standard of value would mirror this basic order. In practice, however, this order is often not observed as he notes:

> According to the utility each man finds in a thing, there are various standards of value, so that it comes to pass that we prefer some things that have no sensation to some sentient beings.[25]

This represents a fundamental distortion which directly relates to present concern over the loss of natural habitats and species, and he continues with a farsighted comment:

> And so strong is this preference that, had we the power, we would abolish the latter from nature altogether, sacrificing them to our own-convenience. Who, e.g., would not rather have bread in his house than mice, gold than fleas? But there is little to wonder at in this, seeing that even when valued by men themselves (whose nature is certainly of the highest dignity), more is often given for a horse than for a slave, for a jewel than for a maid. Thus the reason of one contemplating nature prompts very different judgments from those dictated by the necessity of the needy, or the desire of the voluptuous; for the former considers what value a thing in itself has in the scale of creation, while necessity considers how it meets its need; reason looks for what the mental light will judge to be true, while pleasure looks for what pleasantly titillates the bodily sense. But of such consequence in rational natures is the weight, so to speak, of will and of love, that though in the order of nature angels rank above men, yet by the scale of justice, good men are of greater value than bad angels.[26]

Augustine's Order of Love thus establishes the proper levels of responsibility in our existential situation. For example, we owe love and care to those closest to us: from family, to neighbors, to community, and all whom we are in a position to influence.[27] And we owe respect to other living things as having their own measure of goodness and beauty. This does not preclude our right use of nature, such as the fruits of the field, nor our enjoyment in such use. Our very enjoyment witnesses to their share of goodness and their kinship with us as fellow creatures. "We use what we enjoy and enjoy what we use, et fructibus utimur et usibus fruimor," says Augustine.[28] But according to the Order of Love, nature is a means of satisfying needs as distinct from merely serving our greed or gratification.

For Augustine, this right relationship can only be fully understood and effected in a way that actually influences our way of living in the world, if it is grounded within this major paradigm, that of the *ordo amoris*, the Order of Love. And this not in a vague or merely sentimental manner, but with intelligent insight into the goodness of nature in all its particularities, as the necessary condition for fostering such understanding and appreciation. For while virtue disposes us to use nature well, love does more. It opens one to the "deep down" goodness of things as Gerard Manley Hopkins puts it. It is not an act of the practical or speculative intellect, but a transforming act that discloses the true character of the interaction between human and non-human nature. Without this order of love, it is difficult to make sense of the ways in which Augustine speaks of the goodness of nature.

Here we touch upon the reciprocal connection between understanding and love. Ultimately, profound understanding in the sense of wisdom depends on the insight that only love of the good effects. Plato grasped this when he points to the Form of the Good not only as the source of being, but also as the source of knowledge (*Republic* 6). Augustine, likewise, while grounding the goodness of nature in the goodness of its cause—a transcendent and good Creator—argues that it is a well-ordered love that both gives insight into the true value of the natural world *and* disposes us to act accordingly with restraint and respect for its integrity.[29]

In other words, knowledge or rational argument alone is not sufficient to establish the right relationship and interaction with the environment of which we are an intimate part.Neither is a purely utilitarian approach: "Waste not, want not,"—although Augustine counsels the same. Rather, it is ultimately an ordered love, first for the *summum bonum,* and then for each creature according to its own measure of goodness, that provides insight into its value and engenders that sense of affinity and bondedness with the environment which is rooted in the actual nature of things. Despite their professed spiritual goal, the utilitarianism of the Manichaeans is insufficient. Love of the environment springs from contemplation of the good which requires a life of virtue as its precondition. It is love of nature in this proper sense, a profoundly respectful bond, that alone can establish or restore our proper attitude and relationship with our environment.

Conclusion

Augustine's philosophy is a unified one. It is non-dualistic. Living in integrity, to borrow from the title of Professor Laura Westra's book, requires but one set of principles, not two. The specific material conditions of each nature are to be valued and taken seriously. According to Augustine, the destiny of a human being for life with God after death is neither achieved by an abstraction from matter, nature, or the body, nor hindered by them *per se.* On the contrary, it requires a genuine love and appreciation of nature in and for its own sake, as well as with respect to our use and needs. A well-ordered love enables one to live in the world of nature guided by good judgment or prudence, while preserving and enhancing resources by moderation in their use. This presupposes the proper use of human freedom.It also requires the development of a sensibility for which human beings have an innate capacity, but which needs time and adequate context for its realization. It is in early childhood experience that such a sensibility, an interest and delight in, and an appreciation of, the life-world takes its deepest root, but it requires development of virtue for its realization.

This appreciation or contemplation of the true nature of things belongs to the common good according to Augustine. The defining characteristic of a common good is that the greater the number who participate in it, the more it is available to all. Thomas Merton, grasping the import of this contemplative attitude within the City of God, calls such contemplation a *social activity*, because it creates a "common bond of love for a common object of contemplation," and in this way generates a kind of society.[30] This offers a most interesting and fruitful concept both theoretically and practically with respect to the environment. Those who possess or acquire this contemplative awareness of the goodness of nature make such vision and insight available to others whom it can nurture and guide in practical decision-making.

Finally, in Augustine's view, such contemplative insight and the environmental ethics that flows from it, both with respect to its understanding and articulation, and with respect to its practical implementation, is possible only through the development of human character and virtue. Thus, a theoretical articulation of an environmental ethic has little chance of implementation or influence without its corollary, an adequate level of character in those to whom it is directed.

Notes

1. Augustine of Hippo, *City of God* 11.25, trans. D. S. Wiesen, Loeb Classical Library (1968), v. 3, 526-29.

2. *Augustine, Fathers of the Church: Writings of Saint Augustine; Saint Augustine: City of God* 12.5, trans. Gerald G. Walsh, Daniel J. Honan, and Grace Monahan (Wash-

ington, D.C.: Catholic University of America Press, 1952-1954), reprinted in *Philosophical Classics*, 2nd ed., Baird and Kaufmann, eds, v. 2, 110.

3. *City of God* 8.8, Loeb (1968), v. 3, 39-43.

4. Saint Augustine, *The Catholic and Manichaean Ways of Life* (De moribus ecclesiae catholicae et de moribus Manichaeorum), trans. Donald A. Gallagher and Idella J. Gallagher, in *Fathers of the Church* (Washington, D.C.: Catholic University of America Press, 1966), 2.1.65.See also 2.2.2-3: 66-67.

5. Gallagher, 2.17.55-56: 102-04.

6. Gallagher, 2.17.57: 104.

7. Gallagher, 2.18.65-66: 109-11.

8. Gallagher, 2.13.29: 84-85.

9. Gallagher, 2. 17.63: 108.

10. *City of God* 12.4 (trans. P. Levine), Loeb (1966), v. 4, 19.

11. *De moribus Manichaeorum* 2.16.58, Gallagher 105.

12. Gallagher, 2.17.62: 107-08.

13. Gallagher, 2.19.68: 111-12.

14. Gallagher, 2.19.68; 111-12.

15. *City of God* 8.6, Loeb (1968), v. 3, 31-35.

16. *City of God* 12.4 (trans. P. Levine): "Cuius ordinis decus nos propterea non delectat, quoniam parti eius pro condicione nostrae mortalitatis intexti universum, cui particulae quae nos offendunt satis apte decenterque convenient, sentire non possumus," Loeb Classical Library, v. 4, 18-19.

17. Levine, 19-21.The idea of nature as constituting a whole woven fabric offers a fruitful principle for environmental ethics.

18. Levine, 21.

19. *City of God*, 19.13, in *Fathers of the Church: Writings of Saint Augustine*, trans. Gerald G. Walsh, Daniel J. Honan, and Grace Monahan, reprinted in *Philosophical Classics*, 2nd ed., v. 2, 119.

20. Walsh, v. 2, 119.

21. *De moribus Manichaeorum* 2.17.54, *Augustini Opera Omnia* (Parisiis: Apud Gaume Fratres, Bibliopolis, 1836), 1186; trans. Donald A. and Idella J. Gallagher (above, note 4), 102.

22. Augustine, *Eighty-Three Different Questions*, trans. David L. Mosher (Washington, D.C.: Catholic University of America Press, 1977), Q. 13: 43-44.

23. "Augustine does not make an essential difference between the three Latin words, amor, caritas, and dilectio. All three can be good or evil according to the object loved.The opinion of some authors who thought there was a distinction between them, and especially that dilectio had a positive meaning and amor a negative one, is rejected by Augustine Civ. Dei 14.7 (Tarsicius J. Van Bavel, *Augustine through the Ages: An Encyclopedia*, Allan D. Fitzgerald, O.S.A., ed. Foreword by Jaroslav Pelikan [Grand Rapids, Mich.: William B. Eerdman, 1999] s.v. "Love," 509).

24. Thomas Merton, Introduction to *The City of God*, trans. Marcus Dods (New York: Modern Library, 1950), xiii.

25. *City of God* 11.16 (trans. Dods), 360.

26. Dods, 360.

27. *City of God* 19.14.

28. *City of God* 11.25 (trans. D. S.Wiesen), Loeb (1968), vol. 3.

29. Other thinkers in their own contexts echo similar points. Thomas Aquinas notes that the virtues, e.g., justice, grow and mature under the influence of charity. In the twentieth century, Max Scheler in his essay "Love and Hate" writes: "Love is that movement wherein every concrete individual object that possesses value achieves the highest value compatible with its nature and ideal vocation; or wherein it attains the ideal state of value intrinsic to its nature." *The Nature of Sympathy*, trans. Peter Heath (New Haven, Conn.: Yale University Press, 1954; Archon Books, 1970), 161.

In principle, Augustine's approach breathes a sense that informs the wisdom figures in the Native American tradition with respect for living things under the Great Spirit. Often viewed as mere primitive superstition, the rituals involving prayer to the spirits of the buffalo or the whales that were hunted for food and other needs speak to their awareness of the kinship of living things and their appreciation not only for what these animals provide for human life, but for their own distinctive being. Augustine shares this fundamental appreciation of, and joy in, nature, along with a keen awareness of the interdependence of living things.

30. Thomas Merton, introduction to *The City of God* (trans. Dods), xiv.

II. Medieval Christianity

8

PERCEPTIONS OF NATURE IN POLISH MEDIEVAL AND EARLY RENAISSANCE WRITINGS

Teresa Kwiatkowska

The Concept of *Nature*: Some Linguistic Reflections

The word *nature* that generally designates the totality of things existing around us stems directly from the Latin *natura* derived from the word *nasci* "to be born." Wolfgang Schadewaldt points out that it originally belonged to the vocabulary of the farmer and the breeder, who used the term *natura* in a concrete way to designate "the uterine orifice of a female quadruped."[1] The word *natura* was used quite early to translate the Greek *phýsis.* The term *phýsis* comes from the Greek verb *phýo,* which meant something like "bring forth" and "make to grow," mainly within the botanical realm where the trees grew branches, leaves, flowers and fruits, or the zoological ambit where animals grew hair, horns, wool, and wings. The noun *phýsis* designates the process, the becoming, the flourishing of a thing, and also its "being." The characteristic of growth is that it comes from something, from a common origin, like a uterine orifice. Later, *phýsis* was extended to the totality of the entire *kosmos* that emerges not only as an order (*kósmos)* but also as a living growth striving from form to form.

Contemporary Polish makes a distinction between the idea of cosmological nature (*natura naturans, origo rerum, lex naturae*) and that of *przyroda*—the natural environment (*natura naturata*). The first term refers to the awareness of the universe as an external entity to be comprehended intellectually. It designates the creative origin of everything which is and which reveals the constitution of the thing brought forth. It includes the idea of the human being, a microcosm intimately connected with the universe, a macrocosm. The term *przyroda* comes close to the modern definition of biota, i.e., flora and fauna together, or of all the living organisms at a given location. The historical relationship between the two terms is not clear-cut.

In the wake of numerous human migrations during prehistoric times and the practical absence of literary records, it is difficult to trace accurately the linguistic roots of any concept. Apparently, Poles were the latest of many Indo-European groups who have settled on the territory of present-day Poland. As a result, it is quite impossible to isolate an ethnic core of their culture. The linguistic picture is equally chaotic. Polish, one of the West Slavic groups of languages, is the only surviving "Lechitic" language. It developed in the period between the sixth and the ninth centuries, mainly from the dialects of Great and Little Poland. Non-Slavic loans, i.e., Iranian, Russian, German and Czech, had been inherited through Common Slavic—the ancestor of all Slavic languages. From the Middle Ages Polish was in constant and intimate contact with a number of other languages, borrowing heavily from Latin.

The word *przyroda* evolved from the monosyllabic root *ród, ródź, rod(z), radz*—to give birth to, to produce, bring forth (crops). The prefix, *przy, pri (npu)* that bears the meaning of "to," "toward," "at," and "near," often expresses addition, attachment, adjustment, application (to), or agreement. The related Russian word *priroda* means the totality of all things which are born, i.e., are created or brought into being, and a "set of inborn" (natural) attributes of any given thing. Related Czech and Serbo-Croatian words are borrowed from Russian. While in Russian, Czech and Serbo-Croatian the term *priroda* (природа, příroda, priroda) has the double meaning of nature as the *physical world* and nature as *character*, in the Polish language it designates only living creatures, crops and minerals: namely, the physical universe. The notion of "bearing, bringing forth" is reflected in a semantically wide group of derivatives, many of which share the meaning of being born or created together like a family (*ród*): clan, nation, kind, kin, fellow countryman, parents, siblings, as also natural science, etymology, nation, people, and regeneration.

In the Slavic languages this root supplanted the Indo-European root that can be found in Latin *gignere* (*genere*) to beget, *nasci* (*gnasci*) to be born (English nation, native, nature) and *genus*—birth, stock, kind, sort (English genus, gender, generation, regeneration). *Przy-rodz-enie—prirozeni* (Latin *natura* and Greek *physis*) has a secondary meaning "genitals," i.e., the place through which birth happens and from which the succession of births proceeds.

However, some etymological sources indicate that the root *ród (rod)* present in the word *przy-rod-a* differs completely from the verb *rość* (to be born).[2] The Old Slavic terms *ród* (family, clan) *poród, and rodzić* (to give birth) did not have any physiological connotations. The Slavs, according to Brückner, had no separate expression that would translate the Latin term *nasci.* Originally, the word *ród* (*rod)* designated no more than lucky occurrence, gain, increase, or wellbeing, in the sense of material success. Hence, in the Polish language trees and cereals "give birth." In the twelfth and thirteenth centuries *rod* still designated good luck and the one who bestowed it. Equally, *bog* (god) signified wealth and the one who handed out happiness. With time the terms *rod and rodzina (family)* acquired the meaning of growth or enlargement of a family.

In Polish literary texts of the sixteenth century the Latin word *natura* was compatible with the Polish term *przyrodzenie.* The later had the following meanings: the world (*mundus*), natural laws and activities (*leges naturae, quae naturae propria sunt*). It also meant the natural vital power to create live organisms. In the old Polish language the term *przy-rod-zenie* also designated: human nature, its inclinations (*ingenium*) and its individual characteristics; one of the four elements—building blocks of the entire cosmos and human beings; all earthly and heavenly creatures (including angels); and finally genus (species), sex, and kinship, among others.[3]

Modern use of the term *przyroda* (English nature) entirely discarded the meanings of the Latin (and Polish) word *natura* that were related to the creation and constitution of human beings. Nowadays, its definition includes the totality of the organic and inorganic world, the holistic concept including plants, animals and all physical and chemical components of the environment.

First Visions of Nature

In the seventh and eight centuries, one branch of the Western Slavs, called afterwards *Polanie* or "people of the open fields," settled itself between the Odra and Vistula rivers, founding the nation of Poles. In the earliest record dated approximately 965 C.E. Ibrahim-Ibn-Jacub wrote that (Western) Slavs "*Inhabited the richest limits of land suitable for settlements.*"

In terms of geographic and climatic opportunities that encourage or inhibit human settlement, Poland's location provided many advantages and some obstacles. Its continental climate, with its marked seasons, gave strong summer sunshine without the extremes of summer drought. Hail, winter blizzards, snow damage and spring floods were practically unknown. Extensive forests provided excellent wind cover. The extremely rich native fauna included tarpan, bears, bison and wolves. At the end of the thirteenth century Godzislaw Baszko in *The Chronicle of Great Poland* wrote: "When Lech . . . (the first legendary founder of the Polish state) was crossing vast forests, where presently stretches the Polish kingdom, having come at last to an extremely charming place, with unusually fertile soil, full of fish and game . . . he set up his tent."

Studies of primitive agriculture have concluded that the high medieval period benefited from a more advantageous climate than any time before or since. Accordingly, research in the Karkonosze Mountains has shown that the tree line was 600 feet higher in the fourteen century than in the twentieth, and that apricots and melons grew in valleys where they are no longer. In 1596, Sebastian Klonowicz wrote: "Fair Poland nestles on a fertile sod, / Content as though within the lap of God. . . . Thy fields supply Thy very need."

Nonetheless, it is difficult to explore earlier perceptions of nature, in view of climatic changes, waves of colonization, patterns of settlement and cultural variations. Harsh winters, poor communications, and great distances resulted in the isolation of widely separated communities. The cultural life of Poland under the rule of the Polanian Dynasty (from a legendary past to the recorded history of 1370) is poorly known, thanks to the scarcity of source material. Society was overwhelmingly illiterate. Popular arts were either oral or ephemeral. Artifacts and writings that have survived are mainly religious in nature. The Latin language maintained effective prevalence until the end of the thirteenth century. The earliest written evidence of the Polish language is found in a medieval document written in Latin, the papal "Bull of Gniezno" of 1136. This bull contains 410 Polish names of persons, places and tribes. The ancient *Roczniki*, the chronicles of Gallus Anonimus and of Kadlubek, along with numerous hagiographies, all belong to the universal Latin tradition. The Chronicles of Gaul (Anonymous) glorified the historical past and offered evidence for the expansion of the concept of *nature,* partly as a result of the expansion of a kingdom, and partly as the outcome of the transforming economy. The anonymous author immortalized the twelfth century conquering of the Baltic Sea, and proudly wrote:

> Pisces salsos et foetentes apportabant alii.
> Palpitantes et recentes nunc apportant filii.
> Civitates invadebant patres nostri primitus
> Hii procellas non verentur neque maris sonitus.
> Agitabant patres nostri cervos, apros, capreas,
> Hii venantur monstra maris et opes aequoreas.

Opus Naturae Est Opus Intelligentiae

Since Poland did not possess its own university, young men in search of higher education were obliged to travel abroad, especially to France and Italy. The names of several scholars, such as the historian Martin the Pole in Paris or the physician Nicholas the Pole of Montpellier, bear witness to the cultural connections between Poland and the West. The best known of them was Witelo or Vitellon (1230-1280), a Silesian philosopher who worked with Thomas Aquinas and William of Moerbecke. His essential treatise on the science of optics, the *Perspectiva,* was considered the best and most complete medieval work on the physical properties of light.

Witelo's confidence in experimental and mathematical method influenced his aesthetic view of nature. He contrasted the beauty of nature with the beauty of art and wrote: "Figura etiam facit pulchritudinem. Unde artificiata bene figurate videntur pulchra, magis autem opera naturae." (148) Witelo contemplated the divine intelligence embedded in the natural world, and he enthusiastically cherished its real beauty. His work, free of any neoplatonic influence, showed sensibility to the beauty of the natural world along with a desire to explain all its fascinating phenomena. At the same time, he found art unable to capture the subtle beauty of the natural world. Reflecting on the colorful rainbow, he wrote: "Nec possunt pictores tales colores plenarie simulare." (X, 67) Even the most brilliant human being cannot reproduce the beauty of the divine creation. Witelo's fascination with the phenomena of light reemerged in the verses of the sixteenth century poet Sęp Szarzyński. Nature and its beauty are inseparably related, and both derive from and reveal their transcendent Creator. The beautiful nature of the universe guides the believer to glance through the miserable condition of human existence into the invisible God in his visible Creation. *Vanitas vanitatum et omnia vanitas.*[4]

The philosophy of nature that was developed within the scholastic environment of the Jagiellonian University (established in Krakow in 1364) emphasized the practical rather than cognitive significance of theological investigation. "Rationes theologicae sunt quaedam medicinae," wrote Mateusz of Krakow. Regardless of the dominance of scholastic thought until the late Renaissance, the fifteenth century witnessed the further expansion of empirical studies of nature. It was mainly concentrated on a level of perception found in mathematics and the natural sciences. The economy of nature was a perpetual pre-established harmony defined by the divine intelligence. At the same time, the science of nature quite often responded to a variety of practical demands, such as how to deal with plagues, smallpox and other diseases.

In the early Renaissance, perceptions of nature in formal Polish philosophy still have rigid, scholastic traits. However, at the level of scientific investigation, the question of change figured prominently in two areas of particular importance: the astronomic theory of Nicolas Copernicus (1473-1543) and the growing dominion of the Polish language as a language of theology, philosophy and literature. The new astronomic theory transformed the picture of cosmic nature and of human beings. *De Revolutionibus* bonds together the aesthetic view of the universe and its moral significance. The stars we observe and the beauty of creation are not just to be wondered at and praised: they bring humans closer to the perfection of the divine creator.

The Bounty of Earth: What do you want from us, Lord, for your lavish gifts?

The victory of the Polish language brought descriptions of nature closer to people. Through the translations of the Bible or poetic psalms, the visions of God and his creation permeated the national cultures. The beauty of universal nature unambiguously spoke of its divine source. It revealed itself to human beings outwardly, it manifested its radiance, splendor, and sweetness, so that we might eventually know it for what it has always been: the Beauty of God. The beautiful pictures of nature in all its movements, in its power, in compelling descriptions of majestic mountains and wide plains, had an exceptional appeal. They expressed the universalisality of the human reality, of our emotions and experiences. Translated in 1579 by the brilliant Polish poet Jan Kochanowski, David's Psalms brought closer to popular culture the Creator and His work: the cosmos of nature and the microcosm of human personality.

God resides in changeless and timeless space, the mortal being dwells on Earth like grass, like a flower. In contrast with *aevum,* the cyclical time of nature, *tempus*, the time of human life, is linear and irreversible. The human creature is but a walker on the earth where God is *arbiter naturae*. "In vain man cares here about anything. . . . All this will pass away like the field of grass."[5] Biblical symbols of earth, shadow, grass, flower and wind result from the most elementary life experiences and observance of nature. The translation, called the "miracle" of the Polish culture,[6] poetically blended the original into the earthly landscape of humans whose daily lives were intimately related to nature.

Kochanowski celebrated in song the beauty of the landscape and the joys of rural life. The countryside and rural activities, measured by a peaceful flow of seasons, became the favorite artistic subject for poets and writers of the early Renaissance. They extolled the life and occupations of the ideal country nobleman, their ideal of material and spiritual life. Familiar with nature and inspired by its luxuriant manifestations, the poets painted original pictures of the world, presenting it with simplicity and sincere fascination.

> What do you want from us, Lord for your lavish gifts? . . .
> You are the Lord of the whole world, You built the sky,
> And embroidered it splendidly with gold stars high.
> Of the earth untraversed You lay the foundation,
> And cover it with rich vegetation.
> By your own command the sea stands within its shores
> And is fearful to leap over its assigned course.
> Inexhaustible waters enrich the rivers,
> Bright day and shadowy night keep their hours diverse.

Kochanowski praised the invisible God through the marvels of his creation—the work of art fashioned by *Deus artifex.* He glorified nature, its harmony, and its breathtaking beauty. Kochnowski referred to the "wreaths made from ears of corn," wine and apples of various kinds, yet these gifts, like the spring flowers and the idleness of winter, focus on the admiration of harmony, not the recounting of beneficial crops. Furthermore, he entirely discards the idea that the world and all the wonders of nature had been created for humans: "as it is all Yours, / Whatever in this world man names as his resource." Human beings are but a part of the natural order and subject to its governing laws. The Everlasting Creator assures the cosmological and terrestrial order, offering us his lavish gifts and benefactions, which have no limits.

The Other Comprehension of Nature

Perceiving nature meant different things to a person whose life was daily influenced and determined by confrontation with the natural world, and to the theologian who lived within the monastery walls and dealt with nature intellectually. The connotation of the term was different for those within their *own* nature, and for someone from *outside* the place. When we investigate the history of the concept of nature and its significance throughout the centuries, we should study not only the history of the idea and its perceptions in philosophy, theology and science. We have to look upon the daily life experiences and habits of peasants. When we talk about environmental history we cannot concentrate on the great names from the history of philosophy, religion or literature. The nonarticulated experience of nature might have influenced a far greater number of people than did the statements of philosophers, theologians and scientists.

However, medieval people had to make a living. Between the collapse of the ancient order and the rise of late medieval urban civilizations, people were necessarily "close to nature" in a Europe that was largely covered by untamed forests and wilderness. They had to cope with new and often-hostile environments, to fight wild animals and the everpresent threat of disease, at least in various regions of medieval Poland. The common people often regarded wilderness as distinctly undesirable, an asocial place teeming with spirits. The existence of forest spirits was for many an indication that forests were "ugly," untamed wilderness. The forest and the wetlands, the large lakes and the wild animals, were all potential sources of terror as well as of harvest.

During the early Middle Ages the custodians of learning, monks and ecclesiastics, were generally indifferent and suspicious of pagan interpretations of the natural world. In Poland, as in various parts of Europe, the gap was partly filled by the literature of practical and empirical tradition. Alongside the subtle formulations of poets and philosophers the peculiar zoology of popular bestiaries seemed strangely out of place. Yet, it addressed the relations between natural and supernatural, between human being and other living things. Foremost among the practical arts was medicine: the principal repository of biological knowledge. A significant herbal literature was developed that was most often designed for practical purposes. Recent research indicates that the physicians and healers of the early Middle Ages were not mindless copyists of the traditional sources, but competent practitioners who had to deal with many northern European plants that were previously unknown. Herbal literature contains a good number of accurate observations; indeed, many plants have actually been identified from them.

The strange mixture of facts and fancy in the bestiaries and herbal literature had an inherent purpose: to instruct readers on a variety of different levels. Portraying marvels of nature rich in symbolism and mythology, the articles on animals had moral or theological explanations. Practically everything written in this vein has a symbolic, allegorical sense hidden beneath the literal. The enormous popularity of these tales throughout the Middle Ages suggest the extent to which they provided the "guide" to the natural world, and pointed to the spiritual world beyond it.

The concept of *exemplum* derives from the classic art of rhetoric. It possessed its own literary expression as *commemoratio* in the form of *narratio* or *brevitas.* The expansion of Christianity made the exemplum the most popular medium of Christian education. As the Church fathers said, "Verba docent, exempla trahunt." Popular in Europe, the exemplum played a significant role in Poland. As everywhere else, some medical knowledge could be traced to a number of exempla mainly intended not to teach practical knowledge but to give a moral lesson. Information about the natural world was not very abundant, and much less precise than information about medicine. The audience and the priests themselves instinctively learned the laws of physics while discussing the stars that seemed to grow bigger when looked at through the clouds. Equally the sun rising above the horizon and setting down gave the impression of being apparently bigger than the one observed during the day. Mikołaj of Błonie's collection of 131 sermons, *Sermones de tempore,* written in 1431, contained 245 exempla. The exempla described seawater as salty, greasy, heavy and easy to sail on. He mentioned the other peculiar property of seawater, namely its capacity to ignite fire instead of extinguishing it. The effect was a probable result of the presence of sodium that, in small amounts, brightens the flame. However, all this information was quite a *novum* to Polish listeners. They were not a nation of sailors like their northern neighbors, indeed not even acquainted with the sea. The exempla contained the following practical, if perplexing, gardening information: watering with blood was recommended to keep roses red the whole year around.

Exempla provided a mine of information on the animal world, including species unknown in Polish territory. The fables of unicorns and dragons were the most popular among the collected works of Polish authors like Jacob of Paradyż (1442-1464). Before judging Polish medieval listeners naïve, one should look at the huge bone recovered from the "dragon's" cave that hangs over the entrance to the Wawel cathedral in Krakow. Knowledge about exotic species of animals like lions, elephants or various mysterious birds originated from narratives composed for illiterates or from written bestiaries like *Fizjologus* or *Acta martyrum.*

The descriptions of the animal world are vivid ones, with many detailed accounts of violent relationships amongst species, and only a few depicting a symbiotic bond. Mikołaj of Blonie provided various exempla of the coexistence of humans and animals, finding animals more caring than their human counterparts. Courteous behavior was a distinguishing feature of elephants, that help people wandering in a desert. The female wolf would take care of an abandoned human baby, and the lion would not attack the kneeling homo sapiens. Numerous exempla elaborate on the dog's *ethos* as a faithful friend of humans.[7] A dog and a horse had very particular functions in a human's life; the horse was a companion that shared a destiny with the rider. It had a name and individuality. The dog was a friend and a guard till the death of its owner. Quite often the animal revenged his death. This perception of these two closest companions of humans has persisted through many centuries. None of these animals was considered simply somebody's pet. Nothing certain can be alleged about the human treatment of animals due to the absence of such exempla given by Polish authors. Somewhere along the Mediterranean lies the frontier beyond which the animal loses its divine status, something characteristic of ancient Egypt. It even ceases to be a human being's companion, as it used to be to the desert fathers.

Wilderness and Natural Resources

The first known Polish state (ninth through twelfth centuries) covered a country of imposing wilderness typical of its geographical conditions. And the shapes taken by that wilderness had been manifold. Magnificent, dense temperate woods of mixed conifer and broad-leaved forest covered nine-tenths of the territory, broken by natural pastures and fertile fields. Nature had been an omnipresent phenomenon. The survival of most inhabitants depended on the success of their agriculture. Therefore, the practical use of natural resources led the way to the knowledge of native Polish wilderness. In many historical records the idea of wilderness is that of a resource, in the physical sense of the raw materials it contains.

The first medieval chronicles of Gall (Anonymous, XII century) portrayed Polish natural resources as a real treasure any other country would envy. Physical and biological nature (*przyroda*) seemed to be immeasurable and infinite—at least to Joannis Dlugossii (Jan Dlugosz) in the second part of the fifteen century, when he was writing his geographic and biological supplement *Chorographia* to his great historical magnum opus *Annales Seu Cronicae Incliti Regni Polonias.* The supplement, regarded as outstanding in its own right, described all the natural resources known to the author over the whole of Polish territory.

The *Annals* give a vivid picture of seven main rivers and of major lakes. They provide a very accurate description of the climatic conditions of Poland: harsh climate, rough nature, cold skies, cold strong winds, long lasting winters. Dlugossi also stressed the advantages of Poland's geographical position. Poland, he wrote, is known by the absence of earthquakes, with their disastrous consequences of wrecked cities and villages, and broken mountains. Neither is the country frequented by floods. He emphasized the absence of "poisonous nature," so disagreeable to human beings in many other places. "In quo et felicitas generis Slawonici, quod tam optimas terras sortitum fuit . . . nulle enim terre orbis preter Indiam, quam he a Slawis / primum possesse aurum, argentums, sal, ferrum, cuprum et cetera metalla, que mortals prima ducunt."[8]

These arguments, proudly describing the assets of Polish physical nature, would be repeated numerous times in the future. Dlugossi and his predecessors noticed only wild animals that were valuable for food, clothing and trade. He mentioned the Polish bison, wild boar, deer, moose, elk, beaver, and fur-bearing animals like sable, ermine, mink and fox. While the Polish climate prevented the growth of olives and vineyards, the quality of beer made of wheat and barley was superb, according to the chronicles. He also mentioned another biological phenomenon: the characteristics of resin, the product of the pine trees that in its solid state becomes like silex, with its capacity to start a flame.

Wilderness is invariably depicted as a mighty, unconquered force. In many chronicles, we find evidence of the harsh part it played in molding the lives of those it touched. Natural phenomena such as floods, hail, plagues and droughts, frequently mentioned by the Polish chroniclers, were the doings of nature itself, not a result of the human activity—at least according to the chroniclers. The first ecological thought concerning human impact on the natural environment appeared in the sixteenth century, together with the first legal conservation efforts.[9]

Natural phenomena have always been important in the matter of their descriptions, their interpretation and their meaning. This was particularly so during the Renaissance, when interest in them accelerated. We can observe the systematization and classification of data, and the growing interest in the significance of the environment. This brings to the fore the relevance of national nature, and shows a kind of positive self-identification with one's *own* nature. Representing national nature in this way is to be distinguished from the descriptions of other people's nature.

The posture of pride is clear throughout the writings: feelings of satisfaction and joy at the sight of the richness of the native physical and biological world. In fact, Polish flora, fauna and all the other natural resources had long been a cause of pride for those who describe them. Faith in nature was connected with a conviction that nature could never be destroyed. Worry about the natural environment came after the sixteen century. Polish nature made the kingdom's landscape very attractive and its economy self-sufficient. There was enough food and building materials. Blocks found everywhere in the countryside had been used as a primary building material in the construction of churches and fortresses. "Regio Polonica fecunda frugibus, amena fructibus, deliciosa piscibus, sapida lactiniis, calmosa venacionibus, copiosa armentis et gregibus, dulcis mellibus, comoda equis, referta altibus, dives ferro et plumbo, gloriosa cera, crassa buitro" (Dlugossi, HPI/9).

The chronicles of J. Dlugossi contain almost all the knowledge of the natural world of his times and its evaluation. His monumental history of Poland was based on extensive geographical and economical studies and research. He and his fellowmen celebrated nature as a source of national identity, and as the basis of national power. Nature was emotionally and politically charged, and never detached from questions of nation and identity. The vision of nature in the background of literary works and of chronicles can be seen as symbolic of the good and ideal life in harmony with a divine cosmological order.

Only a few of the many possible concepts of nature have been discussed in this paper. Polish medieval and early Renaissance writings reflect the immense variety of perceptions of nature. The poets turned their attention to the divine beauty of the natural world and to the question of a human existence in accord with the rhythms of nature. The succession of pictures and poetic images gives expression to the bounty of nature as the instrument of God. There was an elaborate correspondence between the little world of a human being and the greater world around him. The chronicles exemplified the pragmatic view of the natural world as a reservoir of resources determined by political and economic necessities of use. Likewise, the attitudes toward nature embodied in Polish tradition are irreducible to any simple expression. However, until the sixteenth century, the poetic expressions and the detached descriptions of landscapes both shared the sense of wonder at God's workmanship in face of the untamed bounty of Polish nature. They all felt the splendor of the extensive woodlands, vast plains, rivers of life, and mountains, as well as that of cultivated nature.

Notes

1. Wolfgang Schadewaldt, "The Concept of Nature and Technique according to the Greeks," *Research in Philosophy and Technology* 2 (1979): 159-171.

2. Aleksander Brückner, *Słownik etymologiczny jezyka polskiego, wiedza* Powszechna (Warszawa: Wiedza Powszechna, 1927, 1993), 459-460.

3. Samuel Bogumil Linde, *Słownik etymologiczny języka polskiego, tom 4* (Warszawa: PIW, 1858, 1910), 676.

4. Andrzej Borowski, J.S. Gruchała, *Lektury Polonistyczne, średniowiecze- renesans-barok* (Kraków: Towarzystwo autorow I Wydawcow Prac Naukowyh "Universitas," 1997), 191-200.

5. Jan Kochanowski, "On human life," *Polish Literature from the Middle Ages to the End of the Eighteenth Century. A Bilingual Anthology*, Selected and Translated by Michael J. Mikos (Warszawa: Constans, 1999), 283-284.

6. Anna Kaminska, *Twarze ksiegi* (Warszawa: PAX, 1981).

7. Teresa Szostek, *Exemplum w polskim średniowieczu* (Warsawa: Instytut Badań Literackich, 1997).

8. Joannis Dlugossi Senioris Canonici Cracoviensis Opera Omnia (Cracow: PWN, 1863-87), Jan Dlugosz, Roczniki czyli Kroniki slawnego Krolestwa Polskiego, J. Dabrowki, eds. (Warsaw: PWN, 1960), 69.

9. Teresa Dunin-Wąsawicz, "Człowiek i woda w średniowiecznej Europie. Stan i pespektywy badań." In Barbara Kuźnicka, ed., *Ekologia człowieka. Historia i współczesność* (Warszawa: IHN PAN, 1995), 47-75.

Bibliography

Galla Kronika Xiega II, 28, *De expeditione in urbem Coloberg facta.* Warsaw: Monumenta Poloniae Historica i, 1968. 447.

Herman, Louis J. (compiler and editor). *A Dictionary of Slavic Word Families.* New York: Columbia University Press, 1975.

Jarosz, Jan Chryzostom. "Zrodla mysli estetycznej Witelona z Polski." *Acta Mediaevalia* VIII. Lublin: Katoliki Uniwersytet Lubelski KUL, 1995. 11-43.

Kwirina Handke. *Rozważaniai analizy językoznawcze.* Warszawa: Instytut Slawistyki PAN, Slawistyczyny Ośrodek Wydawniczy, 1997.

Kowalski Tadeusz (ed.). *Relacja Ibrahim Ibn Jakuba z podrozy do krajow slowianskich w prxekladzie Al Bekriego.* Cracow: Polska Akademia Umiejetnosci. 1946.

Klonowicz, Sebastian Fabian. *Fils* lines 181-84, S. Hrabec (ed.). Wroclaw: Wydawnictwa Zakladu Narodowego im. Ossolinslich, 1950.

Slownik Staropolski, tom VII. Polska akademia Nauk, Zaklad Narodowy Imienia Ossolinskich, 1973-77.

Wolkonsky, Catherine A. and Marianna A. Poltoratzky (compilers). *Handbook of Russian Roots.* Columbia University Press: New York, 1961, 1976.

Vitellonis Thuringopoloni *Opticae libri decem* Instaurati, figuris novis illustrati atque aucti infinitisque erroribus quibus antea scatebant expurgati a Federico Risnero. Basilae: Officina Episcopiana, 1572.

9

NATURE AND RESTORATION IN WOLFRAM VON ESCHENBACH'S *PARZIVAL*

Rosmarie Thee Morewedge

Introduction

Wolfram von Eschenbach's *Parzival* was written at a time when very different conceptions of nature and approaches to nature came into literary consciousness not only in the clerical Latin learned literature, but also in the courtly vernacular literature in Germany. Wolfram's epic, completed around 1210, gives voice to these traditions and new conceptions, showing how new paradigms could coexist with apparently contradictory established conceptualizations. The complexities involved in these at times contradictory conceptions will not be resolved in this essay; it is possible, however, to see them as perspectives informing different levels of meaning and in the development of different figures that assume importance in the work.

In his work *De civitate Dei* Augustine rejected the classical investigation of nature which had studied nature for its own sake; comparing God to an artisan, Augustine viewed nature as the tool of God, designed to reveal God's purpose for man. He proceeded from Romans 1:20, which showed that through visible creatures human beings could see the invisible things of God and could understand His eternal power and Godhead.[1] Although he recognized dangers in natural theology, clergy and laymen alike could read this Book of Nature, he held, which was to reveal the path to God. The Book of Nature did not put a premium on literacy the way the Bible, the Word of God, did. Nature did not exist for its own sake, but for man's salvation.[2] He rejected, for instance, the pagan idea of earth as a mother, affirming instead that the earth is the work of God.[3] Later thinkers, such as Hrabanus, attempted to explore the imago mundi in encyclopaedic terms, advocating the study of nature as an aid for the interpretation of scripture (exegesis) as well as a way of finding in this Book of Nature God's designs for creation (res creata) in a symbolic interpretation. The scientific study of nature was not to be conducted systematically for its own sake, but according to the sequence outlined in the Hexaemeron and in the service of a greater purpose, since simple curiositas was regarded as a vice by the church fathers. In the tenth century the West received through Spain translations of Arabic scientific works, mainly astronomical, astrological and medical, which reflected a mechanistic, deterministic view of the world and a view of nature which saw it as operating according to strict laws of its own.[4] Nature, according to this pagan Arab tradition, was not held to be the tool of God, voluntas Dei, but an organism that had its own autonomy and operated according to its own laws. Thinkers of the twelfth century in the West attempted to reconcile the pagan study of nature as an autonomous pursuit abiding by determined laws with the study of the deeper meaning of these laws in the cosmos. Sturlese points out that in connection with a corpus of works linked to Hermes Trismegistus the study of hermetic texts was carried out with the express objective of observing nature, controlling it and intervening in it.[5] The Aristotelian scientific knowledge that came to the West in the twelfth century as part of the renaissance of the twelfth century and which flourished at the universities, dealt with content in a scientific, rational way, but even more importantly, with scientific, rational procedure and method. While the orthodox denounced the pagan scientific tradition, thinkers like Albertus Magnus made the attempt to keep philosophy apart from theology in terms of methods and goals. A new component was added: personal observation of nature, evident in texts such as a book of Frederick II (1194-1250) on hunting (de arte venandi cum avibus).[6] In her *Physica* Hildegard von Bingen, too, demonstrated a knowledge of nature that appreciated religious perspectives but addressed these in a secular framework of natural phenomena apart from religious questions.[7] Rudimentary forms of experimentation with natural phenomena begin. Although the experimental method is not yet advocated, it is possible to see a new relationship to nature emerging in these different approaches. It is evident from these observations and from other writings that there is no monolithic, unified vision of nature in the Middle Ages.[8]

In Wolfram von Eschenbach's epic *Parzival*, completed around 1210, affairs touching on knighthood and courtly life occupy center stage, moving religion, nature and other human concerns apparently off center. While it is not unnatural for a courtly epic to place the concerns of knighthood, such as proper courtly etiquette, ceremony, battle, tournaments, knightly values, correct thought, courtship, courtly love and proper development ahead of noncourtly themes, it is striking that very special functions are assigned to nature throughout the epic. First, I should like to note that instead of being a backdrop or stage for human activity, nature acquires agency, as its signs by themselves become important indicators of meaning; the human interaction with it reflects, as it were, either a distorted relationship on the part of the human being (or of a specific group of people) to the cosmos or one that betrays a developing consciousness of the proper relationship human beings should have to the cosmos. Interestingly, the relationship to nature can almost be termed to some degree individual—albeit not quite yet subjective. To wit: Upon the death of her husband

Gahmuret, who had died in knightly service, Herzeloyde withdraws from the court and knightly activities to the forest, which becomes from her perspective a "walt zer wâste in Soltâne" (P 117,9),[9] a wasteland, even though there are forest meadows with flowers, birds that sing, brooks and fields that are tilled, planted and harvested. Where many would regard this place as the locus amoenus of classical poetry,[10] she experiences it as a site of deprivation from the court and therefore a wasteland. Her growing son Parzival, however, experiences the same site at the same time differently from his mother as a place that confronts him with natural beauty and yearnings that he does not yet understand, although they move him deeply. First, nature's beauty revealed to him through the song of the birds moves Parzival to tears, although he does not understand why. He is moved by their sweetness, but does not understand the message of nature. Secondly, in his progress, I suggest, specifically through his interaction with nature, nature becomes recognized as a path that leads him to a symbolical understanding, though not an articulated understanding, of the cosmos and his place in it. Third, the symbolical revelation or message introduced by nature needs to be completed or articulated through a specific human or divine communication which relates the symbolical, fragmented human understanding to a larger vision that unites God, the human being, nature and civilization. For Parzival this understanding is completed by instruction from an hermit, who, having lived in nature to atone for the sin of his brother, understands this Book of Nature in which God's overarching purpose is revealed on the one hand, but where astrology, astronomy, and medical lore are seen as following their own determined laws on the other. The function of nature, to reveal God to those who are able to read "natural theology", is related in many ways to thinking associated with the twelfth-century renaissance of the School of Chartres initiated by Bernard de Silvestris.[11] Parzival, who learns to understand nature symbolically, completes this understanding through maturation and experience on the one hand and through specific verbal or written instruction he receives from various guiding figures or objects in the romance on the other. In terms of the twelfth century renaissance, Parzival joins, in effect, the list of Bernard's culture heroes of universal history, who exemplify the idea of the development of the perfect man, who is both human and divine.[12]

Other courtly poets and singers of Wolfram's time and before him had used nature in ways that went back to classical topoi cited in Ernst Robert Curtius, *Latin Literature and the European Middle Ages.*[13] If Virgil had made nature a stage for human activities, medieval poets learned to use it as a code. A recurring element of that code is, for instance, the "linden" tree or the lime tree. A lime tree came to stand for spring time, the setting of love—both of courtly love and lower types of love.[14] Similarly, a verger with a well, a meadow and trees stood for the locus amoenus of pastoral poetry. On the other hand, the silva or dark wood (selva oscura) stood for wildness to be feared and avoided, or used as the site of knightly adventures.[15] King Arthur became identified as the conventional May King, the king of Spring love and knightly adventure, even though Arthur, too, returned to the forest regularly for sacral renewal of his kingship.[16]

Parzival, as has been stated, charts a different approach to nature and comes to hold a different view of it. To be sure, there is still the May King Arthur living in eternal spring evoking representational glamour. The Arthurian level of knighthood is a stage of development through which Parzival passes on his quest to achieve the grail. This is expressed symbolically in the "three blood drops" scene. The falcon, symbolizing the role of the lover in courtly poetry,[17] who leaves the Arthurian realm to join Parzival out in the wintry loneliness, (P 281, 24ff.) is linked symbolically to Parzival and in turn links Parzival symbolically with King Arthur's knights. Like the falcon, who leaves but returns of his own volition in perfect freedom, Parzival leaves the Arthurian realm for the wilderness, but returns subsequently to this court. Parzival comes to Arthur's court, is accepted and honored by it, is cursed by Cundrie la surzière, leaves and is reinstated after an absence of more than four and a half years. But, as shall be shown, when Parzival experiences nature, the view that nature is a code, as it is evoked in connection with Arthur, is often subjected to irony.

> Artûs der meienbaere man,
> swâz man ie von dem gesprach,
> zeinen pfinxten daz geschach,
> odr in des meien bluomenzît.
> waz man im süezes luftes gît!
> diz maere ist hie vast undersniten,
> es parriert sich mit snêwes siten. (P 281, 16-24)
>
> [Arthur is the man of May, and whatever has been told about him took place at Pentecost or in the flowering time of May. What fragrance, they say, is in the air around him! But here this tale is cut of double fabric and turns to the color of snow.][18]

In the romance Parzival and around the hero Parzival a deeper structure of meaning emerges that speaks of the need for and possibility of selected individuals, such as members of the grail community and individuals related to it, who become conscious of flaws in human existence in civilization (the courtly life), to learn about an ordered, harmonious relationship between man, nature and God. St. Augustine, Bernard of Clairvaux, and St. Francis, among others, recognized this goal as a possible road for the clergy, who learn to understand and control nature through labor or interaction with it.[19] For them nature becomes the second book, an alternative to the Book of God, in which it is possible to learn to understand God's purpose for man. What is new in the eponymous romance *Parzival*, however, is that Parzival, a knight who errs—as he believes, because of his apparent incorrect courtly training—remedies this incorrect training not by seeking more advanced training in the laws of knighthood, but by withdrawing from the court into nature.[20]

Sol ich durch mîner zuht gebot
hoeren nu der werlte spot,
sô mac sîn râten niht sîn ganz:
mir riet der werde Gurnamanz
daz ich vrävellîche vrâge mite
und immer gein unfuoge strite (P 330 ,1-7)

[If I am to hear the scorn of the world because I obeyed the law of courtesy, then his counsel may not have been wholly wise. It was the noble Gurnemanz who advised me to refrain from impertinent questions and resist all unseemly behavior.]

Parzival blames his behavior not only on the incorrect training in knighthood he received, but also on God, whom he claims to have served faithfully, but whom he charges with not having kept His part of the feudal contract.[21] By withdrawing into nature, however, Parzival enters into an environment that will reveal God gradually to him (Romans 1:20). He interacts with nature and performs positive knightly deeds which are valorized in the hermitages of Trevrizent and Sigune, i.e., in nature that has become sacred space. For instance, actions such as the restoration of Jeschute to her rightful position culminate in his desire to understand the laws of the cosmos. It is significant that Parzival's understanding of nature is shaped through his interaction with a number of lay persons, specifically Sigune and Trevrizent, who, as was mentioned, withdrew from the court into nature.[22] Their space, too, is centered around stones. (In his cell Trevrizent has an altarstone on which a casket rests that was made of a precious stone given to Trevrizent by Parzival's father. Sigune is buried by a mature Parzival under the tombstone.) When Parzival has come to a deeper understanding of knighthood and of God and nature, and when he is able to reverse his failure and respond correctly to human suffering, he shows reverence to the grail stone that becomes his stone and he shows wisdom in his behavior. (E.g., he does not grant the wish of Anfortas to be separated from the grail for one week in order to be put out of his misery; it is then that Parzival becomes the miles medicus.) And it is also important that Parzival's final understanding of the cosmos leads him to become part of a lay community devoted to both religious and courtly service, namely the grail community, modeled in many ways on monastic communities that established the idea that the recreation of ordo in the postlapsarian world involved the recreation of paradise in the wilderness.[23]

The theme of the importance of acquiring a symbolic understanding of nature in Parzival begins with a demonstration of the harm that occurs from the lack of such an understanding. As a child placed into nature, Parzival fails to understand it or his interaction with it. Parzival spends his childhood in nature in (a figurative) paradise,[24] where he is moved by nature, such as the song of the birds, and turns sad at their failure to continue to sing when he shoots them. (P 118) He clearly lacks the understanding to interpret his emotions correctly. Soltane is not a paradise, since people labor in it, unlike paradise, in which Adam and Eve were free from labor; labor became one of man's punishments following the Fall from grace in paradise, but was recognized by St. Benedict as one of the ways of restoring man to grace.[25] This is not the place to consider Parzival's introduction to knighthood; suffice it to say that he lacks all understanding prior to that event; a symbolic understanding is introduced by his cousin Sigune, who tells him his name and conveys to him the fact that his name has a symbolic meaning., (P 140,16) and by Lady Cunnewère and silent Antanor, who react to his coming to the Arthurian court in highly symbolic ways. At Parzival's entry into the Arthurian court, Lady Cunnewère laughs in an uncontrolled, strange way, in a laugh that was destined for the greatest knight who was to come to the court, and the hitherto silent Antanor suddenly begins to speak for the same reason (P I51,19; 153,25); however, their symbolic understanding is rejected by the Arthurian court and it is not yet understood, except as a censure on the part of the court of Parzival, who is still dressed in fool's garb. After having received instruction and training as a knight, Parzival rides to Pelrapeire, where the conventional setting of the lime tree in front of the court, "a tree trellised for shade", is used as a topos to introduce the topic of a conventional understanding of courtly life and courtly love. After being away from Pelrapeire as a married man, he comes to Munsalvaesche and its marvels, but lacks all understanding of the deeper meaning of what he sees there: a fisher king on a lake who does not fish, a resplendent castle hidden away in the wilderness, a ritual marked by both dazzling radiance and the stench of disease, a bloody lance at whose sight all gathered for the meal weep uncontrollably, a rigidly processional formal meal shared with a man who is carried in lying on a litter. In this strange, marvelous atmosphere, Parzival remains in his thinking on the courtly, conventional surface, without being able to come to a deeper symbolical understanding of what he sees, as P 236, 13-15 states in nuce: Parzival looks on the grail, the "wunsch von pardès" (P 235, 21) the highest paradisical object, yet he thinks only of the coat Repanse de Schoye, the bearer of the grail, had given him. He receives a magical sword with a magical code or magical symbols on the blade, but does not ask about their meaning, assuming that it would be impolite to ask questions and that all that he needed to know would be told to him. The harm his "courtly silence" caused Anfortas and the grail community is conveyed to him later by Sigune (P 255), where he shows deep remorse at not having asked the question of Anfortas. But it is brought home to him only through an introduction of the grotesque, when, at the height of his affirmation at the Arthurian court, (P 308) Cundrie la surzière comes and curses him for not having asked the question by which he would have healed the suffering grail king Anfortas (P 316-17).[26] But instead of seeking higher instruction in knighthood, Parzival rides out into nature with the single purpose of seeking the grail. (P 329) For four-and-one-half years he remains in the wilderness, searching for the grail, until his anger against God begins to turn into the search for a deeper understanding about his relationship to nature, God in nature, and knighthood. The transformation leads to the belief that God will reveal himself through his creature, in this case his dumb horse, and the conviction that he should allow God to lead him through this creature to the place where he would be able to receive further enlightenment.

> Der Wâleis sprach, 'wê was ist got?
> waer der gewaldec, sölhen spot
> het er uns pêden niht gegebn,
> kunde got mit kreften leben.
> ich was im diens undertân
> sît ich genâden mich versan.
> nu wil i'm dienst widersagn:
> hât er haz, den wil ich tragn.' (P 332,1-8)
>
> [The Waleis said, "Alas, what is God? If He were mighty, if God could rule with power, he would never have imposed such disgrace on us both. I was in His service, since I hoped to receive His grace. But now I shall renounce His service, and if He hates, me, that hate I will bear."]
>
> Er sprach, 'ist gotes kraft sô fier
> daz si beidiu ors unde tier
> unt die liut mac wîsen,
> sîn kraft wil i'm prîsen.
> mac gotes kunst die helfe hân
> diu wîse mir diz kastelân
> dez waegest umb die reise mîn:
> sô tuot sîn güete helfe schîn:
> nu genc nâch der gotes kür',
> den zügel gein den oren fiir
> er dem orse legte,
> mit den sporn erz vaste regte. (P 452,1-11)
>
> [He said, "If God's power is go great that it can guide both horse and beast, and men as well, then I will praise His power. If God's art possesses such help, then let it show this Castilian of mine the road that is best for me." And he let the reins fall loosely over his horse's ears and urged it on vigorously with his spurs.]

To demonstrate the importance of the symbolical approach to nature in *Parzival*, it is instructive to take a closer look at several episodes that demonstrate the conventional decoding of nature as an inadequate response, but a symbolical understanding as the proper approach that reveals nature to be an ordered harmonious cosmos with the curative power to overcome a one-dimensional understanding, fragmentation, transgression and alienation. Flaws, false interpretations and errors occur primarily in civilization but also in nature. As a result of having been ejected from Eden, men and women commit errors in both realms—in civilization and in nature—in spite of their best intentions and the strength of their emotions.[27] As a result of sin, the postlapsarian human being can still respond to nature's symbolic signs, but the response is a flawed one, since human nature has been flawed through sin. Nature still continues to reveal God, and man still responds to nature, but to respond correctly, to understand the theophany correctly, instruction is needed from God or His representatives. It was noted that Parzival started his development in nature, that he was moved by nature and began to ask questions about God, but that he still needed specific instructions. Whereas before the Fall Adam and Eve understood nature's revelations directly, the intrusion of sin has confused mankind, so that symbols are no longer interpreted correctly. In *Parzival*, disorientation occurs usually in civilization (in connection with knighthood and the court); however, being in nature is not a safeguard against error or distortion of the message either. It is possible to be disoriented because of a one-dimensional view of one's courtly responsibilities, because of a failure to understand not only the courtly code of behavior but the great underlying symbolic code expressed as a cosmic ordo, of which the courtly code with its sense of decorum should be, but often is not, an expression. A return to nature is invariably accompanied by a reintroduction of the individual to a symbolic reading of the great code of nature that corrects some of the distortion of meaning, but this symbolic response must still be given direction through the word, that is through written or spoken communication, if it is to result in full healing, reorientation, restitution and the restoration of the individual into the cosmic ordo.

The Grail

The grail community is a special lay community called to service to the grail by a message that appears on this stone, which Wolfram calls lapsit exillès (P 469,7), commonly interpreted as "stone fallen from heaven."[28] Whereas earlier courtly traditions, such as Chrétien, represent the grail as a dish or plate, Wolfram represents the grail as a stone with divine and magical properties. It is a stone that has come directly from heaven to earth, not formed by human hands, one whose powers are renewed each Good Friday by a eucharistic wafer brought by a dove from heaven. It is an object on which God reveals Himself and communicates directly with His community in writing that appears on the stone. As a stone (P 469,8), it is a symbol taken from nature through which God communicates His will to his people. It is also a stone that has magical properties, such as the ability to feed masses of people with whatever they might desire; its power to sustain life indefinitely is both divine and magical.[29] (It is expressly prevented from healing Anfortas (P 481), presumably because this process of becoming a healer is as important to Parzival as the healing is to Anfortas.) In prolonging life indefinitely, the grail is associated with Eden, since it returns man to the prelapsarian state he was in before he was subject to death. As stone and symbol of God's presence in the world, it carries a message which is read by the grail community, i.e., by those chosen to serve and decode it. The stone that fell from heaven and entered nature is a special symbol of God's continuing presence in the world, by which He reveals His will for the grail community.

When Parzival first sees the grail stone, he notices its magical, fairy tale elements, namely that everyone is fed by it. The grail is the proverbial horn of plenty, granting to all their favorite foods. He observes the grail as one object among many other magical objects in the refulgence of the great hall at Munsalvaesche, but focuses more on the gorgeous coat given to him and on the courtly lady who gave it to him than on the grail. On his second visit to the grail castle he understands it as a symbol of God's presence on earth; he genuflects before it, showing it the deepest reverence. Fairy tale motifs and structures attend Parzival's early adventures, as was already pointed out by Ehrismann[30] and subsequently by Wolfgang Mohr and Dennis Green.[31]

Anfortas, the grail king, had become horribly maimed in his genitals as a result of not following the prescriptions set for grail knights. Modeled on priestly communities that withdrew into the wilderness to create a monastic paradise,[32] the grail community had a similar enjoinder, in this case obedience to the commands of God written on the stone, which forbade entering into service of a lady or starting a courtly love relationship on one's own without the express sanction of the grail. Instead of following the commandments set for members of the lay grail community, Anfortas transgressed against the commandments set for this Christian lay community by entering of his own volition the service of secular amor and conventional courtly love. In the service of the lady he had chosen, he became wounded by a poisoned spear that caused his testicles to fester painfully. Death would have resulted from this poison, had he not been placed regularly before the grail, which insured his longevity but could not heal him. This stone, a product of nature and heaven, becomes symbolically encoded in carrying out restorative functions, keeping him alive until he could be healed by a knight as was foretold on the stone, who would come to the grail castle (unawares; in a sense magically), who would relieve Anfortas of his suffering, i.e., a miles medicus as Arthur Groos aptly calls him,[33] who would understand humanity, nature, and God as revealed in nature. The healing was to take place magically, since it was contingent on a special question the knight, without being prodded in any way, would have to ask of Anfortas, 'hêrre, wie stêt iwer nôt" (P 484, 27) (Sir, why are you suffering so?)[34] In typical fairy tale fashion, the question was to be effective only once, and then only if asked by the hero without prompting from anyone (P 484, 1-4).

When Anfortas, the ailing grail king, transgressed against the commandments of the grail and became impotent, the grail community stepped in, guided by the grail, to force Anfortas to continue to live by placing him regularly before the grail, and by keeping him alive so that he could wait for the hero who was to come to the grail castle and ask the magical question. Religious symbolism and magical fairy tale elements are initially deeply intertwined in the healing process. For Anfortas the healing was to be magical, at least initially, achieved through a specific ritual question; for Parzival, however, it was to indicate his correct response to symbols and symbolic actions (including incongruous signs, such as a bloody lance), where no commentary and no written or oral instruction was permitted to help him decode the meaning of the sign. For Parzival, a magical response was possible during his first visit according to fairy tale logic, but inadequate in terms of the developmental level required of him by the romance, that he advance beyond the magical question set by the fairy tale paradigm to a symbolical understanding of man, nature, civilization and God. (Gawan comes into a fairy tale setting and establishes control of this setting through reason. Parzival comes into what he regards initially as a fairy tale setting, but must discover that this setting is totally inadequate for dealing with the metaphysical questions he needs to address.)[35] When Parzival fails to ask the question the first time he comes to the grail castle, it becomes evident, through the rhetorical situation and rhetorical progression, that the fairy tale paradigm and magic, i.e., the formulaic, fixed, ritual, fairy tale response, are inadequate in his world and that a different response and a different paradigm are needed. When Parzival is called to the grail for the second time, his response to symbols and symbolic actions is sufficient, assured, and correct. Magic is superseded by a symbolic understanding as the magical qualities of the grail and the magical question that can be asked but once are replaced by tasks of a different order and by the ultimate expansive and compacted symbol—the grail—that speaks to human understanding of ordo rather than to magical ritual. At Parzival's first visit to the grail castle he responds with human, albeit incorrectly focused-sympathy to the pain of Anfortas, but since that is not the magical, ritual, required response, he fails. At the second miraculous visit—miraculous because it contradicted God's first message on the grail and miraculous, moreover, because the precise conditions under which the magical question was to bring healing have been totally reversed, since the terms of the test have been changed totally—instead of being a test of empathy, the test has become one of maturity and wisdom (P 795-796). In fact, the test has become one of demonstrating wisdom and recognition of the symbolic value of the grail in the cosmic ordo, which Parzival has come to understand, to interpret to others with the help of Trevrizent, and to represent as its spokesman to society. At the second visit to the grail castle Parzival's empathy is assumed, and, since he has learned the exact wording of the question, posing the question ("oeheim, waz wirret dier?") (P 795, 28) has become almost superfluous.

Parzival's visits to Sigune stand in the romance as an indicator of his growth or the lack thereof. We recall that she instructed him first explicitly in the symbolical approach to language by telling him not only his name, but also its deeper symbolical meaning. When he visits Sigune's hermitage for the last time after having been called to the grail for the second time, he demonstrates by means of the lime tree and the grave stone that he has learned to work with symbols and to understand their meaning in the cosmos.

During his itinerant years, Parzival returns periodically to Sigune, the pietà in the lime tree, a symbolical site in the forest that is linked to courtly love and penitential religious withdrawal into the wilderness.[36] His growing perception of the symbolical importance of this site provides a test and an objective correlative both of his growth toward the grail kingship and his understanding of his mission It is therefore highly significant that, after he has been called to become grail king, he visits the site for the last time and participates in its symbolical construction as a monument to faithful religious love in nature, by having the tomb stone lifted and the corpse of Sigune placed next to the uncorrupted body of Sch(anatulander in the grave dug by Sigune. (P 804, 27-30) Lifting the stone of this grave and constructing its significance correctly confirm his understanding of the symbolically endowed stone, the grail, to which he subsequently advances. His symbolical task is to separate death and life by separating the stone of death from the stone of life. How did he reach the appropriate level of understanding? Through five years of solitude in nature, by living in nature in isolation and by learning to understand it. But also by a conscious decision to seek divine counsel from the hermit, his uncle, Trevrizent, to whose hermitage in the wilderness he turns on Good Friday, the day of atonement and sacrifice in the liturgical Christian calendar.[37] From his uncle he learns about the cosmic meaning of the signs he observed at Munsalvaesche but did not understand. Symbols relating to the suffering of Anfortas, but also the course of the planets and their effect on men, on the history of salvation and on universal history. And about the symbolic meaning of stones, to which Trevrizent introduces him.

Parzival becomes the divine healer after he understands the ordo of nature. When he becomes the spokesman for the grail, (P 786) his powers exceed those of the grail, since he has been given the power to do more than what the grail stone alone was capable of doing before: not only to keep Anfortas, the ailing fisher king, alive, but to heal him completely. Parzival brings to the grail community the vitality that it has lacked, as the impotent Anfortas is replaced by a king whose wife has just presented him with twin boys, one of whom will become the future grail king. And, learning to read the inscriptions on the grail stone correctly, Parzival can interpret these properly within the sapiential framework he has acquired to guide the lay grail community that strives to combine ideal human and divine values.

The Magical Sword Presented to Parzival at Munsalvaesche

Unawares, as required by the fairy tale, Parzival stumbles upon the grail community, where, as a result of his recent "incorrect" courtly training, he fails to relieve the diseased Anfortas of his pain, having been told that it is impolite and uncourtly to ask questions instead of waiting for one's host to relate what should be known. There at the grail castle, as a symbolic prompt but also a ritual act, a special magical sword with very special virtues is given to him by his host, Anfortas. (P 239, 19-240, 5) When damaged and broken in battle, it can be restored by nature and by nature only, provided one understands this symbolic relationship *and* knows the special spell it requires. On this sword there appears a special message that must be understood as a result of a question, as a result of dialogue, and as a result of communication about it.

> wan do erz enpfienc in sîne hant
> dô was er vrâgens mit ermant. (P 240 5-6)
>
> [For when the sword was put into his hand, it was a sign to him that he should ask.]

It is this dialogue that is to be part of the symbolical accolade into the grail community.[38] The sword becomes paradigmatic for other situations in the epic. He who submerges the broken pieces of the sword in a special spring at its source *and* consciously understands the symbolic message on the sword can restore the broken sword to its original strength (P 253, 25-254, 19). Like the grail stone that assures longevity, the sword assures invincibility, since it cannot be broken, if nature and informed communication work together to keep it strong. (Dennis Green associates it, correctly, I believe, with the magic objects of KHM 92, "Das Wasser des Lebens," where the hero goes out to find the water of life to heal his father, but finds also the sword of invincibility and the loaf of bread that will always be replenished.)[39] While it is of utmost importance to Parzival to learn the symbolic message that will maintain the sword's invincibility, Parzival fails to ask about this message on the sword, thus allowing it to remain incomprehensible and therefore useless to him, just as he fails to ask about the symbolic meaning of the ceremony at the grail castle and the incomprehensible events there, whose incongruousness was to be a signal to him to ask.

The pattern established in connection with this sword is of the greatest significance for us. Wolfram establishes a paradigm: when failures, destruction and problems in the courtly realm occur, nature (understood symbolically) is there to provide healing, restoration and solutions. But to avail oneself of nature's restorative function, one must understand it. To understand it, one must ask. Dialog, communication, instruction are required. Parzival is told:

> You are wearing his sword (that of Anfortas) girded about you, and if you know its magic charm, you may engage in combat without fear. . . . Near Karnant there flows a spring and from it King Lac derives his name. The sword will withstand the first blow unscathed; at the second it will shatter. If

> you then take it back to the spring, it will become whole again from the flow of the water. You must have the water at the source, beneath the rock, before the light of the day has shone upon it—the name of this spring is Lac. If the pieces are not lost and you fit them together properly, as soon as the spring water wets them, the sword will become whole again, the joinings and edges stronger than before, and the signs engraved on the blade will not lose their shine. The sword requires a magic spell. I fear you forgot to learn it there. But if your mouth did learn the words, the power of fortune will sprout and grow with you forever. (P 253,25-254-30)

Gawan, who came into a fairy tale land, might easily have dealt with the fairy tale aspects of the sword, inquiring into its markings and using the power of reason, as he does in all situations that touch on his becoming master of Schastel Marveile. Parzival proceeds differently; reason is not enough for him to obtain control of the Munsalvaesche. He needs to come to a symbolic understanding of what it means to "be in the world in time". The sword serves him well until he fights the battle with his brother, his other self, where the sword breaks, and his brother provides the human solution by throwing away his own sword, a solution that leads to discovery of the fraternal kinship between these two knights, who represent different aspects of an idealized knighthood conscious of its high ethos and knowledge of the cosmos.

The Three Blood Drops in the Snow

When, after his failure at Munsalvaesche, Parzival stumbles unawares upon Arthur's tents at Karidoel, he encounters out in the woods an unseasonal snow, and on this blanket of snow finds three drops of blood which a lone, hunting falcon had produced by chasing and moving in on a goose. On seeing the three drops of blood on the freshly fallen snow, Parzival interprets these as symbols linking him to his wife Condwîrâmûrs, to whom he is connected by a love that is not joyous, like a celebration of Spring, but one that robs him magically of his senses and reduces him to robot-like rigidity. (P 283) The depth of love is conveyed not by the joyous raptures of the union of lovers in May, but by the trance into which the symbols of love, the three blood drops, thrust Parzival.

He discovers in the three blood drops in the snow his personal link to Condwîrâmûrs, his beloved; the symbolic representation in the snow leads him to understand his love as unique, deeply human and embedded in nature and the cosmos. And this symbolic representation on the winter snows, the first symbolic representation he understands and responds to through direct action, has a restorative effect on Parzival, even though it introduces comical elements that threaten to reduce him in stature from the great knight to a puppet. We know that at the grail castle at Munsalvaesche he *under*responded to the symbols that were meant to communicate to him the distress of the fisher king, Anfortas, and that he failed to perform the action that was required to end the suffering of Anfortas. Here, on the wintry field, he overresponds to symbols to the point of loss of consciousness. Just prior to coming to Karidoel, he had gone to Sigûne, his cousin, and had had his honor impugned by her for his failure to relieve Anfortas. Here, in the wintry landscape just beyond the ken of the tents of King Arthur, he begins to become immersed in the symbolical language of nature and to overrespond to symbols. And when he does so, he carries out battles with other knights automatically, appearing to be in a trance, because, while his deeper self seeks the human connection to Condwîrâmûrs, his external courtly self behaves correctly according to courtly mandates on the "courtly" pilot. The text states:

> From its wounds there fell upon the snow three red drops of blood. These brought Parzival great distress, from the trueness of his love. When he saw the blood drops on the snow which was so white, he thought, "Who created this color so pure? Condwîrâmûrs, this color does in truth resemble you. God must wish to give me fullness of bliss, since I have found here something which resembles you. Honor be to the hand of God and to all His creatures! Condwîrâmûrs, here lies your image, for the snow offered the blood its whiteness, and the blood reddens the snow. Condwîrâmûrs, your beau corps is like these colors. That you must confess." (P 282,20-283,9)

Gazing at the three blood drops on the snow, he becomes entranced by the symbol, and in this symbolical trance that connects him to his beloved, he repels Segramors and Keie, the Arthurian knights who had come to challenge him. Humorously, like a mechanical robot moved magically by the symbol which he has interpreted individually (just as Herzeloyde had interpreted the forest as a "desert"), he demonstrates the strength of this symbolic union that allows him to repel—without any consciousness thereof—his Arthurian challengers. It is significant also that he punishes in this repulsion Sir Keie, who had most uncourteously beaten Lady Cunnewère, when Lady Cunnewère had announced symbolically through her laughter the arrival of the greatest knight at the Arthurian court. She had made this announcement at Parzival's first arrival at Arthur's court, when Parzival came to the court dressed as a fool, totally unaware of the laws of knighthood. To Sir Keie's mind, she had shamed the court so much by misappropriating the symbolic function of her gift that he had beaten her publicly for this abuse. By breaking Sir Keie's arm and foot while in this rigid trance, Parzival confirms the correctness of her symbolic utterance, while appearing as a mechanical, robot-like knight, and not at all like the great knight who was to be hailed by her involuntary laughter. The reader knows, moreover, that this supposedly great knight is, at the same time, the knight who had just failed his test at the grail castle. These competing views of his behavior and its symbolic center corroborate but also humorously undercut his status as the greatest knight, while they both suggest and deny the fairy tale interpretation that would place enchantment on the surface but fail to acknowledge the deeper symbolic interconnectedness and consequences of his behavior. The scene corroborates that he is moved by phenomena in nature as he was in Soltâne as a child, but that he has begun to discover a capability within himself for action consonant with this interpretation.[40]

Trevrizent: Hermit in the Wilderness

Trevrizent, brother of Anfortas, withdrew in a penitential mode from the community of Templars at Munsalvaesche into a nature which he constructed symbolically with religious symbols as a hermitage. In its center is the altarstone. In so doing he follows the example of Bernard of Clairvaux and most closely that of St. Francis.[41] In wilderness, at the wild spring, Trevrizent wanted to live a life devoted to God away from human companionship and in abstinence, following the liturgical calendar of prayers and meditations, all in order to find and to give relief to his suffering brother, Anfortas. In the course of his development Parzival visits this site several times, as he visits the symbolically constructed site built by Sigune. Both sets of visits demonstrate an initial lack of a symbolical understanding of nature, but a gradual development on the part of Parzival in this direction.

When Parzival visits the site first, he does so looking for a sacred site to swear an ritual oath to Orilus that Jeschute was innocent of wrongdoing in the loss of the ring and brooch he had snatched from her when he was still a simpleton, before he knew of the laws of knighthood. (P 268) Interestingly, he swore this oath on a casket made of a green stone his father had given to Trevrizent (P 498, 9-12) that rests on an altarstone. (P 459, 23) When he visits the cell for the second time, it is on Good Friday, when he leaves his disorientation behind and emerges into real time, turning his horse on "automatic pilot," trusting God to lead it where he should go to find proper advice and help. And when he visits the hermitage for the third and final time, it is to announce his election to the grail. Let us take a closer look at the moment when he turns to God and nature for guidance.

> Er sprach 'ist gotes kraft sô fier
> daz sie beidiu ors und tier
> unt die liut mac wîsen,
> sîn kraft wil I'm prèsen.
> mac gotes kunst die helfe hân,
> die wîse mir diz kastelân

dez waegest umb die reise mîn:
so tuot sîn güete helfe schîn:
nu genc nâch der gotes kür.'
den zügel gein den ôren für
er dem orse legte,
mit den sporn erz vaste regte,
gein Fontân la salvâtscheez gienc (P 452,1-13)

[He said, "If God's power is so great that it can guide both horse and beast, and men as well, then I will praise His power. If God possesses such help, then let it show this Castilian of mine the road that is best for me. Thus His kindness shall show its help. Now go, whichever way God chooses." And he let the reins fall loosely over his horse's ears and urged it on vigorously with his spurs. It took the path toward Fontane la Salvatsche.]

Fontane la Salvatsche is the site of Trevrizent's hermitage not far from the grail castle, a wilderness with a wild fountain, rather than the fountain of life, where Parzival's guilt is taken away from him, assuring him of eternal life. And here Trevrizent gives Parzival instructions on the mysteries of the grail, laws of the cosmos and the movements of the planets: [42]

mit der sternen umbereise vart
ist gepüfel aller menschlîch art. (P 454, 15-16)

[To the circling course of the stars man's affairs and destiny are linked.]

Trevrizent formulates theories about nature set forth in our introduction that support both views of nature we outlined: (1) nature as a mechanism following its own laws to which man's destiny is linked [here nature is viewed as Geo or the Mother of Adam (P 463, 23- 30; 464,10-20) and the Grandmother of Cain and Abel; the movements of the planets, moreover, are linked to the festering of the wound (P 489, 24; 490, 12)] and (2) nature revealing God and God's message for his elected lay community through the grail stone's proclaiming God's message to those elected to serve the grail. Trevrizent speaks also (3) of God's ability to intervene directly in the history of man through the grail and its knights. To replace the neutral angels that served the grail before, God calls men and women through messages that appear on the stone to serve the grail community, but God also sends out from this community knights and virgins to become lords and mistresses of countries, as Herzeloyde was sent to king Castis. Trevrizent mentions theories of nature that were current at the time.

Conclusion

We have observed in Wolfram's *Parzival* that nature has a special effect on figures in the work, and that key figures make an effort to seek out nature in order to seek a remedy for problems arising in civilization. We have observed that the interaction can move from magical ritual to a symbolic response and even to a fully articulated understanding of the laws of nature. Magic and the fairy tale paradigm are shown to be less adequate in bringing a protagonist to an understanding of nature than the symbolic paradigm, through which even God can reveal himself. For those destined to progress to high levels of human existence and sapiential levels, magic needs to be replaced by a symbolical experience that is linked on the highest levels to an existence in nature andto objects originating from nature. The experience of nature, according to twelfth century philosophical thought, was there to reveal God's grandeur. But what is observed in Parzival is that nature, too, is an inadequate, flawed symbol. A symbol can be interpreted in a variety of ways, such as in traditional (e.g., religious, courtly), conventional and individual ways. The interchangeability of meaning became a danger, where one and same nature could be desolate desert for one person and a locus amoenus for another, and where three blood drops could be viewed simply as a part of a hunting scene by some and a special representation of the beloved by another, or the grail could be seen as a cornucopia by some and the symbolic representation of God by others. The danger from such interchangeability of meaning is a lack of all meaning and a lack of commitment to meaning. Revealing God and Heilsgeschichte (the path to human salvation) and the possibility of divine intervention (the miracle) in destiny on the one hand and following deterministic laws on the other, nature is given an ultimate standard or assurance of meaning by divine authority, namely in the grail, where it is shown that all who are elected into this community can agree on its meaning. Such a standard and a guarantee of the possibility of commonality of meaning in the world of this narrative is established in the grail. The grail becomes a symbol of the continued possibility of communication with God. God renews the power of this symbol through the dove that brings the wafer each Good Friday, but God speaks directly through the writing on the grail, which communicates a message that can be understood by the elect.

> ûf einem grüenen achmardî
> truoc si (die maget) den wunsch von pardîs
> bêde wurzeln unde rîs.
> daz was ein dinc, daz hiez der Grâl,
> erden wunsches überwal. (P 235, 20-24)

> [Upon a deep green achmardi (green silk from Arabia) she (the queen, a maid) bore the perfection of Paradise, both root and branch.

That was a thing called the Grail, which surpasses all earthly perfection.]

Flegetânîs der heiden
kunde uns wol bescheiden
ieslîches sternen hinganc
er jach, es hiez ein dinc der grâl:
des namen las er sunder twâl
inme gestirne, wie der hiez.
'ein schar in ûf der erden liez:
diu fuor ûf über die sterne hôch
op die ir unschult wider zôch,
sît muoz sîn pflegn getouftiu fruht
mit alsô kiuschlîcher zuht:
diu menscheit ist immer wert,
der zuo dem grâle wirt gegert.' (P 454, 9-11, 21-30)

[The heathen Flegetanis could tell us how all the stars set and rise again. . . . He said there was a thing called the Grail whose name he had read clearly in the constellations. "A host of angels left it on the earth and then flew away up over the stars. Was it their innocence that drew them away? Since then baptized men have had the task of guarding it, and with such chaste discipline that those who are called to the service of the Grail are always noble men."]

The grail is the most general, unspecific, abstract object with a heavenly history that has come to earth and, as a stone it ispart of nature. As a "thing" it appears to have cosmic, fairy tale and religious powers, as was stated before, but it also has a power to concretize the invisible and to transmit it as meaning, as the written word of God that appears on its side. With such a meaning spelled out, the grail becomes the vehicle—albeit the most expansive one and compacted one—of a metaphor which affirms the communication of God and man. In the age of nascent literacy and of uncertain access to literacy for the knighthood, God writes on his stone and the lay community serving the grail reads. Wolfram involves Parzival in the work on stones, giving to each stone its function. There are several stones that he needs to heed in his life: the stone of his father on which he restores Jeschute's honor through his oath, the stone of death and the stone of life-the stone covering the grave of Schianatulander which needs to be opened so that Sigune can be laid in it as a saint of love, and the grail stone, which Parzival must show reverence to, decipher and represent in order to bring healing to the wounded fisher king. (It is possible that in this reflective work on the meaning of stones Wolfram is making reference to yet further stones, not simply the stone Petrus on which he was to build his church,[43] but also the stone mentioned in the poem of Walther von der Vogelweide, which reflects on the meaning of life and how one should live one's life: wie man zer welte solle leben as one who is sitting on the stone or the rock of life.[44]

Ich saz ûf eime steine,
und dahte bein mit beine:
dar ûf satzt ich den ellenbogen:
ich hete in mîne hant gesmogen
daz kinne und ein mîn wange.
do dâhte ich mir vil ange
wie man zer welte solte leben:
deheinen rât kond ich gegeben,
wie man driu dinc erwurbe
der keines niht verdurbe.
Diu zwei sint êre und varnde guot,
daz dicke ein ander schaden tuot:
daz dritte ist gotes hulde,
der zweier übergulde.
Die wolte ich gerne in einen schrîn (I, 8, 4-19)

In becoming grail king, Parzival, as is well known, is able to attain these goals of life: honor, prosperity and God's grace. He comes to this position as spokesman of the grail through a maturationin nature marked by symbolic stones that reach from the stone of his father Gahmuret that was placed on the altar stone in Trevrizent's hermitage to the grail stone endowed with meaning by God.

Notes

1. "For the invisible things of him from the creation of the world are clearly seen, being understood by the things that are made, even his eternal power and Godhead; so that they are without excuse."

2. Augustinus, *De civitate Dei* XXI, 8 ed. Bernardus Dombart et Alphonsus Kalb, *Corpus Christianorum, Ser. Lat.* 48, (1955) 771 ff.; Doris Rube, "L'ymage du monde qui commence a Dieu et a Dieu prent fin. Zur Rolle der Theologie in französischen Enzyklopädien," in *Geistliche Aspekte mittelalterlicher Naturlehre*, ed. Benedikt Konrad Vollmann (Wiesbaden: Dr. Ludwig Reichert Verlag, 1993), 69; Loris Sturlese, "Die Sonderstellung der Kosmologie in der antiken und mittelalterlichen Naturlehre," in *Geistliche Aspekte mittelalterlicher Naturlehre.*

3. Clarence J. Glacken, *Traces on the Rhodian Shore* (Berkeley: University of California Press, 1967), 197-198; Augustinus, *De civitate Dei* VI, 8.

4. Sturlese, 54; Karen Gloy, *Das Verständnis der Natur: Die Geschichte des wissenschaftlichen Denkens* (München, 1995), 147-150.

5. Sturlese, 55; Glacken, 175,183-185, 312, passim.

6. Ed. Carl A Willemsen, parts I-II (Leipzig: Insel Verlag, 1942).

7. Benedikt Konrad Vollmann, "Hildegard von Bingen: Theologische versus naturkundliche Schriften?" in *Geistliche Aspekte mittelalterlicher Naturlehre*, 40-47.

8. Benedikt Vollman, ed., *Geistliche Aspekte mittelalterlicher Naturlehre*, 170-172.

9. *Wolfram von Eschenbach*, ed. Karl Lachmann (Berlin: de Gruyter, 1926) 6th ed.

10. Ernst Robert Curtius, *Europäische Literatur und Lateinisches Mittelalter* (Bern: Francke, 1948) 4th ed., 202-206; Jacques le Goff, L'imaginaire médiéval (Paris: Gallimard, 1985), 61-67.

11. Glacken, 208-215.

12. Curtius finds this thinking in Bernardus de Silvestris and in Alan de Lille's Anticlaudianus, 129-131.

13. Curtius, 116-137; cf. also Wolfgang Mohr, "Die Natur im mittelalterlichen Liede," *Geschichte, Deutung, Kritik: Festschrift W. Kohlschmidt*, ed. Paul Zinsli (Bern: Franke, 1969).

14. Walther von der Vogelweide II, 39,11-40,18:

Under der linden
an der heide,
di unser zweier bette was,
di mugt ir vinden
schône beide
gebrochen bluomen unde gras.
vor dem walde in einem tal,
tandaradei,
schône sanc diu nahtegal.

Die Gedichte Walthers von der Vogelweide, ed. Karl von Kraus. 13th ed. Hugo Kuhn (Berlin: Vereinigung von Freunden der Bremer Presse, 1965).

15. Everett U. Crosby, "The Subjugation of Nature in the Development of the Medieval Hunt and Tourney," in *Man and Nature in the Middle Ages*, ed. Susan J. Ridyard and Robert G. Benson (Sewanee, Tenn.: University of the South Press, 1995), 173-175. Cf. Dante Alighieri, *La Divina Commedia*, ed. C. H. Grandgent, rev. Charles S. Singleton (Cambridge, Mass.: Harvard University Press, 1972).

Nel mezzo del cammin di nostra vita
mi ritrovai per una selva oscura
che la diritta via era smarrita
Ahi quanto a dir qual era è cosa dura
esta selva selvaggia e aspra e forte
che nel pensier rinova la paura!
Tant' è amara che poco è più morte; (1,1-6)

16. Le Goff, *The Medieval Imagination*, tr. Arthur Goldhammer (Chicago: University of Chicago Press, 1988), p. 58.

17. cf. Der Kürenberger, in *Des Minnesangs Frühling, 1: Texte*, Karl Lachmann ed., eds. Hugo Moser and Helmut Tervooren (Stuttgart: S. Hirzel, 1977), p. 25.

Ich zôch mir einen valkenmêre danne ein jâr.
dô ich in gezamete,als ich in wolte hân,
und ich im sîn gevideremit gold wol bewant,
er huop sich ûf vil hôheund vlouc in ánderiu lant. MF 6, 1-4.

18. Translated by Helen M. Mustard and Charles E. Passage. *Parzival, by Wolfram von Eschenbach* (New York: Vintage, 1961).

19. Glacken, 213-218, 302-309.

20. In so doing, his actions parallel those of other members of his family, who withdrew into nature to atone: his mother, Herzeloyde, his cousin Sigune, and his uncle

Trevrizent. Le Goff comments on this, "Penitence and revelation: this is the profound apocalyptic Christian significance of the forest-wilderness." (*The Medieval Imagination*, 58)

21. Parzival's understanding should have become sensitized and his curiosity should have been raised by the paradoxes presented to him: a fisher king on a lake who does not fish, a castle in the wilderness built to stay almost invisible, tension at the reception of a guest that almost ends in a fight, a bloody lance that is carried around the room and causes a great display of sorrow and woe, a strange stone that is carried into a hall and that feeds the masses, etc. However, Parzival fails because he does not pay attention to the symbolical significance of these paradoxes. He sees the fisher king on the lake, but thinks only of finding lodgings for the night, he is angered by the tension at the reception, but does not inquire into its cause, he sees the grail, but thinks only of the lovely woman, Repanse de Schoye, andof the special coat she gave him, without considering that this honor was meant to indicate symbolically the passing of the mantle to the new grail king, he sees the bloody lance that is carried around the room and the crying that breaks out, but he does not ask why, he receives the sword with magical markings (almost as if it were a ritual Schwertleite), but he does not ask about the strange markings, he sees the strangely ailing host shivering in spite of the fires, yet he does not ask the question of sympathy that is on his lips, thinking that it would be a discourtesy to ask inappropriate questions

22. Gabenis should also be mentioned in this connection, although he withdraws from the world for pilgrimages only at certain times, such as Good Friday.

23. Glacken describes how religious orders, seeing themselves as partners of God, attempted to recreate paradise in the wilderness. See especially the discussion on the monastery at Clairvaux. (214, 303)

24. Walter Johannes Schröder, "Die Soltane-Erzählung in Wolframs *Parzival*," *Studien zur Darstellung und Bedeutung der Lebensstufen Parzivals* (Heidelberg, 1963). Thomas Kerth, "Parzival in Eden," *Neophilologus* 63 (1976): 260-268, disagrees strongly with the view that this is an Eden.

25. Glacken, pp. 304-309.

26. For the importance of the introduction of the grotesque that becomes visible in the contrast of Parzival's angelic beauty and Cundrie's repulsive features, cf. Rosmarie Thee Morewedge, "The Grotesque in Wolfram von Eschenbach's *Parzival*," Diss. UCLA, 1974.

27. Le Goff points out that the wilderness became not only a paradise but a site of temptation, where one met Satan and his demons. *Medieval Imagination*, p. 51.

28. Interpretations that have been made include lapis elixir (the philosopher's stone), lapis ex caelis "stone from heaven," lapsit ex caelis "it fell from the heavens." Cf. Martin (359-360) for all variant readings in manuscripts. Wilhelm Stapel ("Wolfram von Eschenbach's Parzival," in *Wolfram Jahrbuch* 1955, 9-27) suggests that the full phrase (which Wolfram may have quoted from memory) might have been "lapis lapsus ex caelis," "a stone fallen from heaven." For a review of the literature and the many excellent interpretations offered, see Bumke, 250-268. A separate study will be necessary to focus on the grail stone in this work, particularly in its links to other stones to which we have connected it.

29. It is a common fairy tale motif, seen in many tales, such as Grimms' fairy tale, KHM 97, "The Water of Life;" but it is also found in the Bible, where Christ, the Word of God made flesh, becomes the means of eternal life.

30. Gustav Ehrismann, "Märchen im höfischen Epos," *Beiträge zur Geschichte der deutschen Sprache und Literatur* 30 (1905): 14 ff.

31. Wolfgang Mohr, "Parzival und die Ritter. Von einfacher Form zum Ritttere-pos," *Fabula* 1 (1958), 201- 213; Dennis Green, "Parzival's Departure—Folktale and Romance," *Frühmittelalterliche Studien*, 14 (1980/81), 352-409.

32. Le Goff, *The Medieval Imagination*, 50; Glacken, 213-14; Roger D. Sorrell, *St. Francis of Assisi and Nature: Tradition and Innovation in Western Christian Attitudes toward the Environment* (New York: Oxford University Press, 1988), 14-28.

33. Arthur Groos, "Treating the Fisher King (Parzival, Book IX)," in *German Narrative Literature of the Twelfth and Thirteenth Centuries. Festschrift Roy Wisbey*, ed. Volker Honemann, Martin H. Jones, Adrian Stevens, and David Wells (Tübingen: Niemeyer, 1994), 298.

34. It is Trevrizent, the hermit and uncle of Parzival, who tells him what question he should have asked and in so doing prevents the question from being effective in the future, since its magic was good only the first time it was asked without prodding or aid from anyone. Dennis Green points out that in citing the question, Trevrizent prevents Parzival from being in a position to ask it in the future. See "Trevrizent's 'lie'," in *The Art of Recognition in Wolfram's 'Parzival'* (Cambridge: Cambridge University Press, 1982), 337-341, but cf. also 320-336.

35. Green, *Recognition*, pp.160-175.

36. See Groos, "Sigune auf der Linde and the Turtledove in *Parzival*", *JEGP* 67 (1968): 631-645, esp. 636 for Mariological associations with the pietà.

37. For the importance of the liturgical and astrological calendars, cf. Arthur Groos, *Romancing the Grail: Genre, Science and Quest in Wolfram's "Parzival"* (Ithaca, N. Y.: Cornell University Press, 1995). See also Wilhelm Deinert, *Ritter und Kosmos im "Parzival." Eine Untersuchung der Sternkunde Wolframs von Eschenbach* (München: Beck, 1960).

38. Bumke, 232.

39. Green, "Parzival's Departure—Folktale and Romance," *Frühmittelalterliche Studien*, 360 correctly cites important motifs in KHM 97, "The Water of Life," namely the water of life, the loaf that will keep on feeding the multitudes and the sword with which one is invincible.

40. Morewedge, "Wolfram von Eschenbach's Comedy of Errors: The Blood Drops Scene," *Mediaevalia* 15 (1993), 127-144.

41. Sorrell, 18-19.

42. Greene, *Recognition*, 176-222; Groos, *Romancing the Grail*, 222-226.

43. As my colleague, William Snyder, correctly pointed out in conversation.

44. Karl Lachmann, ed., *Die Gedichte Walthers von der Vogelweide.*

Bibliography

Augustinus, *De civitate Dei*. Bernardus Dombart and Alphonsus Kalb ed. *Corpus Christianorum. Ser. Lat.*, 1955.

Bertau, Karl. *Deutsche Literatur im Europäischen Mittelalter* II: 1195-1220. München: Beck, 1973.

Bumke, Joachim. *Die Wolfram von Eschenbach Forschung seit 1945: Bericht und Bibliographie*. München: W. Fink, 1970.

Curtius, Ernst Robert. *Europäische Literatur und Lateinisches Mittelalter*. 4th ed. Bern: Franke, 1963.

Dube, Waltraut F. *Medieval Medicine in Middle High German Epics*. Diss. University of Indiana, 1981.

Ehrismann, Gustav. "Märchen im höfischen Epos," *Beiträge zur Geschichte der deutschen Sprache und Literatur* 30 (1905): 14 ff.

Glacken, Clarence I. *Traces on the Rhodian Shore: Nature and Culture in Western Thought from Ancient Times to the End of the Eighteenth Century*. Berkeley: University of California Press, 1967.

Gloy, Karen. *Das Verständnis der Natur: I Die Geschichte des wissenschaftlichen Denkens*. München: Beck, 1995.

Green, Dennis H. *The Art of Recognition in Wolfram's* Parzival. Cambridge: Cambridge University Press, 1982

———. "Parzival's Departure—Folktale and Romance." *Frühmittelalterliche Studien* 14 (1980/81): 352- 409.

Grimm, Reinhold R. *Paradisus Coelestis Paradisus Terrestris: Zur Auslegungsgeschichte des Paradieses im Abendland bis um 1200*. München: Fink, 1977.

Groos, Arthur. "Treating the Fisher King (Parzival, Book IX)." *German Narrative Literature of the Twelfth and Thirteenth Centuries*, ed. Volker Honemann, Martin H. Jones, Adrian Stevens, and David Wells. Tübingen: Niemeyer. 1994, 275-304.

———. *Romancing the Grail: Genre, Science, and Quest in Wolfram's "Parzival"*. Ithaca, 1995.

Kerth, Thomas. "Parzival in Eden." *Neophilologus* 63 (1979): 260-268.

Knapp, Fritz Peter. "Der Gral zwischen Märchen und Legende." *Beiträge zur Geschichte der deutschen Sprache und Literatur* 18 (1996): 49-68.

Lachmann, Karl. *Die Gedichte Walthers von der Vogelweide*. 13th ed., Hugo Kuhn using ed. of Carl von Kraus. Berlin: de Gruyter, 1965.

—ed. *Wolfram Von Eschenbach*. Berlin: de Gruyter. 1926.

Le Goff, Jaques. "The Wilderness in the Medieval West." In *The Medieval Imagination*, tr. Arthur Goldhammer. Chicago: Chicago University Press, 1988, 47-59.

———. L'imaginaire médiéval. Paris: Gallimard, 1985.

Martin, Ernst, ed. *Wolfram von Eschenbach "Parzival" und "Titurel"*. Halle: Waisenhaus, 1903. Part II: Kommentar.

Mohr, Wolfgang. "Die Natur im mittelalterlichen Liede." In *Geschichte, Deutung, Kritik*. Festschrift W. Kohlschmidt, ed. Paul Zinsli. Bern: Franke, 1969.

———. "Parzival und die Ritter. Von einfacher Form zum Ritterepos." *Fabula* 1 (1958): 201-213.

Morewedge, Rosmarie Thee. "Wolfram von Eschenbach's Comedy of Errors: the Blood Drops Scene." *Mediaevalia* 15 (1993) publ. 1998: 127-143.

———. "The Grotesque in Wolfram von Eschenbach's *Parzival.*" Diss. UCLA, 1974.

Ruhe, Doris. "L'ymage du monde qui commence a Dieu et a Dieu prent fin. Zur Rolle der Theologie in französischen Enzyklopdien des späten Mittelalters." In *Geistliche Aspekte mittelalterlicher Naturlehre*. Wiesbaden: Reichert, 1993.

Schaefer, Hans-Wilhelm. "Die Planetennamen in Wolframs Parzival." *ZfdSp* 21 (1965): 60-68.

Schroeder, Walter Johannes. *Der Ritter zwischen Welt und Gott. Idee und Problem des Parzivalromans Wolframs von Eschenbach*. Weimar: Boehlau, 1952.

Sorrel, Roger D. *St. Francis of Assisi and Nature: Tradition and Innovation in Western Christian Attitudes toward the Environment*. New York: Oxford, 1988.

Sturlese, Loris. "Die Sonderstellung der Kosmologie in der antiken und mittelalterlichen Naturlehre," In *Geistliche Aspekte mittelalterlicher Naturlehre*. Ed. Benedikt Konrad Vollmann. Wiesbaden: Dr. Ludwig Reichert Verlag, 1993.

Vollmann, Benedikt Konrad. "Ausblick." In *Geistliche Aspekte mittelalterlicher Naturlehre*. Wiesbaden, 1993.

Zinsli, Paul, ed. *Geschichte, Deutung, Kritik. Festschrift Werner Kohlschmidt.* Bern: Franke, 1969.

10

NATURAL LAWS AND THE LAWS OF NATURE IN ARISTOTLE AND AQUINAS

Laura Westra

The role of nature in all laws is as pervasive as the role of philosophy is, in both antiquity and the Middle Ages. It is not my intention at this time to duplicate the arguments arising from virtue ethics and the quest for the "good" found in Plato and in Aristotle, and its importance for the establishment of a solid environmental ethics (Westra, 1998). At this time I want to explore what the classic approaches to natural law in Greek and Medieval thought may have to offer in support of a sound public policy and a better world governance.

There is no question that there are great disanalogies between the polis/city and the ancient and medieval forms of governance, and today's situation. Simply, the main disanalogy is perhaps the size and composition of today's cities and nations. Aristotle himself notes that when a population is very large, it is hard to find laws that such a population will respect:

> Experience shows that it is difficult, if not indeed impossible, for a very populous state to secure a general habit of obedience to law (Aristotle, *Politics* 1325 b33- 1326b2; Baker, 291).

Aristotle goes even further in the *Ethics:* "a state cannot be made out often citizens, and one which is made out of ten times ten thousand is no longer a state?" (Bk. IX, c.1, no.3). This is not only defensible on Aristotelian principles, that is, following Aristotle's argument that there is an appropriate size for a ship, for instance, and that something that exceeds that size is no longer a ship, and that this is true of natural organisms. In addition, human ability can reach only as far as a person is capable of reaching, and this limits also the size of what a ruler can control and direct.

From the point of view of international human rights and environmental protection, the same conclusion must be reached: a state cannot meet the appropriate or best standards and results simply through self-governance. Maurice Strong argues that there are at least ten major areas of laws that *must* be global, in order to be effective, hence they cannot be left to individual national states (Strong, 2000). The ability of local governance is exceeded by the magnitude of the sheer number that must be justly governed, and also by the magnitude of the sheer number of the problems to be controlled.

On the latter point, however, Aristotle cannot provide an argument. Another problem with proposing a modern place for natural law, at least in Aristotle's version, is the lack of homogeneity among today's citizens. For Aristotle, the polis was made of citizens whose conceptions of right and wrong were basically the same. It is clear that even in small to medium-sized towns, this prerequisite of both morality and just governance no longer exists: in a sense we are all what Aristotle called "barbarians," and neither citizenship nor community can be based on similar ethnicity or background.

After admitting to such grave differences between ancient and medievals on one side, and modern day realities on the other, what can still be learned from the past and natural law? I believe that it is precisely in the forgotten connections between nature and laws that we can find both inspiration and principles to help us better understand our immense current problems. As ecologist William Rees reminds us, after Descartes humankind has tended to accept a strong dualistic division between intellectual, rational things, and material ones. The latter have been viewed as ours to use, control and manipulate; all nature belongs to that category (Rees, 2000). In the ancient world we find the root of Descartes' position in the work of Plato, whose general lack of interest in all things natural is well known. Yet Plato's vision, like that of Aristotle after him, was based on the primacy of the good, a "good" that is only comprehensible against the background of man's own nature.

When we turn to Aristotle, nature regains its role as the fundamental standard of rightness of all things, from the size of populations, to the best constitution, to the laws most appropriate to bring about the full flowering of humankind. In the next section we will look at Aristotle's *Politics* in order to tease out the role of nature in the best laws and the best governance. In the following (third) section, we will consider the work of Thomas Aquinas, seeking answers to the same questions.

Nature is central to Aristotle's argument in the *Politics.* This is routinely accepted by Aristotelian scholars: Aristotle conducted his study of things human in the fields of politics and ethics (and also of logic, poetry and oratory), side by side with a study of things natural (physics, medicine, and general biology) (Baker, 1973: xxvii).

In addition, his "inclination towards the Ionic 'becoming'—the genetic doctrine of phusis" (xxix)—ensures that nature will be and remain foundational for all his arguments, from the admiration he evinces for the beauty of perfected forms, to the presence of design in nature as such *(Parts of Animals* 1, c. v, #3, 6 and 7). We note that governance, citizenship and the polis itself were discussed with reference to natural standards (of size, of completeness and the like). In the same sense, the constitution of the State will provide its "essence," the explanation of its identity as a "quasi-juridical person" (Baker, 1973: 100.101). The constitution is analogous to the natural laws governing physical organisms (Book III, Ch. VI, 1278a40 ff.).

Like all natural entities, the State has two main ends (in this case, not just one end), for the association it represents. Aristotle starts with the basic "natural impulse" according to which "men desire to live a social life"; the other end is represented by the common interest: "The good life is the chief end, both for the community as a whole and for each of us individually. But men also come together, and form and maintain political associations merely for the sake of life" *(Pol.* III, 6. 1278a40 ff.).

Hence the *essential* nature of a State; the laws that regulate it exist for the sake of maintaining (1) life; (2) social association; and (3) the good life (Baker, 1973: iii). This simply reelaborates the theme clearly stated in Book I of the *Politics,* that "every polis exists by nature," and that the "nature of things consists in their ends or consummation," since "the end, the final cause, is the best" (Bk. I, ch2, 1522b9 ff.; cp. Baker, 5). The polis exists "by nature," and man is meant "by nature" to live in a social environment.

If we consider the modern, liberal democratic state, we find something that is in direct conflict with the Aristotelian view of *The State.* It does provide social association, so it satisfies at least one condition Aristotle finds essential to the nature of the State. But note that the other two "ends" or reasons why men join together in political association are missing or under threat. In glaring contrast with the Aristotelian emphasis on the State's support of the "common good," or the happiness that is based on the "natural end of man" as a moral ideal, in modern times even a token quest for that sort of good has been completely eliminated from present political institutions (Westra, 1998).

In the support for the basic goal "life," we find the greatest modern problem. The rhetoric remains the same in all modern states: the safety and the protection of all citizens should be taken for granted, as there are government bodies, armies, health professionals to ensure these ends. But the reality is quite different: modern environmental violence, fostered by government-sanctioned corporate activities represents the antithesis of a "common interest" based on the primacy of life protection (Westra, 1998; Westra, 2000).

Neither man's essential self, whose moral end is the intellectual pursuit of "happiness," nor yet man's biological, animal self, are well served by today's State and its "constitution." Aristotle did not envision asking for human preferences to establish final ends, as these are the fixed, proper ends of a well-organized, well thought-out state. As Aristotle clearly argues in the *Nicomachean Ethics* (Ch.7), the final end of man is not a question of private choice: it is a matter of universal, principled understanding: asking men what they prefer is only appropriate for the *means* to the ends that describe the common good, based on the presence of life itself.

Aristotle's chapter on Kingship emphasizes the reasons of his position: what is required is an "aristocracy" to govern, that is, "a government vested in a number of persons who are all good men, provided that such men can be found"

(Pol. Bk. III, Ch. XV, 1285b26 ff.). It is understood that those who govern are "best" in a sense that is entirely foreign to today's states: they are chosen solely for their moral qualities and prudence. They are not to hold office by heredity; by contrast, they are to be viewed as "law guardians" or "ministers of the law" (Ch. XVI, 1287a 18 ff.). The law is intended to retain these men, who eventually use what they have learned in the best possible way: "He who commands that law should rule may thus be regarded as commanding that God and reason alone should rule" (Barker, 1973: 146).

As we study Aristotle, the connection between nature and law becomes clear. Human nature is a universal, essential principle, as it defines what is good not only for individuals, but also for states, their constitutions, organizations and governance. But it is not only human nature, but nature as it applies to natural nonhuman organisms and processes that still provides the standards and the measure of what is right and appropriate. Fred Miller, Jr. speaks of the "political naturalism" present in the *Politics,* particularly with reference to justice. Justice is central to Aristotle's political theory, and it is necessary, together with "virtue and practical wisdom," for the "full realization of human nature" (Miller, 1997: 67).

The "aristocracy" Aristotle indicates as the best form of governance must fulfill its mandate by fostering the perfection of human nature, precisely through virtue and wisdom. Hence the political constitution employs justice to help achieve the *natural* ends of men. Miller also points out the similarity between the polis and a living organism (or that which exists by nature), and how it is another clear indication of Aristotle's naturalism: "An organism can function well and be healthy or function badly and be sick; hence it can live in a natural condition *(kata phusin)* or in an unnatural condition *(para phusin).* Similarly, the polis can exist in a natural condition or an unnatural condition" (Miller, 1997:15).

In essence then, Aristotle supports a "theory of natural justice." Much of what Aristotle believes is also taken up by Thomas Aquinas, who, after reading the *Politics* and Augustine's *City of God,* designed his own doctrine, one that, making also use of several Roman jurists, emerges especially clearly in the *Summa Theologiae.* The main tenets that emerge are summarized by Baker: the doctrine that law is the true sovereign and that governments are the servants of the law; the doctrine that there is a fundamental difference between the lawful monarch and the tyrant who governs by his arbitrary will; the doctrine that there is a right inherent in the people by virtue of their collective capacity of judgment to elect their rulers and to call them to account (Baker, 1973: lxi).

In the next section we will turn to Thomas Aquinas, and continue to emphasize the *natural* within his doctrine of law and justice.

Thomas Aquinas, Nature, and Natural Law

As we move to consider natural law in Thomas Aquinas, we necessarily pass from antiquity to the Middle Ages, a very different historical period. Yet it would be simplistic to assume that the difference is simply one of adding Christianity to Aristotle, or eliminating from his doctrine whatever is contrary to Christian thought. We need to understand how the concept of natural law evolved, as it did not leap a thousand years from the great Philosopher, to a great Philosopher Theologian, without maintaining some sort of continuity. We find the thread of this continuity quite early in our own epoch, in the definition attributed to a Roman jurist, Domitius Ulpianus (c.170-228): "jus naturale est quod natura omnia animalia docuit." This definition was also adopted by Justinian in the *Corpus Juris Civilis* (Crowe, 1974: 261). Ulpian was known as a "great name" in Roman jurisprudence and, unlike other contemporaries, he distinguishes clearly between the "natural law" and the "jus gentium." Gaius (180 AD), by contrast, "distinguishes only two kinds of law, the jus civile and the 'jus gentium', the latter being the work of natural reason" (Crowe, 1974: 262).

What nature teaches animals, freely translated from Ulpian, is "to reproduce (Ulpian adds, 'that is what we call marriage'), to educate one's offspring, and the like." *Jus gentium* is the law used by humans, which is different "because it is held in common solely by human beings." Finally, there is civil law. This division, surprisingly, was the one preferred by St. Thomas, rather than Isidore's two-way division within *jus naturale*, incorporating whatever is natural to mankind, and thus common to all nations and civil law. The former is "natural" because it is "independent of human conventions" (Crowe, 1972: 64).

It is easy to believe that St. Thomas would have wanted to preserve as much as possible the Aristotelian principles concerning different levels of law. But, if we accept that the generic tenet of natural law is "based upon the natural inclinations common to all animals," as Ulpian does, then—for instance—"the distinction between fornication and marriage becomes uneasy" (Crowe, 1974: 267).

Eventually Bonaventure, who does not write specifically on laws, adopts Ulpian's definition in his own *Commentary on the Sentences.* The tripartite definition can be roughly translated as follows: in the first sentence, natural law represents what is found in both Gospel and laws; in the second sense, it is the law common to all nations, and it is mandated by right reason; finally, in a third sense, it encompasses, most appropriately, what nature teaches all animals *(In IV Sent.,* d. 33, a.1, q.1, Bonaventure *Opera Omnia,* ed. Berton, Paris, 1856, t. V. V. II, c.17).

There is no need to pursue further the history of natural law, interesting and varied though it is. The main point, at least according to Ulpian, Bonaventure and St. Thomas, is the notion of nature, as nonhuman, being a firm component of a true understanding of natural law. Nature remains the standard, the starting point, the basis for helping us understand what natural law might mean, when we apply it to humankind. It is implicitly acknowledged that man and nonhuman animals (to insert the use of modern terminology) have several common characteristics: they are created and they are subject to identical or similar biological laws, so that a Cartesian split between nature and human reason becomes impossible. We are co-natural with whatever is alive, though it might not be possessed of reason, at least insofar as we are considered as biological beings.

The presence of biological nature is thus ensured in this conception of natural law. But another problem arises. Does St. Thomas rely on a "non-ethical statement about the nature of the good," and does that mean that the claims of natural law are flawed (Donagan, 1969: 327)? Contemporary analytic philosophy would view this as a fallacious claim, sufficient to invalidate all the claims of natural law arguments. But, as Alan Donagan argues, St. Thomas does not simply claim that a factual good or "whatever we in fact seek" is the basis of natural law. His claim instead follows a different path: man is a rational animal, hence he seeks, like all other natural creatures, that which is the good appropriate to his nature (as rational animal) (Donegan, 1969: 327). Not a factual, but a moral claim is implicit in the description of the good as that which all desire (rationally).

But there is another aspect of natural law that is even closer to the aims of an environmental ethic of respect for nature. First, it permits us to acknowledge that "human reason is subject to the laws of reality, which come from divine reason" (Donagan, 1969: 329). But the importance of these laws is guaranteed by their origin and their source, so the respect and acceptance of such laws goes without question. Even more significant is the fact that the laws of nature entail a final causality and a direction and goal to all natural processes. Hence, their single and collective "natural ends should not be thwarted. Hence, to interfere with the natural unfolding of these processes must be—at least *prima facie*—not only prudentially, but also *morally* wrong. Speaking of the wrongness of lying, according to St. Thomas in the S. T. II-II, 110.3, Donagan says: "This argument plainly presupposes an unstated principle, namely, that if an activity has a natural end, then it is unnatural and wrong voluntarily to engage in that activity in such a way as to prevent the attainment of its end" (Donagan, 1969: 331).

We can now affirm that there is an inseparable connection between the laws of nature and any moral theory based on natural law, and that becomes even more evident when we consider environmental morality. The connection remains strong even if one prefers not to accept a theological dogma in its defense. One simply needs to be prepared to accept Aristotelian arguments, as well as later legalistic and moral arguments, that support natural law in addition to, and independently of religious argument.

Conclusion

We have traced briefly the role of the laws of nature, and of the concept of nature in natural law doctrines, from ancient philosophy through the Middle Ages, looking at Aristotle and Thomas Aquinas. We were able to show the presence of several important principles linking morality and law through nature and to nature. If we are to understand the direction our laws should take today, in order to help correct the inability of modern governance to enact laws and regulations that are environmentally sound and that protect citizens, we should reconsider the doctrine of natural law.

We found a number of principles and arguments tying the historical, powerful natural law doctrine to nature, its processes and its laws. Particularly important, yet mostly absent from today's understanding of the proper role of governance and the law, are the following:

1. The conaturality of human and nonhuman life, with the clear acknowledgement that the same laws and processes apply to both.
2. The necessity, in view of this, that the legal and regulative part of modern governance equally reflect that reality in its mandates.
3. Because of this reality, it is wrong, at least in principle, to act in ways that prevent the actualization of natural entities, according to their own natural unfolding. Preventing such entities from reaching their final form cannot be done routinely, being as it is morally wrong (as well as prudentially suspect, according to environmental ethics and the precautionary principle).
4. Objections aiming at discrediting the validity of natural law can be answered, and the common attacks on it from analytic philosophy can be refuted.

In the final analysis, whether implicitly or explicitly, much of the content of natural law, its core meaning including the value and importance of natural laws and functions, is present in today's civil and criminal laws. Of course it is not fully understood, and the debt to past traditions is never acknowledged or accepted.

It is therefore imperative to reexamine and clarify the full import and meaning of natural law doctrines, so that their implicit message can be rendered explicit.

Bibliography

Baker, Ernest, ed. and tanslator. *The Politics of Aristotle.* Oxford: Oxford University Press. 1973.

Crowe, Michael B. "St. Thomas and Ulpian's Natural Law." In *St. Thomas Aquinas 1274-1974: Commemorative Studies.* Toronto: Pontifical Institute of Medieval Studies. 1974.

Donagan, Alan. "The Scholastic Theory of Moral Law in the Modern World." In *Aquinas: A Collection of Critical Essays,* ed. Anthony Kenny. Notre Dame: University of Notre Dame Press. 1976.

Hiskes, Richard P. *Democracy, Risk and Community.* New York: Oxford University Press. 1998.

Miller, Fred D., Jr. *Nature, Justice and Rights in Aristotle's Politics.* New York: Oxford University Press. 1997.

Rees, William. Chapter in *Ecological Integrity: Integrating Environment, Conservation and Health,* eds. D. Pimentel, L. Westra, and R. Noss. Washington, D.C.: Island Press. 2000

Strong, Maurice. *Where on Earth Are We Going?* Toronto: Knopf. 2000.

Westra, Laura. *Living in Integrity.* Lanham, M.D.: Rowman Littlefield, 1998.

———. "The Disvalue of Contingent Valuation and the Accounting Expectation Gap" In *Environmental Values.* Lancaster, U.K.: White Horse Press. 2000.

11

LA TUTELA AMBIENTALE DEL LAGO TRASIMENO IN ETA MEDIOEVALE

Environmental Protection of Lake Trasimene in the Middle Ages

Valentina Vincenti

[Summary]

[Lake Trasimene lies about 30 km west of Perugia and is surrounded by low hills. The lake is almost circular in shape and has three islands, Maggiore, Minore and Polvese. It is a very shallow lake, no more than three meters deep on average, and, because there are no tributaries, the depth and level of its waters depend entirely upon precipitation and evaporation. So the lake's ecosystem is a very fragile one; exploitative human activities have had a very negative impact upon it.

In the medieval period the lake was extremely rich in both flora and fauna. Today, many of the earlier species are still present, but overall its biodiversity has been severely reduced. The lasca, for instance, a fish well known as the symbol of the lake, no longer exists, and many of the small local mammals are also extinct.

The area has a long history, dating from the twelfth century B.C.E., because it was always a prosperous agricultural and fishery center. Thanks to these natural riches, it was viewed as an area desirable to appropriate, and over time it became annexed politically to Perugia. The presence in it of varied and abundant fish was deemed to be particularly important from an economic point of view. During the medieval epoch it was vital to secure the presence of fish for Lent and other days designated by the Church as meatless. The presence of these economic advantages based on the natural bounty of Lake Trasimene helped expand and consolidate the power of Perugia.

It is instructive to consider that even in those times a number of regulations were put in place to protect and conserve nature and to restrain various human economic activities. Fishing, for instance, was only permitted during the winter months, so that the fish could continue to enjoy their natural reproductive cycle during the summer. In addition, several fishing techniques that produced indiscriminate catches were forbidden, to ensure that young fish, which had not reached maturity, would not be taken.

Significant fines were imposed on those unwilling to abide by these regulations. In 1490, indeed, the authorities decided to outfit a vessel with both oars and sails and to place armaments on board, so that the crew could enforce the regulations if necessary, and so protect the lake.

Not only were fish protected, but hares and other wildlife were also protected by restrictions on hunting. It is surprising to find a fairly sophisticated understanding of the "rhythms of nature" and the ecology of the area so early in the history of the region. Clearly the regulations were intended to preserve flora and fauna, and to ensure that fishery, agriculture and other economic activities of the citizenry would not conflict with the natural cycles of the area.

Descriptions of the lake from between 1558 and 1575 wax eloquent about the beauty and productivity of Lake Trasimene, and, generally, of the idyllic conditions present there. They extol its pure waters (though they add that the water is undrinkable!), its "delicate" and rich-tasting varieties of fish, and the abundance of wild birds there, from ducks to swans.

Given the increasing recent ecological damage to the lake (even swimming from the beaches is not recommended today), it is instructive to turn to the inspiring wisdom of the environmental laws put in place by medieval Perugia.]

Il lago Trasimeno, situato a circa 30 km ad ovest di Perugia, è circondato da basse colline ed ha una forma pressappoco circolare, al suo interno vi sono tre piccole isole: la Maggiore, la Minore e la Polvese; con i suoi 126 km^2 ed il suo perimetro di 54 km, è il quarto piu grande lago dell'Italia insulare ed è il risultato di un processo geologico relativamente recente cominciato circa 2 milioni di anni fa. In tale periodo l'Italia centrale era costellata da grandi specchi d'acqua che occupavano le vallate interne fino a quando il sollevamento della penisola non ne causò il prosciugamento; il lago Trasimeno può dunque essere considerato, assieme al lago di Chiusi, ciò che rimane di un vasto bacino che nel passato occupava l'intera Val di Chiana. Sua caratteristica principale è quella di avere una scarsissima profondità (attualmente circa 4 m. in media) e di non avere immissari di portata notevole, tanto che il suo livello ed il ricambio delle acque dipendono essenzialmente dalle precipitazioni e dalla evaporazione; ne consegue che la sua superficie e il suo livello sono estremamente variabili dipendendo così strettamente, non solo dall'andamento stagionale, ma anche dalle fluttuazioni delle precipitazioni che di anno in anno possono subire forti cambiamenti.[1] Tutto ciò rende molto delicato ed instabile l'equilibrio ambientale del lago che ha costantemente richiesto un'attenta tutela affinchè le attività dell'uomo, da sempre dedite allo sfruttamento delle sue risorse, non ne compromettessero l'ecosistema. La fauna del lago, come la sua flora, è ancora ricca sebbene la situazione attuale non sia paragonabile a quella del periodo medioevale: nelle acque sono presenti anguille, tinche, carpe, lucci, e granchi, mentre è scomparsa alla metà del XX secolo la lasca, il pesce che era un po' il simbolo del lago stesso, a causa di una errata immissione di pesce persico che ne ha distrutto la popolazione. Anche la martora e la lontra sono state sterminate nei secoli passati.

Le rive del Trasimeno sono state abitate fin dal paleolitico superiore a causa del favorevole microclima che tempera i rigori dell'inverno e le calure dell'estate in un territorio così lontano dal mare, a questo si aggiunge la ricchezza della sua fauna composta da un discreto numero di pesci e di uccelli lacustri, sia migratori che stanziali, nonché la fertilità dei terreni che le circondano.

La frequentazione delle sponde non si è mai interrotta nel corso dei millenni: sono state recentemente rinvenute le testimonianze anche di un insediamento di età protostorica nei pressi di S. Savino dove sono venuti alla luce frammenti ceramici databili tra XII-X secolo a. C. Poche sono le notizie inerenti al Trasimeno per l'età etrusca e per quella romana,[2] sappiamo comunque che le sue rive dovevano essere costellate di piccoli insediamenti dediti alla pesca ed all'agricoltura.[3]

Vista la contiguità geografica tra il territorio di Perugia e il bacino lacustre, da sempre le vicende storiche della città si sono unite a quelle del Trasimeno, è però soltanto a partire dal periodo medievale che con certezza sappiamo dell'inclusione del lago nei suoi domini. L'acquisizione da parte del commune di Perugia di questo prezioso ecosistema è stata lenta e graduale: nell'817 Ludovico il Pio concede a papa Pasquale II "Perusiam cum tribus insulis suis"[4] includendo, in tal modo, tutta la zona nei possedimenti della Chiesa. Alla fine del X secolo d. C. la situazione non era ancora stabilizzata e Perugia ed Orvieto si contendevano Chiusi ed il suo fertile circondario. Nel 997 l'imperatore Ottone III dona al monastero di Campoleone, a poca distanza di Arezzo, Castiglione e la costa occidentale del lago; contemporaneamente Perugia si impossessa lentamente di altre parti dello specchio d'acqua: nel 1139 le si sottomette l'isola Polvese e nel 1174 la Minore. Pochi anni dopo, nel 1184 l'abate Ugo di Campoleone cede i suoi diritti sul lago a Perugia, cessione sancita nel 1212 da papa Innocenzo III che assegna il territorio di Chiusi e tutto il Trasimeno al libero comune.[5]

L'inclusione nei propri domini della fertile zona di Chiusi e del bacino lacustre segna una svolta fondamentale per il comune: la prosperità garantita dai raccolti di grano, coltivato in modo estensivo e la rendita derivata dalla pesca, consentono a Perugia di imporsi sui centri limitrofi divenendo in breve la città più potente del territorio corrispondente all'Umbria attuale.

Immediatamente comincia un programma di bonifica delle rive occupate da estese paludi e contemporaneamente, si inizia a incamerare i profitti dati dall'appalto dei diritti della pesca che costituiscono una delle fonti di guadagno più ingenti per la città. A questo proposito nel capitolato d'appalto del 1388 si dichiara che: "il laco de Peroscia è quella comunanza la quale più fructo rende al Comuno che niuna altra comunanza che et dicto Comuno aggia."[6]

La raggiunta ricchezza si manifesta nel grandioso programma urbanistico che caratterizza i decenni a cavallo tra XIII e XIV sec. che vedono la costruzione della fontana maggiore nel 1278 e del palazzo dei consoli iniziato nel 1293. Proprio il programma iconografico della fontana di Giovanni e Nicola Pisano rivela l'importanza dei nuovi domini del comune: infatti a fianco dell'allegoria della città, raffigurata come una donna con una cornucopia tra le braccia, vi sono le rappresentazioni del Chiugino, con le spighe in mano, e la così detta *domina laci* che tiene dei pesci nel pugno.

L'importanza vitale del lago per il comune perugino era dovuta non solamente alla resa pecuniaria assicurata dal suo sfruttamento, ma anche dalla possibilità, fornita dal Trasimeno di procurarsi una grande quantità di pesce durante la Quaresima e i giorni di vigilia prescritti dalla Chiesa che, in un anno solare, erano in tutto circa 150.

L'approvvigionamento del pesce non era cosa da poco considerando che, nello statuto del comune redatto nel 1342, si prescriveva, per chi avesse mangiato carne durante la Quaresima, una multa di 400 libre e si poteva arrivare addirittura al rogo.

L'immenso valore del bacino lacustre per la comunità perugina è dimostrato dalla costante attenzione che la legislazione della città dedica allo sfruttamento delle sue risorse che è compendiata negli statuti e nelle così dette cedole, cioè nei capitolati d'appalto; in sintesi lo statuto può essere definito la fase statica della legge, mentre la cedola ne è la fase applicativa.[7]

La più antica attestazione della regolamentazione dello sfruttamento del Trasirneno, è la prima cedola del 1276 seguita dallo statuto del commune, redatto nel 1279, con gli articoli dal 234 al 252.[8] Seguono nel 1342 un nuovo statuto con ulteriori normative descritte nel IV libro agli articoli 119-127 e numerose cedole redatte in volgare, che si susseguono a partire dalla metà del XIV secolo.[9] Durante il XV secolo se ne contano 45, tutte scritte in volgare. Fondamentale è anche la cedola, emanata nel 1568 da papa Pio V, composta da 115 articoli che costituisce un regolamento organico di tutte le attività legate al Trasimeno. Seppure redatta in un periodo che esula da quello di nostro interesse, questo documento è di grande importanza poiché recupera e riassume gran parte della legislazione precedente.[10]

Come fonte di notizie per la vita de lago e delle attività legate alla pesca merita di essere citato anche il poema, detto *Trasimeniade,* composto da tre libri in esametri latini dell'umanista perugino Matteo dall'Isola, attivo nell'ultimo quarto del XV secolo. Questa opera singolare contiene anche diverse illustrazioni che rappresentano i vari metodi utilizzati dalle popolazioni rivierasche per la cattura del pesce.[11]

Fin dalla prima cedola e dal primo statuto a noi giunti possiarno osservare alcuni regolamenti atti a preservare il patrimonio ittico del lago e le sue caratteristiche ambientali e tale indirizzo è quello seguito da tutta la legislazione seguente. Le normative sono capillari e riguardano ogni aspetto, anche il più minuto, dello sfruttamento delle acque, delle isole e delle rive. Una regolamentazione così ferrea e dettagliata non può non essere stata dettata anche dalla consapevolezza della delicatezza dell'equilibrio ecologico (per quanto anacronistico sia questo termine) dello specchio d'acqua, reso ancora più instabile dalle continue variazioni di livello della superficie.

Sarebbe lungo e forse eccessivo citare tutte le norme elaborate dal Comune di Perugia nei suoi statuti e nelle sue cedole, menzioneremo dunque quelle che principalmente sono inerenti alla tutela dell'ecosistema lacustre.

Innanzi tutto gran parte delle norme regolavano la stagione della pesca confinandola ai mesi invernali e impedendo il suo svolgimento durante l'estate, periodo di riproduzione dei pesci, e consentendo la cattura solamente del pesce detto albo,[12] considerato di scarsa qualità, dall 1° maggio al 31 agosto.[13]

Erano inoltre proibiti tutti i sistemi di pesca che potessero nuocere troppo alle specie ittiche (a questo proposito l'elenco delle reti illegali è contenuto nello statuto del 1346) e nel caso che ve ne fosse stata la necessità, erano stabilite le reimmissioni di pesci nel lago di specie e in quantità ben definite.

Sempre per tutelare il pesce gli abitanti del lago, detti *Lacosciani,* erano tenuti a "rifrascare" il lago ogni tre anni cioè a gettare sui fondali numerose fascine dove i pesci potessero nidificare e riprodursi con maggiore tranquillità. Si proibiva altresì la cattura di avanotti e di pesci che non avessero raggiunto un'età completa di sviluppo.[14] Nel caso che, fuori della stagione della pesca, nelle reti rimaste nel lago fossero rimaste prigioniere delle tinche, vi era l'obbligo di rigettarle in acqua e per i contravventori era prevista una multa.[15]

Le pene pecuniarie per i trasgressori delle norme, specialmente per i pescatori di frodo, erano assai severe, nonostante questo le attività illecite dovevano essere frequenti tanto che il commune, con la cedola del 1490, istituì un battello, precisamente un "brigantino a la marinescha" fornito "di vele, reme et altre artiglierie neciessarie per dicta guardia" che pattugliasse le acque del lago allo scopo di far rispettare le normative in vigore. Già nelle cedole precedenti comunque si regolamentava la sorveglianza del lago: ad esempio in quella del 1406 al paragrafo 23 si decreta che gli officiali incaricati di sorvegliare l'applicazione della cedola stessa dovevano stare al lago dal 1° novembre al 1° giugno.

Gli stessi pescatori erano soggetti ad un regime giuridico particolare in quanto tutori dell'equilibrio del lago e garanti del rifornimento di pesce per la città: erano dunque esentati dal servizio militare in caso di guerra né dovevano partecipare alle così dette "cavalcate" cioè alle esercitazioni a cui invece erano obbligati gli altri cittadini.

L'interesse della legislazione non era rivolto solamente al patrimonio ittico: la rubrica 246 della cedola del 1276 vieta la caccia dei conigli selvatici nelle isole, per maggior salvaguardia si proibisce di introdurvi cani e si nomina un pubblico ufficiale che garantisca il rispetto delle norme.[16] All'articolo seguente si decreta invece l'impianto di vigne nei terreni demaniali delle isole Polvese e

Maggiore: "Quoniam vinum letificat cor hominum, et hominibus insularum Lacus potest parere sanitatem,"[17] ma in realtà anche per bonificarne ulteriormente i terreni.

L'attenzione si appuntava anche sulle così dette pedate, cioè sulla fascia costiera compresa tra la zona di massima e di minima espansione delle acque, dove i canneti erano protetti poiché i pesci vi andavano a depositare le uova.

Non veniva trascurata nemmeno la regimazione dei corsi d'acqua che sfociano nel lago, al capitolo 27 della cedola del 1414 si stabilisce una spesa di 200 fiorini a carico dell'appaltatore, per regolare l'afflusso delle acque dei torrenti Triesa e Rio Maggiore e per "reparare che el aqua de la dicta Triesa e del dicto fossato o veramente qualunche altra acqua non entreno en lo dicto lacho."

Da tutto ciò si evince che già in un'epoca così antica era chiaro il complesso sistema di rapporti e di interdipendenze dell'ecologia lacustre. Erano regolate anche le coltivazioni delle sponde come la potatura e l'eventuale taglio delle piante vicine al lago. I proprietari delle selve attorno alle rive non ne potevano cioè disporre liberamente, ma dovevano eseguire una potatura nei mesi prestabiliti per fornire le fascine e i giunchi necessari alla fabbricazione delle ceste per il trasporto del pesce e per l'allestimento degli impianti fissi di pesca che, nel medioevo, sono costituiti dai così detti tori o tuori.

Vale la pena a questo proposito fare un inciso descrivendo questo ingegnoso sistema di cattura del pesce poiché esso sembra essere stato ideato adeguandosi, e di conseguenza rispettando, i ritmi della natura e non quelli richiesti dallo sfruttamento e dalla convenienza a breve termine, così consueti nella nostra epoca.

La necessità di rifornire la città e le campagne, soprattutto in tempo di Quaresima, di pesce aveva reso necessaria l'ideazione di impianti fissi di pesca che rendessero meno aleatorio il rifornimento di un alimento indispensabile per il rispetto delle norme ecclesiastiche la cui infrazione comportava, come si è detto, pene gravissime. Il Trasimeno era diviso in zone pertinenti alle varie comunità di pescatori delle sponde e delle isole: Ogni gruppo di abitanti disponeva, nella zona lacustre a loro pertinente, un numero prefissato di impianti di pesca che venivano sfruttati durante la stagione consentita dalla legge cioè dal 1 novembre al Sabato Santo che solitamente cade tra la fine di marzo ed i primi di aprile. Il toro era composto da fascine di quercia che venivano tagliate subito dopo la fine della stagione della pesca, in primavera, e poi messe in acqua per acquistare peso. Le fascine venivano poi caricate su dei barconi e trasportate al largo e qui affondate sul luogo dei tori dell'anno precedente nei mesi di giugno e di luglio.[18] Il riconoscimento e la memorizzazione della giusta posizione dei tori era affidata ad un sistema semplice ed ingegnoso che usava come coordinate dei punti fissi di riferimento posti sulle rive. Dopo questa operazione il lavoro tornava a terra con la raccolta della canapa che si svolgeva ai primi di agosto, i gambi delle piante venivano lasciati macerare nelle acque ormai calde del lago e poi filati. Nella stagione estiva uomini e donne tessevano delle lunghissime reti di 9 x 40 m. dalle maglie tanto sottili da non far passare un dito tra di esse. Con i primi freddi autunnali i pesci cercavano rifugio tra le fascine dei tori in modo che, ricominciata la stagione della pesca, ai pescatori non restava altro da fare che circondare volta a volta i vari tori con la lunghissima rete, togliere la fascine accatastate e catturare così tutti i pesci che vi si erano annidiati.[19] La pesca durava cinque mesi, ma in realtà si dovevano escludere le giornate di tempesta, quelle con le acque gelate e infine quelle di nebbia essendo impossibile ritrovare la posizione dei tori senza vedere i punti di riferimento sulle sponde.

Come si vede, il complesso meccanismo che si svolgeva nell'arco di un anno coinvolgeva tutta la popolazione (pescatori, boscaioli, contadini, donne) e molteplici aspetti della flora e della fauna lacustre creando un'armonia vera e propria tra l'attività dell'uomo e la vita delle altre specie.

Conclusioni

Dall'esame della legislazione di età medioevale del comune di Perugia risulta chiaramente che tutti i regolamenti inerenti il Trasimeno avevano, come fine principale, il mantenimento del patrimonio costituito dal lago stesso senza trascurare nemmeno la tutela dell'aspetto estetico. Seppure i moventi di tale atteggiamento siano diversi da quelli attuali non possiamo non considerare i risultati delle politiche amministrative medievali che per secoli sono riuscite a preservare intatto il delicato ecosistema del lago. Sicuramente l'armonia con la quale sembrano aver convissuto le esigenze degli uomini e quelle delle altre specie viventi sono dovute ad un diverso approccio alla realtà e a finalità diverse: non va dimenticato che tutte le attività umane erano condizionate in modo preponderante dai ritmi dell'anno liturgico che pero ricalcavano quelli della natura stessa, sovrapponendosi ad essi senza contrastarli.

Nel XX secolo la presenza massiccia dell'uomo e l'agricoltura intensiva che ha sostituito le antichissime colture del lino e della canapa, scomparse dalle rive attorno agli anni Sessanta, nonché sbagliate immissioni di specie ittiche che hanno distrutto la lasca, hanno compromesso l'habitat del lago. Cipriano Piccolpasso ci ha lasciato una descrizione del lago, fatta all'incirca tra il 1558 ed il 1575,[20] che ci fa comprendere come, nonostante il Trasimeno rimanga un complesso floristico, vegetazionale e faunistico tra i più importanti d'Italia, abbia comunque subito un impoverimento delle specie in esso presenti sia per varietà che per numero di individui, impoverimento del resto condiviso, purtroppo, da tutto il resto del territorio della penisola italiana.[21] Riportiamo qui qualche passo esemplificativo:

> "le acque di questo lago sono quasi sempre chiare e limpide e dolci al gusto, ma non molto sane usandole per bere." "Et pur veggiamo il suo pescie assai dilicato como sonno i lucci...; fannovi de bone tinche, ottime lasche, grosse anguille et di dilicato sapore e vi fa anco

> di una sorta di pescie che i Perugini gli dicono albi, non molto grossi...Questo pescie è insipido e di non grande pregio; ve ne è poi di un "altra sorte che li dicono scarpete et altri scarbete, queste si salano e seconsi al fume etmangiansi per cosa delcata et fanvi anco una sorta di granci ma non di molto pregio, vi si veggano anco di una sorta di gamberi piccolissimi, vi fanno ancora una sorte di cappe dette da quegli huomeni talleni." "Vi si veggiono in riva di questo lago et per il lago diverse sorti di uccelli, como focole, germani, anatre, et il verno cigni e grue in grandissima copia." [22]

Fortunatamente la saggia politica dei comuni che si affacciano sulle acque e l'istituzione del Parco Regionale del Trasimeno e delle oasi faunistiche dell'Isola Polvese di Valle e di Punta Navaccia ha, negli ultimi decenni, arginato e rimediato alcuni dei danni avvenuti negli anni immediatamente seguenti la fine della Seconda Guerra Mondiale. Nonostante ciò il patrimonio di saggezza, contenuto nelle leggi della Perugia medievale, può ancora costituire una fonte di ispirazione anche per il terzo millennio.

Note

1. Per arginare i danni delle piene del lago nel 1420 Braccio Fortebraccio da Montone, signore di Perugia, aprl un condotto, che aveva funzione di emissario, allo scopo di regolare l'eccesso delle acque. Per una accurata trattazione cfr. V. Castellani, W. Dragoni, "L'emissario medioevale del lago Trasimeno," s.l., s.n., 1981. Questo canale, lungo 1057 m., correva in galleria per circa 900 m. sotto le colline di S. Savino e di Monte Petreto per gettarsi infine nel torrente Caina, affluente del Tevere. In realtà l'opera non ebbe successo a causa di difetti della sua costruzione che rendevano troppo esiguo lo scarico delle acque. Nel 1895 fu progettato un nuovo emissario, realizzato nel 1898, che corre parallelamente a quello precedente, e che ha una lunghezza di 7.314 m. Si è sempre ritenuto che il canale voluto da Braccio Fortebraccio sostituisse uno più antico di età romana: a parte il discusso passo di Strabone (vedi a nota 2), durante i lavori della fine dell'Ottocento per l'apertura del nuovo emissario, furono ritrovati resti di un cunicolo più antico, strumenti da scavo e monete di epoca romana risalenti ai tempi dell'imperatore Claudio che aveva decretato lo scavo di un canale per il regolamento delle acque del bacino del Fucino in Abruzzo. Tutti questi dati, andati purtroppo distrutti o dispersi, possono far supporre che una regolamentazione del livello del Trasimeno in età romana non sia solamente una leggenda.

2. Esula dal nostro argomento il discorso storico, basti qui accennare al fatto che le poche fonti, tutte di età romana, riguardano per lo più la famosa battaglia tra Romani e Cartaginesi, svoltasi nei dintorni di Tuoro nel 217 a.C. nel Corso della Seconda Guerra Punica. Un accenno al Trasimeno si ha in Silio Italico che parla dei sistemi di pesca del lago dicendo che era consuetudine catturare il pesce con reti di lino ed in Strabone, V 226 che però dice il Trasimeno affluente del Tevere. Questa affermazione è sembrata un sicuro indizio che già in epoca romana esistesse un emissario che scaricasse le acque in

eccesso del lago negli affluenti del Tevere, ma nello stesso passo il geografo dichiara tali anche il lago di Bolsena e quello di Bracciano.

3. Recentemente è stata riportata alla luce una villa romana che fornisce preziose informazioni sulla tipologia di questi insediamenti: P. Bruschetti, T. Ercolanelli, *Passignano sul Trasimeno. Una villa sul lago: la residenza romana di Quarantaia* (Ponte S. Giovanni: Quattroemme, 1997).

4. R. Chiacchella, "Perugia e il Lago," in *Storia illustrata delle città dell'Umbria, 2* (Milano: Elio Sellino, 1993) 385-400.

5. A. Bartoli Langeli, *Codice diplomatico del Comune di Perugia* (Perugia, 1983); S. Caprioli, *Statuto del Comune di Perugia, I* (Perugia: Deputazione di Storia Patria, 1996) 231 ss.

6. U. Nicolini, in G. Moretti (a cura di) in *Lingua, storia e vita dei Laghi d'Italia.* Atti del Convegno dell'Atlante linguistico dei laghi italiani, lago Trasimeno 23-25 settembre 1982 (Rimini: Maggioli, 1984) 391-414.

7. Riprendo qui la felice definizione di U. Nicolini, op. cit. alla nota precedente, p. 392.

8. In realtà la prima attestazione dello sfruttamento da parte del comune del lago e un documento del 1259 dove il podestà viene esautorato dalla vendita dei frutti del Trasimeno ed al suo posto vengono nominati appositi uffici ma in tal caso non si può parlare di una regolamentazione generale. *Archivio storico del comune di Perugia, Consigli e Riformanze* reg. 4, c. II.

9. Le cedole in questione, inerenti al XIV secolo, risalgono agli anni 1385, 1388, 1391 e 1394.

10. La bolla papale recupera in gran parte la normativa di una cedola più antica andata perduta alla quale viene attribuito il nome di *cedola vetus* e che dovrebbe essere stata redatta nel 1379, cfr. M. Tabarrini, *L'Umbria si racconta, Dizionario* (Foligno: Porziuncola, S. Maria degli Angeli, 1982), s. v. Trasimeno. La pubblicazione integrale della bolla di papa Pio V è contenuta in O. Polimanti, *Raccolta della legislazione sul lago Trasimeno* (Perugia, 1931). Per un elenco dei manoscritti e delle pubblicazioni a stampa della cedola del 1568 cfr. U. Nicolini op. cit. alla nota 6, p. 393. L'ultima legislazione inerente al Trasimeno prima dell'annessione dell'Umbria al Regno d'Italia è del 1822 quando papa Pio VII emanò un altro complesso di norme.

11. Il manoscritto della Trasimeniade è conservato alla biblioteca Augusta di Perugia (Ms. 1085). Per una sua descrizione generale cfr. C. Conti, "La 'Trasimeniade' di Matteo dall'isola e la pesca nel lago Trasimeno" in G. Moretti (a cura di) op. cit. alla nota 6, p. 415 ss.

12. Il pesce albo è il cavedano (*Leuciscus cephalus*) considerato di qualità inferiore rispetto a quello che era pescato durante l'inverno cioè lucci (*Esox lucius*), tinche (*Tinca tinca*), anguille (*Anguilla anguilla*), e lasche (*Rutilius rubilio v. trasimenicus*).

13. Cedola di Pio V del 1568, art. 10.

14. Nella cedola del 1406 al paragrafo 6 si proibisce ad esempio di pescare la tinca e la lasca il cui peso sia rispettivamente minore di 4 once e di un'oncia, *Archivio Storico di Perugia, Consigli e riformanze*, 51, cc, 16r-18v. Una sintesi in italiano di tale cedola si trova in U. Nicolini op. cit alla nota 6, p. 396-398

15. Cedola di Pio V del 1568, art. 13

16. S. Caprioli op. cit. alla nota 5, I, 238. Nulli liceat venari vel capere cuniculos stantes in insula Maiori, in insula Minori et insula Puluese, nec canes immittere, nec

etiam retinere. ...Et potestas et capitaneus faciant eligi unum bonum et idoneum hominem de civitate Perusii super custodia cuniculorum in ipsis insulis facienda.

17. Ibid. p. 238 s.

18. Bolla di Pio V del 1556, art. 99.

19. La pesca mediante i tori andò declinando a partire dalla fine del Medioevo a causa di un progressivo innalzamento delle acque sostituita da altri impianti fissi detti "porti" e dalla pesca effettuata con reti da lancio dette "ghiacci" o a strascico.

20. C. Piccolpasso, *Le piante et i ritratti delle città e terre dell'Umbria sottoposte al governo di Perugia*, edizione a cura di G. Ceccini (Roma: Istituto Nazionale di Archeologia e Storia dell'Arte, 1963); l'opera, mai data alle stampe durante la vita dell'autore e nota da tre codici autografi: il Vittorio Emanuele n° 550 della Biblioteca Nazionale Centrale di Roma, L'Urbinate Latino n° 279 dell'Apostolica Vaticana, il n° 3064 della Biblioteca Augusta di Perugia.

21. Per una sintesi del patrimonio naturale del Trasimeno cfr. E. Orsomando, G. Bini, A. Catorci, *Aree di rilevante interesse naturalistico dell'Umbria* (Perugia, Regione dell'Umbria, 1998), 84-89.

22. C. Piccolpaso, op. cit. a nota 20, pp. 90-91, tav. LII. Per *scarbeta* si intende la scardola (*scardinius erytrophtalmus*), per *cappa* la anodonta (*Anodonta cygnea*); i granchi e i gamberetti si trovano nelle specie *Patamon edule* e *Palaemontes varians*. Tutti i pesci elencati si trovano ancora nel lago, tranne la lasca, come pure le folaghe (*Fulica atra*), il germano reale (*Anas platyryncos*) e l'anatra in varie specie. Sono invece scomparsi quasi del tutto il cigno selvatico (*Cygnus cygnus*), la gru (*Megalornis grus*) e la lontra (*Lutra lutra*) che pure non è menzionata nel brano di Piccolpasso.

III. Medieval Islam

12

ISLAMIC ECOLOGY: THE DE-ALIENATION OF PERSONS FROM NATURE

Parviz Morewedge

Metaphysics of the Self as a Framework for Ecology

Contemporary ecological stances often depend on a choice between two implicit metaphysical presuppositions: (a) the state of personhood requires a context of "being-in-the-world" (including the world's physical dimensions), but (b) human beings (persons) and the physical environment is fundamentally alienated from one another. If nature were construed as an essential dimension of personhood, ecology would emerge as a dimension of self-preservation; nature would become, in fact, a manifestation of the "extended self." As this essay will demonstrate, such an ecological perspective actually exists within the intellectual tradition of Islam.

Islam is not alone in this regard, of course; the concept of the extended self presents itself in many ordinary connotations of "personhood." Soldiers going to war, or persons sacrificing themselves for a religious cause, vividly illustrate the dynamics of the phenomena of the extended self. The love of parents for children shows that the extended self is indeed universal and holds in all cultures. A parent feels lost without her/his children; when a child eats, the mother is totally attentive and is unaware of her own hunger. Indeed, in a nonsyntactical and a phenomenal sense, a child is more his/her parent than a parent is her/himself.

In such contexts, actions of persons extend beyond the ordinary language notion of a person as restricted to the field of her/his body. For example, in most nomadic cultures, from East Asian to Middle Eastern, Native American and African, the notion of a person extends beyond the immediate family, extended family, or the tribe; as the experience of a journey is entangled with the natural environment through which one travels, persons and nature become essentially connected. Nor are nomads alone in their regard for nature. In cultures in which worship is carried out in sacred spaces such as temples and mosques, the sacredness of the physical entities is iconic functions for the invisible spirit.

By contrast, if a "person" is conceived to be alienated from his/her natural environment, then ecology needs some suprapersonal justification, such as the belief that nature is a gift of some divine entity. Furthermore, if the physical dimension of nature is depicted as evil, or persons are viewed as pure disembodied spirits—with an implicit implication of inferiority of their body—then one needs special arguments for extending "care" to material entities; thus justification of ecological concerns needs secondary and not primary sui generis considerations.

The Notion of Person and Nature in Islamic Ethos

Notwithstanding the transcendent elements of the divine in Islamic religious tradition, this essay points to a very strong core of Islamic intellectual tradition that logically supports an ecological perspective of nature. By "Islamic intellectual tradition" I mean both a dimension of its formal theology as well as its philosophical tradition. Being grounded in the naturalism of Greek philosophical tradition and the monistic mysticism affected by Zoroastrianism, Islamic philosophy often takes a nonmonotheistic stand, such as adhering to the cosmogony of emanation instead of creation. Islamic theology too shades positive light on nature, teaching that nature is a gift of the divine, partaking in the positive norm of its maker. (Qur'an 29:60-62; 51:58; 52:28) From a more mystical standpoint, Shabistari argues that even idols are good, because whatever comes from The Good is also good.[1] Constructing a theoretical framework for the de-alienation of persons from the ground of their being as well as nature, the monism embedded in Muslim emanationism contradicts the dualistic ontology of the God/world distinction in monotheistic systems.

In this chapter, I argue against the interpretations of several contemporary scholars such as S. H. Nasr and S. Inatai who, in my opinion, mistakenly either identify the concept of "persons" with nonworldly spiritual entities or view evil as a dimension of nature.[2] To support my position, I draw from the work of R.C. Zaehner and his categorization of mysticism into the "theistic, isolation type" and the "monistic, integrative type." Here, Zaehner argues that in the integrative, monistic, nature-oriented type of mysticism, mystics aim to integrate themselves within nature, including its physical constituents.[3] In contrast, in the theistic, isolationist type of mysticism, the so-called soul needs to isolate itself from its embodied nature; only in such as separated state can the soul be connected in some sense to a supranatural, immaterial type of entity. A paradigm case of such isolation is proffered by Zaehner in regard to the crucifixion of Christ: "Man, having crucified the 'ego' on the cross, ascends into heaven where he is eternally united with the Father through the force of attraction which is the Holy Ghost Who is substantial love and substantial joy."[4]

Not all types of mysticism have religious significance. In this vein, W. T. Stace asserts, "There are several grounds for insisting that intrinsically and in itself mystical experience is not a religious phenomenon at all and that its connection with religion is subsequent and even adventitious."[5] His basic reason for the distinction between mysticism and religion is based on his assumption that mystical experience points to an undifferentiated unity among all entities. I read him as follows. Monotheistic religions presuppose a dualism between a transcendent God and a phenomenal world. In contrast, mystical experience dealienates persons from the world in the light of its monistic vision. Since dualism and monism are incompatible, mysticism in its monistic mode is incompatible with a dualistic interpretation of monotheism.

These concerns are not mere lofty philosophical conceptual games; they have implications for existentially significant everyday life issues such as the physical pleasures of food, sexuality and our attitude towards the feminine. Noteworthy is the implication of the attributes of "physical" and "natural" to the so-called feminine archetype.[6] For example, in some types of theistic mysticisms, the ideal woman as the positive archetype of the great mother is the immaculate virgin praised for avoiding sexual relations.[7] In contrast, for nature mystics the feminine archetype is represented by an "earth mother" who fully participates in sexual relations as part of nature's vegetation mysteries as the so-called fourth element.[8]

An interesting contrast between these two interpretations is found in the views of C. G. Jung and R. C. Zaehner. For Jung the feminine principle has its roots in the so-called anima dimension of man's archetype. During his process of individuation, which is Jung's ethics of self-realization, a man should integrate within himself those characteristics that society has labeled as feminine, such as nurturing children. When a person violates integration, Jung argues, by following Nietzsche "to kill the feminine within himself," the result is insanity. As he himself puts it: "She [the anima] is not an invention of the conscious, but a spontaneous product of the unconscious." In his nonnormative account of the negative and the positive effects of the female counterparts, Jung makes no reference to God.[9] In contrast, Zaehner directly attacks the Jungian framework as follows:

> The symbolic significance of the dogma of the Assumption is not [Jung's view that] the deification of the "eternal feminine," a collective unconscious, or whatever it may be, but the deification of the human soul as represented by Mary, who is common with all human beings, is the daughter of the One Father, and is, in her own right, the spouse of the Holy Ghost and Mother of the Son. Through Immaculate Conception she is sinless and therefore "whole," an integrated personality already.[10]

At issue is the value of the human body. Does the greatest human fulfilment come from perfection of the body's peculiar functions, including the heterosexual relations that culminate in having children so the human species continues? Or, in contrast, is there a "higher" state of existence that involves rejection of sexuality, as practiced by celibate monks and exemplified in the virgin birth? Of course there is a counterargument that celibacy is for a select chosen few. But one cannot deny the negative normative implication of this perspective for sexuality. The degradation of sexuality is often connected with degradation of the physical environment to a so-called higher realm which can receive only out separated soul-self. In religions such as Catholicism and Manichaeism, the chosen elite—namely the clergy—is required to practice celibacy. An extreme asceticism, in the sense of attributing evil to matter, is found in Mani's teaching as follows:

> the doctrine of the two primary elements, God and matter, stood at the center of Mani's system. The two eternal substances, that never pass through creation, could also go by the names of Light and Darkness or Truth and Lie. Thus the impersonal concept of Truth and Light could be regarded as a personal being, God, whilst correspondingly Lie and Darkness received not only the impersonal appellation Matter but were also personalized as "the Prince of darkness."[11]

I claim that there is a common misunderstanding that Islamic spirituality is ascetic and antiphysical. Many facts belie such an interpretation. Take, for example, the notion of temporary marriage, the spirit behind polygamy in Islam, and the emphasis on the economic rights of women in both inheritance laws and in marriage.[12] In spite of the nonspiritual dimensions of these practices, no guilt is associated with sexual relations as long as they are practiced in accord with religious laws. In Islamic formal theology, physical pleasures are an aspect of the gracious gift of the Divine to creatures. Most Muslim philosophers are more influenced by Greek thinkers than monotheistic cosmologies, and thus shy away from the view of evil and asceticism that is well grounded in some Christian types of monasticism. Readers familiar with my earlier criticism of application of the Zaehner's view may wonder if I have changed my mind about the specific argument I presented against his views.[13] I have not. In spite of my criticism of the application of his model to Sufism, in my opinion the general account of his "monistic mysticism" shows an insightful grasp of the connections between normative views on nature and self-realization ethics.

When one turns to Islamic perspectives on the issue of alienation from nature, as to be expected there is no agreement on this issue. On the one hand we have the official orthodoxy depicting God as a transcendent entity. In this vein, Qur'an reads that "God is Absolute, there is nothing like it. It does not beget and it is not begotten" (Qur'an, 112:1-4). Along with other monotheistic creeds, Islamic theology teaches that God is independent of the World, as He created the universe out of nothing. This act of creation is a gift, a graceful blessing (*karama*) of God; God is most merciful and most kind (Qur'an 9:117 -118).

Is this a universal theme in the Muslim tradition? The answer, at least in formal theology, is yes. But, as is to be expected in all of the world's great religions, there are diverse tendencies. Accordingly, in the rich realm of Islamic theology, one finds some themes that may be interpreted or misinterpreted as monism connecting the world and a notion of an Ultimate Being, which is more akin to The One of Plotinus than to the God of Islam.[14] Here again, the tendency is to assert that the entire world is an emanated reflection of the hidden world, which has a divine constituent. I realize that this move is more "all is Godism" than "all is nature." In the schema of "all is Godism" the alienation between humanity and its source (*arche*) disappears.

If in fact the salient features of what Zaehner labels as "monism" are found in classical philosophy and mystical poetry, one may "Why philosophy?" Here, the answer is obvious. Transcendent monotheism has a number of philosophically serious problems exemplified by the following questions. Prima facie, it is meaningless to make sense of "nothing"—thus how can the world be out of nothing? Since a transcendent deity is in the Kantian noumena, there are epistemological, ontological, and semantic difficulties with the designatum of this concept.

In addition to these issues there is a serious normative problem in transcendent monism. Suppose, as Marxists, psychoanalysts, and existentialists agree, alienation is a prime problem of humanity. In one sense of the term, "alienation" signifies a separation between persons and their source, such as the ground of their being, the Greek *arche* and the Arabic-Persian *al.* There are two senses in which an Ultimate Being emerges as the ground of an entity. First, in the light of monistic cosmogony, an Ultimate Being such as the One of Plotinus or the Necessary Existent of ibn Sina is the source of all entities, including the souls of persons. Second, the Ultimate Being as the ultimate partner in the process of mystical union is the last phase of ethics of self-realization; in a process language, the last phase of persons would be indistinguishable from the One.

Traditional Sufic models point to two aspects of person—the ephemeral self that is annihilated in the process of mystical union; and that dimension of the self, which reaches a persisting mode of eternity via its mystical union with the One. This cyclical model is best clarified by the analogy of a river, which descends from an ocean and returns to it. As we have pointed out in substance-event ontology, a union between a transcendent substance and a finite self-substance would be a categorical mistake; the only permissible substantial change is in context of the pair of generation and destruction.[15] In the light of this restriction, prima facie a metaphysical system has only one option. If it adopts a substance-event language with time as an accident, then it is resigned to a state of alienation between human beings and God. It could, however, choose another type of metaphysics—such as a phenomenological one—where the divine is an incarnation of the monadic self. In the language of Shabistar, the divine is then a reflection of a soul-self. Through depicting mystical union as the last phase of a series of processes that culminates in the merging of the soul-self into an Ultimate Being, I have argued that such a model is a more adequate interpretation of ibn Sinan metaphysics than the religious creation model.[16] Being a universal theme, the doctrine of emanation and return is found in most ancient myths; but where is the philosophical root of cosmogony? If we translate the Greek term *ousia* as substance, as A. H. Armstrong does, then the following passage in *The Enneads* illustrates the doctrine's prototype. Here Plotinus talks about the ascent of the soul towards the One:

> [The soul] will arrive, not in something else but at itself, and in this way since it is not in something else it will not be in nothing, but in itself alone and not in that being, it is in that; for one becomes, not substance, but "beyond substance" by this converse.
>
> The Enneads [9, 10][17]

It should be noted that such a mystical union does not constitute annihilation of the self, but rather the annihilation of the ego dimension of the self that seeks otherness with the One. Islamic mysticism uses the terms (*)*fana'* (ego annihilation) as opposed to *baqa'* (persistence). Plotinus alludes to both the genetic as well as to the joyful features of such a journey through the analogy of the soul's desire for such as union being like the love of the daughter for the father.18 In Islamic circles the germ of this process theory began in the systems of ibn Arabi and in ibn Sina; later it fully developed in the philosophies of S. Suhrawardi and Mulla Sadra.[19] As I have indicated, a major ontological issue here is that time is treated not as an accident but as substantial.[20] The root of this interesting perspective is in fact Neoplatonic, a tradition that influenced Augustine. As observed by M. Wagner,

> Plotinus maintains that a properly philosophical conception of time would denote the cause (aitia) and source (arche) of real existents which justify various of our temporal concepts and statements.[21]

Suppose we can verbally abstract the temporal dimension of an entity. If so, it does not follow that time in itself is an accident, but only that the hypothetical absoluteness of the temporal dimension of an event is questionable. It is true that (as Leibniz argues) temporal dimensions of a set of events in the same neighborhood are experientially relational and not substantial.[22] But the immediate temporal aspect of each *Dasein* is not accidental but experientially related to a specific phenomenon. There is no contradiction here. One refers to a scientific model in a realistic ontology; the other is a dimension of existential experience. None of these ideas is new. A variation of the objectivity of time was present in the pre-Islamic Iranian religion of Zurvanism, and continued after ibn Sina.

The ontological implication of the above discussion to ecology is that the tripartite space-time-matter nature of nature is also an essential dimension of the human experience. In the same manner, the notion of the spiritual aspect of a person may be abstracted verbally from other phases of human experience. The logical possibility of this linguistic move does not imply usefu1ness or adequacy in identifying the inner essence of a person as a nonphysical entity. By contrast, the bodily dimension of a person is related to its individuation.

Let me go back to varieties of monism in the Islamic tradition. Monistic themes are often expressed by depicting the ultimate being in the language of allegorical and symbolic theology, instead of affirmative or negative theology.[23] In poetry, icons are frequently employed to express the unity between persons and ultimate being without explicitly refuting orthodoxy or logical contradiction. Sometimes a mystical poet is explicit about an unorthodox position. For example, M. Shabistari (c. 13th century) questions whether or not the soul is the reflection of the phenomenon of the ultimate being or the phenomenon of the ultimate being is the reflection of the soul.[24] Another significant dimension of Shabistari's discourse is his replacement of the fearsome image of God by the joyful begetter of happiness through the beautiful gift of nature. Shabistari concludes his argument by recognizing there cannot be a duality in a true unity; for him, the doctrine of "unity" implies that essentially the expression "soul" and the ultimate being designate the same entity.[25]

This affirmative vision of return to God is found in the Qur'an (6:67,72; 10:45-46). Allegorically God is depicted as the Light of Lights in the Sura of Light *(Mishkt al-Anwar* in the Qur'an xxiv: 35-36). This light imagery is used in mystical poetry to depict a monistic ontology as follows: God is like the sun; cosmogony is like glow of the sunlight; faith is the heat of this sun in our hearts; love is the fire that returns to its origin. In a previous study, we showed how this light motif of emanation and return is applied to Rumi's mystical poetry.[26]

This latter theme is a mere repetition of Proclus's principle that "All that proceeds from any principle reverts in respect of its being to that from which it proceeds."[27] Since the Ultimate Being is the ultimate remote cause of the world, then mystical union is a mere return of entities to the ground of their being. Let us note Martin Buber's brilliant depiction of man-God encounter in the context of I and Thou. Here the Jewish theologian notes that only a glimpse of an infinite may make us aware of ourselves as finite beings; in this vein Buber asserts, "The human person is quite probably conceivable without the possibility of meeting with other men, but without that with God I cannot conceive of it."[28] After all, as Wittgenstein stated, one can never directly sees one's eyes. The self is never an object of its own experience. Through love, a lover empathizes in the *Dasein* of the beloved in such a way that she/he can inspect her/himself, as the beloved would experience her/him. Such an experience is a common one. Imagine a person who may sacrifice himself for her/his country, her/his children, or some religious cause. In such as context, she/he identifies more with his extended self then his personal self. Buber's insight may be restated as follows. Only in our glimpse of the infinite—going beyond the circle of our own finite existence—can we formulate a notion of a finite being as "the other." In ordinary experience we become aware of our age when we note the growth of our children and their evolving relation with us.

The emphasis in Islamic mysticism is close to but is still fundamentally different from Buber's vision, which as a religious monotheist cannot identify the I of the self with the Thou of the divine. Sufic vision follows the Neoplatonic theme that the soul seeks "no otherness than the One"; Plotinus states that "the One, therefore, since it is has no otherness, is always present, and we are present to it when we have no otherness" [V I9, 8-30-40]. The Islamic union goes beyond I and Thou as the finite merges into the one It, such that there is no otherness. In a sense similar to a mother and child encounter, where the former finds her in the latter, in Sufic love the finite, contingent entity finds its essence in the necessary indefinite entity. I have already proposed that, using Islamic mysticism, Descartes's *Meditations* should be reread not as a set of proofs of existence of this or that, but as a hermeneutic journey towards the ground of *Dasein.*[29] Accordingly, the ontological argument in this sense does not prove existence of an independent entity but the dependence of contingent existents. Freedom, as depicted by Spinoza, is not our independence of the world, but the discovery of the sources of our independence.[30]

Indeed, there are traces of such a monism in Islamic theology itself. In this tenor, the first primary principle of Islam reads as the so-called doctrine of unity expressed in various places (Qur'an 2:163; 6:19; 16:22; 23:91-92; 37:1-5; 38:65-68; 92:1-4). This concept has two senses. In its primary sense, the notion of unity points to God as simple entity.[31] If God were a complex of simpler constituents, then It would had been caused by these constituents. For example, the material cause of water consists of its oxygen and hydrogen. Consequently, because it is composed of simpler constituents, water is neither self-sufficient nor omnipotent. Thus the attribute of unity has been adopted as a principle of religion in Islam. But this doctrine has its mystical counterpart in the cosmos as expressed in the doctrine of the unity of existents held by a number of philosopher mystics.[32]

Such a position is analogous to Spinoza's monism, which asserts that the notions of "the Divine," "the World," and "Substance" refer to the same entity.

Accordingly, what may be called a person is in fact a mode of the world-nature. Thus one may either consider the environment as a mere extension of a person or the self as a spatial-temporal modification of the entire reality. I am not trying to push the complex set of Islamic doctrine to a finely-toned Spinozaic ontology. Conceiving later Islamic ontology predominately as process metaphysics, the primary metaphysical primitive is not a substance of integrated processes in which a human being's experience is grounded in nature—"nature" referring here to A. N. Whitehead's connotation of the word as being that which is given to experience.[33]

A paradigm case of Islamic mystical depiction of the self as a process is found in ibn Sina's phenomenological ontology. For him (as opposed to that of Hegel), development is not ontologically prior to the Absolute. First, in an intentional language, being is encountered in experience. Second, in the intentional phenomenological account, what is experienced is the subject not as a substance but in the light of "being-in-the world"; this process in mysticism may be described as a series of transformation of phases, which consists of stations and states. Third, the last phase of this process-path can be viewed as an incarnation into a mystical union with the Necessary Existent, which is the ground of the being of persons. Finally, there is an urge for a de-alienation through a vision of the unity of existents. A common allegorical theology points to the image of persons as a river, which returns to its oceanic source, or a flame, which ejects towards its source, the sun.

The above position, linking a mystical depiction of the self with an ecologically friendly view of physical nature, faces two prima facie objections by an alternative tendency in Islamic scholarship, as I will illustrate. The first objection holds that in some sense the essential self is a disembodied spirit; consequently, the bodily dimension of the person is an unworthy appendage, which should finally be "isolated" prior to salvation of the soul. This argument does not make a linguistic metalanguage distinction between the spiritual and the physical terms; it fails to note that one is in space while the other is not. Aristotle never made this type of mistake, as he demonstrates in his doctrines that neither form nor matter exists in nature in isolation. But we still often encounter the common platitude that the spirit is in some sense "higher" than the physical. Obviously such a notion alienates a person from her/his own bodily constituents as well as from the physical pleasures of the material world.

The second family of objections points to matter as a kind of "evil," which devalues any care for the physical dimension of nature which has no immediate concern to the so-called spiritual person. Next I shall turn to counter objections to these theses.

Depiction of Spirit and the Alienation of Persons from Nature

One danger of postulating a transcendent realm for all values lies in the shortchanging of nature and the physical world; on such an agenda, the care of nature takes a back seat to the preparation of the self for salvation. Very cleverly John Dewey points out that often values are not imposed from the outside but they are embedded in human nature. Accordingly, Dewey notes:

> The fundamental conceptions of morals are, therefore, neither arbitrary nor artificial. They are not imposed upon human nature from without out of its operations and needs . . . the framework of moral conception is as permanent as human life itself.[34]

On the surface, this position may appear to be contrary to Plato's dictum that the soul is justice, depicted as a harmony between parts of the soul in which we are supposed to control our appetites.[35] This division between thinking and other faculties (such as feeling) has been challenged many times in the history of philosophy, such as in Nietzsche's thesis of "will to power" and Rousseau's doctrine of "sympathy." An example of such a tendency is found in contemporary philosophical psychology where "passions" and "feelings" are depicted as essential constituents of any rational process. In this vein, Antonio R. Damasio argues that in fact the so-called passions and feelings are essential constituents of process of reasonability; he cites a number of cases of persons who accidentally lose the functionality of the part of their brain that deals with feelings and passions. Such persons totally lose their sense of rationality that includes the Aristotelian notion of practical wisdom (*phronesis*). Damasio asserts:

> Feelings do seem to depend on a dedicated mulicomponent system that is indescribable from biological regulation. Reason does seem to depend on specific brain systems, some of which happen to be feeling.[36]

Reasoning as applied to human experience is often not the application of logically valid schema to syllogisms, but deliberations illustrated by John Dewey's following account of end-means process of inquiry:

> The science that is our distinctively human use is that in which warranted ideas about nonhuman world are integrated with emotions as human traits. In this integration not only is science itself a value (since it is the expression and the fulfillment of a special human desire and interest) but it is the supreme means of the valid determination of all valuation in all aspects of human and social life.[37]

In sum, both in Dewey's pragmatism and contemporary psychology, human values about nature are construed as essential constituents of both reasonability and scientific knowledge. The opposition to this view is found in the writings of those (often religiously motivated) who attempt to de-materialize values and thus strip nature of its intrinsic worth. They often maintain that persons are embedded with a divine spiritual ingredient, which is contaminated by the urges of the body. Even though the body craves "worldly goods," it should be scolded, as "true happiness" lies in our spiritual dimension. I take this reading to be a misinterpretation of the Islamic ethos which connects Islamic with ascetic monasticism. Seyyed Hosein Nasr proffers an example of this position below.

> Men no longer climb spiritual mountains—or at least rarely do so. They now want to conquer all mountain peaks. They wish to deprive the mountain of all of its majesty by overcoming it . . . Christianity by the spiritual experience of the Divine Comedy and in Islam by the nocturnal ascension of the Prophet Mohammad (upon whom be

> peace) is no longer available to man, there remains the urge to fly into space and conquer the heavens.[38]

If the reader has depicted an antimodern, antiscientific tenor accompanying Nasr's spirituality, she/he is correct. Note how Nasr places Alchemy over Chemistry.

> The traditional sciences such as alchemy, which can be compared to the celebration of a cosmic mass, became reduced to a chemistry in which the substances had lost all their symbolic intelligibility, a fact that is mostly responsible for the crisis which the modern scientific world view and its application brought about.[39]

What are the etymological and historical contexts of this view? Let us reflect on the etymological roots of the concept of "spirit"—the English term is derived from the Latin "spiritus," semantically rooted in the Greek *pneuma.* One major occurrence of this term is in the *New Testament,* which reflects *ruhwach* in Hebrew and *ruh* in the Qur'an. The religious version of this familiar allegorical imagery points to the act of the divine breathing life into clay.

While this beautiful story is a part of the sacred monotheistic tradition linking human beings to a divine origin, it cannot seriously be presented as a scientifically credible point. By "credible" I mean that it is not reasonable to say that because sacred monotheistic texts use such a symbolic account of generation of life, "spirit" in fact exists as a designatum of a human person. The theme of creation of the world or human being by a mediator from the divine appears in many mythological accounts of religious beliefs; Ancient Egyptian mythology portrays a beautiful image of human beings being creating from the weeping of the eye of the All-Lord, Re."[40]

The philosophical roots of the term are clarified in at least two dimensions. The first rests with the conjecture of ancient historians who point to a family of similar concepts: the motion of sperm in early orgiastic religions; Indic "agni" (fire); Indic-Iranian "mithra," which are embedded with the "light motif" expressed later in notions such as "the inner light of reason," and self-evident analytical truths. It is well known that philosophers like Aristotle and ibn Sina use this concept as a dimension of the nonphysical aspect of a person that comprises of the soul (*psyche, nafs*), the spirit (*pneuma, ruh*) and intelligence (*nous, aql*). In the light of these tripartite aspects of the mental, it is intelligence rather than spirit that is referenced as the candidate for supraspecial status of human beings.

Several key passages in Aristotle points to the independent sources of the mental aspect of humanity.[41] In the Aristotelian sense, this material is presented as a description of human nature using a certain set of complex concepts, as well as a proof for the existence of a notion. An example of the latter is his proof for the prime mover.

Often in western philosophy proof of the soul is described in the light of the Cartesian attempt to prove existence of the soul-self; this is indeed riddled with many philosophical problems. One difficulty lies in the logic of the argument, which at best he can assert to an activity. What Descartes should have asserted is that whatever I state implies that there is an activity which prima facie implies participation of an agent; we may not know which specific body belongs to such an agent, but this does not prove that the agent is or can be disembodied.

Another objection rests on the celebrated logical possibility of a "private language," posited by Wittgenstein.[42] His well-known position is based on the definition of language as a societal game, in which criteria for following the rules of the game must come from outside, in the sense that a ruler cannot be used to measure itself. Noteworthy here is the fact that there is no way the notion of a person can be construed without reference to bodily behavior in a social physical setting. At best the so-called spiritualist must presuppose a moral dualism in which a spiritual dimension of the person for some reason has a "higher" function than the physical part. Even if this is the case, the physical part partakes some of the moral aspect of the physical, as it becomes a necessary constituent for persistence of the spiritual dimension.

These ascetic tendencies are present in Western philosophy as demonstrated in Neoplatonism as well as later Christian asceticism. In Neoplatonism, however, the body is ultimately referred to as instrument, played by the musician (the soul), and discarded after its use. It is highly questionable if such an attitude finds many supporters in Islamic philosophy.[43] Ironically, however, the development of Islamic philosophy, closely associated as it is with the religion of Islam, is also falsely associated with asceticism; consequently, the reader looks and finds asceticism in any Islamic doctrine including the notion of person.

Being careful to avoid mistakes, philosophers such as David Hume and Immanuel Kant do not follow the Cartesian error of the substantial theory of the soul. In light of his primitive tendency to assert contingent knowledge or impressions as the basis of matter-of-fact statements, and his rejection of the possibility of experiencing self as a substance, Kant is also careful to depict the phenomenal self in the light of the transcendental unity of apperception, which is a container of experience rather than a substance. His entire theory of substance is a transcendental concept, which places it as a dimension of talking about experience rather than a discovery.

The same is true with very careful Muslim philosophers. Ibn Sina's conundrum of the flying man does not prove existence of the substantial soul, but similar to Heidegger depicts a field of experience. A few interpreters like Leon Goodman misinterpret this position as the Cogito of Descartes. In my opinion the best treatment of this view is found in the recent work of Nader El-Bizri who compares the phenomenological views of ibn Sina and Heidegger on being and persons. In this light el-Bizri writes:

> Avicenna's consideration of the encounter of being through an existential analytic of the existence of al-nafs (anima, Dasein) is hermeneutic and . . . is not based on subjectivity . . . [but] of how *al-nafs* is the limit of the world . . . [and] . . . does not exist as a metaphysical subject.[44]

Obviously the notion of "spirit" as a metalinguistic tool may be useful to clarify certain aspects of activities of a large number of believers. Just because "spirit" might be a more adequate tool than the materialistic reduction of human behavior, it does not prove the following two themes: it does not show that "the spirit" is an object-language term designating some actual entity in the physical world; and it does not prove that in order to overcome simplistic mechanistic materialism, we have to appeal to the spiritual. We could also use some non-physical notion such a psychological attitudes.

In sum, nature is an essential dimension of an operational notion of persons. Verbally the concept of "a person" may be abstracted from the actual world; in the actual world, however, a person is inseparable from nature, including its physical dimensions. Obviously there is no need to censor any quality ascribed to the complex activities of a person, including the notion of the "spiritual," to account for religious, mystical, aesthetic, and other aspirations of persons, even though these may be "caused" in some models from sexual, economic, and other more "basic" drives. Prima facie, there is no basis for the supposition that in some sense the spiritual dimension of a human being is morally superior to other dimension. Our perspective construes nature to be an essential dimension of a person. Consequently, preservation of nature is necessarily connected with self-preservation. As we have shown, the prima facie presumption of spirituality and "antimatter" asceticism is not compatible with a dominate sense of naturalism in either major Greek or classical Islamic philosophy.

Notes

1. Shabistari, *Gulshan-i Ras,* ed. J. Nourbakhsh (Tehran: Ferdousi Press, 2535 A.H.), 56. Shabistar argues as follows. As the divine is a transcendent entity, each person can mystically point to the divine from her/his perspective. Thus an idol should be viewed in the light of the love of the believer. Moreover, since the divine is the Perfect Good and an idol as the divine generates a reality, and only good comes form Good, then an idol is also a positive entity.

2. See Parviz Morewedge, "The Transcendent Spirit, Private Language Fallacy, and Islamization of Ibn Sina: Reflections on the Works of S. H. Nasr," in *The Philosophy of Seyyed Hossein Nasr*, ed. Lewis Edwin Han, Randall E. Auxier, and Lucian W. Stone Jr. (Chicago: Open Court, 2001).

3. R. C. Zaehner, *Mysticism, Sacred and Profane* (Oxford: Oxford University Press, 1960).

4. Zaehner, 207.

5. W. T. Stace, *The Teachings of the Mystics* (New York: Macmillan, 1960), 23.

6. The most comprehensive study of the so-called feminine archetype is found in Erich Neumann, *The Great Mother*, tr. Ralph Manheim (Princeton: Princeton University Press, 1972).

7. Carl G. Jung notes "I consider the Assumption as a cautious approach to the solution of the problem of opposites, namely, to the integration of the fourth metaphysical figure into the divine totality. The Catholic Church has almost succeeded in creating a quaternity without shadow, but the devil is still outside. . . . Being a natural and a spontaneous symbol, the quaternity has everything to do with human psychology, while the Trinitarian symbol (though equally spontaneous) has become cold, a remote abstraction." C. G. Jung, *The Symbolic Life: Miscellaneous Writings*, tr. R. F. Hull (London: Routledge, 1977), 714.

8. See E. Neumann, *The Great Mother*, 73-83.

9. C. G. Jung, *Aion*, tr. R. F. C. Hull (Princeton: Princeton University Press, 1968), 13-14.

10. Zaehner, *Mysticism, Sacred and Profane*, 120.

11. George Widengren, *Mani and Manichaeism* (New York: Holt, Rinehart and Winston, 1965), 43.

12. See Qur'an, various citations.

13. P. Morewedge, "Sufism, Neoplatonism and Zaehner's Theistic Theory of Mysticism," in *Islamic Philosophy and Mysticism*, ed. Parviz Morewedge (Delmar: Caravan Books, 1981).

14. Parviz Morewedge, "The Neoplatonic Structure of Some Islamic Mystical Doctrines," in *Neoplatonism and Islamic Thought*, ed. Parviz Morewedge (Albany: State University of New York Press, 1992), 51-76.

15. Parviz Morewedge, "Substance and Theories of the Self in Islamic Mysticism," in Parviz Morewedge, *Essays in Islamic Philosophy, Theology, and Mysticism* (Oneonta: Oneonta Philosophy Studies, 1995).

16. Parviz Morewedge, "The Logic of Emanationism and Sufism in ibn Sina," *The Journal of the American Oriental Society*, Part I, 91:4 (1971): 467-476; Part II, 92:1 (1972): 1-18.

17. *Plotinus*, trans. A. H. Armstrong, Vol. vii, 345.

18. Armstrong, *Plotinus*, 337.

19. All of these Muslim thinkers rejected the substance-event theory of Aristotle. For ibn Arabi, the cosmos is depicted in the light of phases of unfolding from the Absolute One. Ibn Sina, instead of opting for the Qur'anic cosmogony of creation or the Aristotelian model of co-eternity, chose the neo-Platonic doctrine of emanation. Accordingly, he depicts cosmos in the light of an eschatological layer of entities—the One, the Intellect, the Universal Soul, the individual souls and bodies. Moreover, ibn Sina proffers a model of return of the soul to the Necessary Existent. (See *The Metaphysics of Avicenna* (*Ibn Sina*), tr. P. Morewedge [New York: Columbia University Press, 1970], chapter 37.) S. Suhrawardi's full-fledged ontology of illumination depicts the cosmos as layers of light, in which the One is identified as a light of lights (nur al-anwar). (See *Suhrawardi's Philosophy of Illumination*, tr. John Walbridge and Hossein Ziai [Provo: Brigham Young University Press, 2000]; also Majid Fakhry, "Suhrawardi Against the Peripatetic Philosophers," in *Philosophies of Existence*, ed. Parviz Morewedge [New York: Fordham Uni-

versity Press, 1972], xxx-xl.) Finally, an explicit process-type of philosophy is found in Mulla Sadra's ontology of layers of existence, God being "pure absolute existence." (See *The Metaphysics of Mulla Sadra*, tr. Parviz Morewedge [New York: SSIPS, 1992].)

20. See *The Metaphysics of Mulla Sadra*, tr. Parviz Morewedge (New York: SSIPS, 1970).

21. See Michael F. Wagner, "Real Time in Aristotle, Plotinus and Augustine," in *The Journal of Neoplatonic Studies* (IV: 2): 81.

22. See *The Leibniz-Clarke Correspondence*, ed. H. G. Alexander (Manchester: Manchester University Press, 1956).

23. See Parviz Morewedge, "Mystical Icons in Rumi's Metaphysical Poetry: Light, the Mediator, and the Way," in *Essays in Islamic Philosophy, Theology and Mysticism*, 195-236.

24. Shabistar, *Gulshan-R*, 51-52.

25. *Gulshan-R*, 51-52.

26. P. Morewedge, "Mystical Icons in Rumi's Metaphysical Poetry: Light, the Mediator and the Way," in Essays in *Islamic Philosophy, Theology and Mysticism*, 195-236.

27. *Proclus: The Elements of Theology*, ed. and tr. E. R. Dodds (London: Oxford University Press, 1953), 35.

28. *The Philosophy of Martin Buber*, Paul Arthur Schlipp, ed. (London: Cambridge University Press, 1967), 694.

29. See Parviz Morewedge, "A Third Version of the Ontological Argument in the ibn Sinan Metaphysics," in *Islamic Philosophical Theology*, ed. Parviz Morewedge (Albany: State University of New York Press, 1979), 188-222. Here I argue that the so-called Ontological Argument of Augustine and Descartes can be reconstructed as a hermeneutic search towards various phases of the self-world, as "being"—"the subject as the beholder of experience, the Necessary Being as the ground of experience and ultimately a search for the unity of existence."

30. See Parviz Morewedge, "Ibn Sina (Avicenna) and Malcolm and the Ontological Argument," *The Monist* 54, no.2 (April 1970): 234-249. Here I argue that the primary sense of the Necessary Being is not as the most independent entity, but, following Spinoza, as the ground of our dependency.

31. See Parviz Morewedge, "Theology," in *The Oxford Encyclopedia of the Modern Islamic World*, ed. John K. Esposito (New York: Oxford University Press, 1995), 218-224.

32. For an example of controversy concerning this notion, see Al-Taftazani's criticism of ibn Arabi in Alexander D. Knysh, *Ibn Arabi in the Later Islamic Tradition: the Making of a Polemical Image in Medieval Islam* (Albany: State University of New York Press, 1999), 146-153.

33. Alfred North Whitehead, *The Concept of Nature* (Ann Arbor: University of Michigan Press, 1957). Whitehead states, "Nature is that which [is] observe[d] in perception through the senses. . . . Nature is not thought" (3). His main premise is to show that in experience we directly encounter nature and not "thought." In light of this model, nature is inseparable from the self through sense perception.

34. John Dewey and James H. Tufts, *Ethics* (New York: Henry Holt, 1936), 344. A salient point in Dewey's ethical theory is that human nature should be taken as the primary source of morality and not as a compendium of habits and needs to be corrected by some transcendent yardstick.

35. In the *Republic*, Plato never depicts an ascetic position that unconditionally degrades physical pleasure. Instead, his view of justice is that of a harmony like the "proportion of a musical scale, the highest and lowest notes and the mean between them," stating that the just man may "be ready to go about whatever he may have to do, whether it be making money and satisfying bodily wants, or business transactions of state." *The Republic of Plato* [iv.433], tr. F. M. Cornford (London: Oxford University Press, 1941).

36. Antonio R. Damasio, *Descartes' Error: Emotion, Reason and the Human Brain* (New York: G. P. Putnam's Sons, 1994), 235.

37. John Dewey, "Theory of Valuation," in *Foundation of the Unity of Science* (Chicago: University of Chicago Press, 1970), 446.

38. S. H. Nasr, *The Encounter of Man and Nature* (Albany: State University of New York Press), 19.For our criticism of Nasr's position, see Parviz Morewedge, "The Transcendent Spirit, Private Language Fallacy and Islamization of Ibn Sina: Reflections on the Works of S. H. Nasr," in *The Philosophy of Seyyed Hossein Nasr*, ed. L. E. Han, R. E. Auxier, and L. W. Stone, Jr. (Chicago: Open Court, 2001), 735-753.

39. Nasr, *The Encounter of Man and Nature*, 21.

40. See Hans Bonnet, "Re" in *Reallexikon der ägyptischen Religiongeschichte* (Berlin, 1952), 626-630.

41. See *The Metaphysics of Avicenna (ibn Sina),* tr. Parviz Morewedge (London: Routledge, 1970). This text contains a glossary of these terms in English, Persian, Arabic, Greek, and Latin.

42. See Ludwig Wittgenstein, *Philosophical Investigations*. Wittgenstein defines private language as a language in which only the speaker can know the worlds (PI I, 243). Then he shows that words do not name a sensation such as "pain" (PI I, 244). Words are learned in experience of language games (PI I, 281, 304). Now the logic of the game is that criteria for correctness need to be outside of the game, as no one can see his/her eyes directly; and the same ruler cannot be used to measure it.

43. Plotinus is indeed not against the physical dimensions of person; after all, the genesis of the body is the result of the contemplation of the soul. It follows that one needs to attend to the body, and any discipline is a constructive one to augment the use of the body not to punish it [I.4, 4,25-30, 16. 13-29; I.4, 14]. To a happy sage, the body is like a musical instrument, which is needed to express the music of life. Graciously at death we should be ready to give up the lyre which has served us well. [I.4, 16, 13-29]

44. Nader El-Bizri, *The Phenomenological Quest between Avicenna and Heidegger* (Binghamton, N.Y.: Global Publications, 2000), 150.

13

THE UNIVERSE ALIVE: NATURE IN THE *MASNAVÍ* OF JALÁL AL-DÍN RÚMÍ

L. Clarke

This essay offers a glimpse, in the heart of that period of history we reckon from our perspective to be "mediaeval," of a non-European ecology in a part of the Western world outside (though not far removed from) Europe. That world is the Islamic world, and the ecology is a product of the Islamic tradition of mysticism known as Sufism. Why include such an essay in a volume otherwise concentrated on Greek and Christian traditions? The answer, of course, is that Islam is heir and kin to both. Without Islam, the view is incomplete. Born in the same region and choosing from a similar stock of materials and ideas, Islamic civilization constructed its own, distinctive edifice, which can be usefully compared to those of its neighbors.

Jalál al-Dín Rúmí, the poet and mystic of the title, was born in Balkh, in ancient Bactria (now Afghanistan), at the beginning of the thirteenth century. The greater part of his life, however, was spent in Anatolia, chiefly in the town of Konya, where he died in 1273. Thus he lived in the midst of that epoch from the twelfth through the fourteenth centuries which, not only in Islam but also in Christendom and among the Jewish peoples, saw an unparalleled efflorescence of mystical thought.[1] Rúmí inspired the foundation of the *Mevleviyah* order of Sufis, famous in the West as the "Whirling Dervishes." But more important, he composed a very large quantity of mystical poetry. His lyrics are collected under the name *Díván-i Shams* or "The Poetical Works of Shams," after a mysterious dervish who, before he suddenly disappeared without a trace, was Rúmí's first saintly "mystical beloved." The *Díván-i Shams* is an outpouring of the ecstasy of mystical experience. Rúmí's theosophy, on the other hand, is expounded in the 26,000-line *Masnaví* (literally, "poem in rhymed couplets"). The *Masnaví* is a didactic work filled with colorful parables and allegory, and most of this essay depends upon it.

The essay begins by reconstructing Rúmí's vision of nature. This part of the discussion is divided into three sections: first, the universe in general; second, the animal world; and third, the workings of Eros (*'ishq*). My liberal use of quotations here and throughout the discussion is intended to illustrate not only the substance but also the tenor of Rúmí's teaching. In the fourth section I go on to describe the metaphysical context of these views and to locate Rúmí's vision of nature at a particular juncture—between the antimaterialist, idealist impulses of mysticism and Gnosticism on the one hand, and the positive, natural realism of the "orthodox" Islam of the revelation on the other. I finally attempt to evaluate Rúmí's ecological message. What can we learn from this master of theosophical Sufism for the purposes of our modern thinking about the environment? I find that, while the poet's primary purpose is, without doubt, to make a statement about God and Man and not about nature, he does, nevertheless, suggest an intuitive, ecstatic mode of *experiencing* nature that may have something to teach us. This essay is also intended as a contribution to debate about the ecological potentials of monotheism and mysticism. Monotheism, since it implies anthropocentrism, has been accused of desacralising nature; while mysticism, since it appears to be world denying, has sometimes been seen as rejecting the value of a natural world thought to be illusory. The *Masnaví*, I think, challenges both these propositions.

I

We are able to speak of Rúmí's "ecology" because his mystical worldview is, above all, holistic. His theosophy embraces, as systematically as mystical inspiration allows, the whole universe; there is no more appropriate translation of the title of his poem, *Masnaví-ye Ma'naví*, than "The Meaning of All Things." This includes the totality of interrelations of organisms—although it should be understood that, as with the Greeks and Romans, nature for Rúmí implies everything around us, not just organic, natural or tangible things. The universe moreover, when seen as the mystic possessed of insight sees it—as a totality (*kull*) rather than in this or that part (*juz'*)[2]—is ordered, harmonious, purposive, and good. This view is partly an inheritance from the Greeks, driven as they were by the search for intelligibility and order in the cosmos. The order the Greeks imagined, however, was mechanistic, to the point of being mathematically calculable; whereas the order of Rúmí's cosmos, since it directly depends on the Grace and Mercy of a Living God, is moral and beyond calculation.

Rúmí's mystical worldview is shaped by the belief, on which he so often insists on—even commenting at one point that it is this with which "the whole of the Quran is concerned" (III, 2520)—that there are no secondary causes (pl. *asbáb*). Secondary causes are an illusion. This view derives from Islamic occasionalism—a metaphysics expounded by the orthodox, Asharite Islamic theology to which Rúmí was attached, but turned by him to mystical purposes. Thus nature is not subject to any necessary mechanical law. Rather, every thing is created anew and sustained by God at every moment; "all the atoms of earth and heaven are God's army" (IV, 783) and "in all the earth and heavens not an atom moves a wing, not a straw turns, / Save by His eternal and effectual command" (III, 1902-3). Rúmí recites in Book One of the *Masnaví*:

> What is the meaning of this Arabic word "cause"? Say rather, "cord."
> This cord came into the well of this world by Divine artifice.
> The revolution of the waterwheel causes the cord to move, but not to see the mover of the waterwheel is an error.
> Beware imagining that these cords are moved by the giddy wheel of heaven.
> (I, 847-9)

That is to say, one should not imagine anything like a set of "laws of nature" that functions by itself. God may, if and when He chooses, make the "waterwheel" (or "the wheel of heaven," that is causation) turn in a certain way; but it is nevertheless still He and He alone who turns the wheel that moves the rope (or the "cause," the Arabic word *sabab* having both meanings). If nature is constant, it is only because God, by His Mercy, lets it be so; the course of nature could equally be inverted:

> Know that the subtlety of water is not derived from the water; it is only the gift of the Bounteous Originator.
> If He makes air and fire low in place,
> and if He lets the thorn surpass the rose,
> He is the Ruler—God does as He wills. (II, 1617-19)

The universe is, moreover, *alive*. This recalls Plato's idea, expounded in the *Timaeus*, of the universe as a living being regulated by the World Soul. Rúmí's occasionalism, however, gives rise to significant differences between himself and Plato. For while the *Timaeus* deems the world a "visible living being"[3] merely by analogy between its functioning and the functioning of organisms, the *Masnaví* tells us that the world is alive because it is given life directly by God, He being the real and direct cause of every thing. Moreover, while according to Plato the world as a "living being" is also "single,"[4] with one part set in motion by another, for Rúmí, *each separate part* is animated by God's continual and separate creative acts.

Rúmí's verses on the living universe can be appreciated only if we keep in mind that all this is for him literal truth. "Earth and water and fire are His slaves," says the *Masnaví*, "with you and me they are dead, but with God they are alive" (I, 838). This is not to say that their "aliveness" is metaphoric—that most grave error of interpretation committed by the rationalist Mu`tazilites.[5] It is not merely that they are subordinate to God to a degree best expressed through metaphor. Rather they are alive actually, in as real a sense as any reality of this contingent world. But this evident truth is hidden from those without mystical insight, and the poet often reproaches the philosopher and skeptic who depend upon intellect rather than heart, and thus fail to see. For if one is not misled by the senses and the illusion of secondary causes, that nature is alive and even percipient will not seem more amazing than that humans should be so, since we also are alive only through God's intervention at each moment.

Because God arranges it so, nature is also articulate. Again, the literal truth of this reality is not to be doubted, even though it is veiled from the skeptic:

> The speech of water, the speech of earth, and the speech of mud are apprehended by the sense of them that have hearts [that is the mystics].
> The philosopher who disbelieves in the moaning pillar[6] is a stranger to the sense of the saints;
> He says that melancholia brings many phantasies into people's minds.
> Nay, but the reflexion of his wickedness and infidelity cast this idle fancy of skepticism upon him! (I, 3279-82)

The speech of nature is continual and multidirectional; Rúmí describes it as "an uproar" (*ghulghulí*). Some of these conversations are carried on between the natural things themselves, suggesting that the processes of nature, far from being mechanical, are intelligent, intimate, and affective:

> You yourself [the reader] know [instinctively] what words the sun, in the sign of Aries, speaks to the plants and the date-palms;[7]
> You yourself, too, know what the limpid water is saying to the sweet herbs and the sapling. (VI, 1068-9)

But most such conversation, or the ultimate conversation, is speech between nature and God:

> The doing of God toward all the particles of the world is like spells breathed by enchanters.
> The Divine attraction holds a hundred discourses with the effects and the secondary causes, without uttering a word or moving a lip.
> Not that the production of effects by the Divine decree is not actual; but His production of effects thereby is inconceivable to reason. (VI, 1070-72)

The import of the "hundred discourses" of God with nature becomes clear when we remember the place in Islam of the Word of God as revelation. Thus, we might think, each thing receives revelation in its own mode; to each thing is delivered its own Truth. And indeed, nature does have its own and particular wisdom. To one gifted with sense as was Solomon, nature does speak and communicates those truths. Rúmí tells how Solomon used to come each morning into the Furthest Place in Jerusalem (*al-Aqsá*, here meaning Solomon's Temple) and question the herbs growing there:

> He saw that a new plant had grown there; then he would say, "Tell your name and use—
> What medicine are you? What are you? What is your name?
> To whom are you hateful and to whom are you useful?"
> Then every plant would tell its effect and name, saying, "I am life to that one, and death to this one
> I am poison to this one, and sugar to that one: this is my name inscribed on the Tablet by the Pen of the divine Decree."

And this, according to the *Masnaví*, led to Solomon teaching the physicians, who then compiled their pharmacopoeia (IV, 1287 ff.). Nature yields its wisdom to those who understand and care to inquire; and this wisdom may perchance be heard by those whose focus is on practical use.

There are, however, morally instructive differences between nature and humankind.For instance, unlike Man, nature constantly uses its speech to praise God. "All particles of phenomenal being," declares the *Masnaví*, "whether in movement or at rest, are speakers, and declare: "Verily, to Him we are returning" / The praises and glorifications of the hidden particles have filled heaven with an uproar" (III, 465-6). Nature, in fact, is in close conversation with the divine: "Stone and earth and mountain have their invisible recourse to Him" (VI, 2420). Although humankind may doubt and is unaware of it, everything on earth glorifies God:

> Inasmuch as Thou has made everything a glorifier of Thee—both the discerning and undiscerning entity—
> Each glorifies Thee in a different fashion, and that one is unaware of the state of this one.
> Man disbelieves in the glorification uttered by inanimate things, but those inanimate things are masters in performing worship. (III 1495-7)

The Quranic inspiration for this passage, and likely for the idea of an articulate world in general, is found in the chapter of the "Ascension at Night": "The seven heavens and the earth and their inhabitants," says the Quran, "praise Him. There is nothing that does not praise Him—but you do not understand their praise" (Q. 17:44).

Nature is exemplary above all because it submits wholly to the Divine Will. So also should we give up our own will, in order to become like fire, "standing ready to do God's behest, writhing continually day and night, like a lover" (I, 839). But Man repeatedly fails to reach the standard of the natural world (even though his potential is far greater). Thus Rúmí likens the "universals" (*kulliyát*) to a ball that prostrates itself before God's polo mallet, and then he poses the question: "How should you, O heart, you who are but one of these hundred thousand particulars, not [also] be in restless movement at His decree?" (VI, 926-7).[8] The consciousness of the elements, unlike human consciousness, is never diverted from their Lord. The elements, Rúmí says, are unacquainted with us, but acquainted with God, while we are aware of things other than God, but heedless of God and the many prophets He has sent us (II, 2371). In fact, it was because they did not wish to disturb this perfect relationship that they were reluctant to accept the trust that humankind accepted: They said, "We are averse to this life—that one should be living in relation to created beings and dead in relation to God" (II, 2373). On the other hand, the elements and heavenly bodies will not be rewarded by God for this obedience, since it does not involve choice:

> This celestial sphere revolves involuntarily
> Hence its revolution has neither reward nor punishment, for free-will is (accounted) a merit at the time of Reckoning.
> All created beings indeed are glorifiers of God, but that compulsory glorification is not wage-earning. (III, 3287-9)

Nature does, nevertheless, have a moral sense. Its activity in this world is not automatic; it is purposive and meaningful. In order for nature to have this quality, it must, of course, be able to relate to the moral drama here on earth. And to relate, it must be percipient; it must literally see and hear. And so it does, by the command of God—in exactly the same way and no less so than we do. From the mountains to the wind to the stones, all nature declares: "We have hearing and sight, and are happy" (III, 1019). Only an unenlightened mind that imagined the eye to be the necessary organ of sight would think nature to be unseeing. The eye is not, in fact, the organ of sight at all. Rather, it is God alone who enables sight, as the poet explains:

> Deem not the fat [the white of the eye] to be the cause of sight, O son; otherwise none would see [visible] forms in dream. . . .
> The genie and the demon see the like, and there is no fat in the sight-organ of either.
> In fact, there was [originally] no relationship between light and the fat [of the eye]: the loving Creator gave them relationship (IV, 2403 ff.).[9]

Thus nature, through the direct intervention of God, sees and witnesses and is a moral actor. Nature's moral action is evident most strikingly in its interventions in favour of the prophets. "If I relate the help," says Rúmí, "given rationally [*'áqilánah*, that is with conscious intent and understanding] to the prophets by the inanimate things of the world, the *Masnaví* will become of such extent that if forty camels carry it, they will be unable to bear the full load" (IV, 789-90). The poet reproaches those who fail to appreciate this truth and thus deny nature's real moral sense as it works in concert with God:

> If God did not give the wind vision without eye, how did it make a distinction among the people of 'Ád?[10]

> How did it know the true believer from the unbeliever . . . ?
> If the fire of Nimrod has no eye, how can it be explained that it takes care to show respect to Abraham?
> If the Nile had not possessed that light and sight, how should it have picked out the Egyptians from the Israelites? (IV, 2411-15)[11]

Nature also observes and remembers the deeds of humankind, in order to act, as it is said in the Quran itself, as witness on the Day of Judgement:

> At the Resurrection, how should this earth give testimonies concerning good and evil without having seen?
> For [it is said in the Quran] that "she [that is the earth] will relate her experiences and informations" (Q. 94:1): the earth will reveal her secrets to us (IV 2421-2)

In a charming etiology, Rúmí attributes his ritual prostrations in prayer to a desire to make the earth his witness:

> For that reason I am laying my head [humbly] on the earth, so that she [the earth] may be my witness on the Day of Judgement.
> On the Day of Judgement, when "she shall be made to quake mightily" (Q. 98:1) this earth will bear witness to all that passed [in and from us];
> For "she will plainly declare what she knows" (Q. 99:4): earth and rocks will begin to speak.
> The philosopher, in his [vain] thought and opinion, becomes disbelieving; let him go and dash his head against this wall! (I, 3275 ff.)

Here we see that the natural world is not only obedient and good in itself, but also capable of distinguishing—and thus, in a measure, judging—the qualities of our acts.

II

Animals are a natural target of symbolic discourse about human behavior because they are animate and in close contact with us, which prompts us to attribute to them personalities as a way of speaking about ourselves—while at the same time, since we approach them as species rather than individuals, we are able to fasten to them certain characteristics, which they then exemplify. Rúmí does use animals and animal fables in this way as an ordinary didactic device. His stories are populated by timorous, foolish mice, cunning foxes, brave lions, wise elephants—and most famously, the stubborn, gluttonous donkey, representing the appetitive soul. On the level of hidden reality, however, animals in the *Masnaví* are more than simply ciphers used by the poet to construct allegories. They have their own metaphysical truth *qua* animals, from which the aspiring mystic may learn. They are, for instance, content. Their trust and reliance on God is implicit:

> In this world thousands of animals are living happily, without anxiety
> The dove on the tree is uttering thanks to God, though her food is not yet ready.
> The nightingale is singing glory to God, saying, "I rely on Thee for my daily bread, O Thou who answerest prayer." . . .
> You may take every animal from the gnat to the elephant: they all have become God's dependents...
> [While] these griefs within our breasts arise from the vapor and dust of our existence and vain desire. (I, 2291-6)[12]

Most important, the natural, God-given instinct of animals is not obscured, as is ours, by intellect and false imaginings:

> Sheep know the smell of the harmful wolf and creep away in every direction.
> The brain of animals knows the smell of the lion and bids farewell to grazing.
> You have smelled the wrath of God. Turn back! Consort with prayer and dread! (II, 387-9)

Instead the animals follow, intuitively and without confusion, the basic instinct and motive force of the universe, Love (though the unenlightened may deny that this is so):

> Wolf and bear and lion know what love is: he that is blind to love is inferior to a dog!
> If the dog had not a vein of love, how should the dog of the Cave have sought to win the heart of the Seven Sleepers. . . .[13]
> You have not smelt the heart in your own kind: how should you smell the heart in wolf and sheep? (V, 2008-11)[14]

Because animals in myth often take on the role of mediator between human and divine, their mysterious "speech" is thought to contain divine wisdom. This is the impulse behind the story in Jewish and Islamic lore of King Solomon who understood the speech of the birds and beasts.Rúmí relates the tale of a man who demanded of Moses that he teach him the language of the birds and beasts "that perchance I may get a lesson concerning my religion" (III, 3267). The man reasonably proposed: "Since the languages of the sons of Adam are entirely for the sake of acquiring water and bread and renown/ It may be that the animals have a different care, namely that of taking thought for the hour of passing away from this world" (III, 3268-9). Moses taught him what he asked, and the speech of the animals did reveal to him the future. But this knowledge, which is suited only to the enlightened saints, brought him nothing but grief, as what he finally heard was the animals' conversation about his own imminent death.In this story, nature is invested with an elemental occult power. Nature, or aspects of it, are become taboo, are become sacred. And the sacred yields its power only to those who have the wisdom and insight to properly deal with it—while those who overstep the bounds (even, it is implied here, if their intentions are good) are destroyed.

III

For Rúmí, as for Plato and Aristotle, the activity of all mortal things stems from *Eros* (*'ishq*). *Eros* is life; *Eros* is at once the Mover and the Cause:

> Know that the wheeling heavens are turned by waves of Love: were it not for Love, the world would be frozen, inanimate.
> How would an inorganic thing disappear by changing into a plant?
> How would vegetative things sacrifice themselves to become endowed with spirit? . . .
> Each one of them would be as stiff and immovable as ice; how should they be seeking and flying like locusts? (V, 3854-6)[15]

The dynamic power of *Eros* or Love is manifested in a web of mutual attraction. The skies, for example, yearn for the earth and the earth for the skies; "unless these two sweethearts are tasting delight from one another," says the poet, "then why are they creeping together, like mates?" (III, 4412). Humankind is equally caught in this system of mutual attraction, not only in relation to its own fellows, but to all that it needs and desires:

> No sound of clapping comes forth from one hand of thine without the other hand.
> The thirsty man is moaning: "O delicious water!" The water moans too, saying, "Where is the water-drinker?"
> The thirst in our souls is the attraction exerted by the Water: we are Its and It is ours.
> The Wisdom of God in destiny and in decree made us lovers of one another.
> Because of that fore-ordainment, all the particles of the world are paired as mates and each is in love with its own mate.
> And every particle of the universe is desiring its mate, just like amber and the blade of straw. (III, 4397-402)

Mutual attraction animates the whole universe as the meeting of causes continually produces effects—for instance, sound, or nourishment through drinking. The attraction of *Eros* also results, of course, in the effect of generation; God, says Rúmí, "implants the desire of every part for another part [so that] from the union of both an act of generation results" (III, 4416). The ultimate end of generation, in turn, is to perpetuate the great cycle of life; as Aristotle says, since "being is better than non-being, and living than non-living" and an organism cannot be eternal in itself, it is "eternal in the way that is possible for it,"[16] that is through attempting to perpetuate its kind. Thus the process of the universe animated by Love is that of a continually recurring cycle. And Man is an integral part of this great cycle of life, of the "caravan of spirits incessantly arriving from heaven, that they may traffic on the earth and go back again"(III, 4191):

> The grace of God bestows a throat on the earth, to the end that it may drink water and make a hundred herbs to grow.
> Again, He bestows on the animals a throat and a lip, in order that they may eat the earth's herbage and desire.
> When the animal has eaten its herbage, it becomes fat: the animal becomes a mouthful for Man and disappears.
> In turn it becomes earth and becomes a devourer of Man when the spirit and the sight are separated from him.
> I beheld the atoms (of created existence) with their mouths all open: if I should tell of their food, the tale would become long. . . .
> Know that all the world is eating and eaten. (III, 22-30)

But within this cycle, there is a linear, upward-moving process in which material is made to ascend toward spirit. Through this process, all being, including natural things, proceeds heavenward. In Platonic terms, we might say that such motion results from the defects of matter as it seeks to fulfill itself by moving closer to perfection, only the Perfect being fully at rest—the principle of plenitude. The *Masnaví*, however, vigorously communicates a sense that the movement of natural things is driven by emotion—that it is even, in some way, voluntary. All nature, Rúmí says, is impelled upward by its own aspiration for a higher state of being, which it achieves by gladly—even rapturously—sacrificing its life so as to join with that which stands above it. Thus for every "mineral that aspires toward the vegetable"—that is the vegetative state—"life grows from the tree of its fortune/ Every plant that turns its face toward the [animal] spirit drinks . . . from the Fountain of Life" (VI, 126-7). "Every mote," says the *Masnaví*, "is in love with that Perfection and hastening upward like a sapling/ Their haste is saying implicitly "Glory to God!" They are purifying the body for the sake of the spirit" (V, 3858-9). Nature's strenuous, purposeful ascent is exemplary for humankind. Man must try, just as nature eagerly does, to "die" to himself and then to welcome Death itself in order to attain to a higher state of being: "You have seen this life," says the *Masnaví*, "to be implicit in previous deaths; how, then, are you so attached to the life of the body?" (V, 807).

Rúmí's scheme at the same time integrates humankind into nature. Constituted as he is from the natural world, Man continues to be unconsciously tied to it even as he turns away to reach toward formlessness and spirit. The craving of the animal soul for animal things—for stinking dung and "fodder"—is repeatedly condemned by the *Masnaví*. But the longing for vegetable origins is portrayed in a most positive way—apparently because it is not directed, avariciously, at any particular object of desire, but represents the stirrings of a wholly natural affinity:

> First he came into the clime of inorganic things, and from the state of inorganic things he passed into the vegetable state.
> Many years he lived in the vegetable state and did not remember the inorganic state because of the opposition between them.
> And when he passed from the vegetable into the animal state, the vegetable state was remembered by him not at all,
> Save only the inclination that he has toward that state, especially in the season of spring and sweet herbs—
> Like the inclination of babes toward their mothers: the babe does not know the secret of its desire for being suckled. (IV, 3637 ff)

This instinctive affinity of the human to the green world is, in fact, parallel to that of the soul for its original sustenance: "The desire of the body for green herbs and running water is because of its origin from those.../ The desire of the soul is for wisdom and the sciences; the desire of the body is for orchards and vines." (III, 4436-8).

The enlightened mystic, however, *consciously* remembers his secret origins in nature and understands their significance.This insight allows him to accept his own death as the glad culmination of plenitude and so to contemplate his destiny after:

> I died to the organic state and became endowed with growth, and [then] I died to [vegetable] growth and attained to the animal.
> I died from animality and became Adam [man]: why, then should I fear? When Have I become less for dying?
> At the next remove I shall die to man, that I may soar and lift my head above the angels;
> And I must escape even from [that state of] the angel: "everything is perishing except His Face" (Q. 55:26).
> Once more shall I be sacrificed and die to the angel;
> I shall become that which enters not into the imagination.
> Then I shall become non-existence; non-existence saith to me, (in tones loud) as an organ: "Verily, unto Him shall we return" (Q. 2:156). (III, 3901-6)[17]

IV

Like Sufism in general, the *Masnaví* has antimaterialist overtones. This antimaterialism is centered on the body. The lesson most repeated by Rúmí, through a variety of figures and allegories, is that the aspirant must begin by conquering the fleshly appetites of the lower, animal soul (*nafs*) that fix it to the material world. We are, says Rúmí, trapped in a "disgraceful body" (*nang-i tan*, recalling Plotinus's "shame at being in a body" famously reported by Porphyry) (V, 2279). Inhabiting the body is like nothing so much as being trapped in a cage with loathsome companions;[18] our ambition should be to escape this trap to become instead "simple and all one substance . . . knotless and pure like water" (I, 686-7). The death of the body is "a welcome gift to the adepts of the mystery: what damage is done by the scissors to pure gold?" (IV, 1681). One should determinedly demolish the house of the body in order to discover the spiritual treasure beneath it; if it simply falls into ruin itself, that is if natural death intervenes without ascetic exercise, "the treasure will not be yours, since the spirit receives that Divine gift as wages for destroying the house" (IV, 2450-4).

Rúmí derides the material world somewhat less. Still, it is described as a "dark and narrow pit," while we within it are embryos, gladly drinking blood and disbelieving in the real world outside (III, 53-68).[19] The mystics know that this world, while it might seem spacious to others, is uncomfortably cramped, narrow and hot, like a bathhouse; Spirit needs a wider space to soar (III, 3535 ff). The world is a "rotten walnut," the walnut symbolizing a worthless plaything (VI, 3471); it is a phantom (III, 314 ff; IV, 1367-69); it is a deceitful ghoul (III, 216-226). The world is a loathsome old woman who imprisons the falcon of the soul (IV, 2628 ff); it is an old witch with a stinking vulva who manages to enthrall the young prince, the Spirit of Man (IV, 3085 ff.).

Nevertheless, it is very clear from the *Masnaví* that it is not nature qua nature that is at fault. The problem is not nature, but our incorrect relations with it. For the enlightened soul who experiences the whole of nature as it really is rather than grasping at this or that part, it is a foretaste, replete with blessing, of Paradise to come. In fact, God has diverted trickles of the rivers of that Garden into this world, which, though defiled here by "the poison of mortality and indigestion," can lead us toward their paradisiacal source:

> God has given milk and nourishment for babes: He has made the breast of every wife a fountain.
> He has given wine to drive away grief and care: He has made of the grape a fountain to inspire courage.
> He has given honey as a remedy for the sick body: He has given the inward part of the bee a fountain of honey.
> He gave water universally to high and low for cleanliness and for drinking.
> The object is that you should follow the track of these derivatives towards the origins; but you are content with this offshoot. (I, 1630-8)

Thus, consistent with the emanationist worldview of neo-Platonic Sufism, the world is seen as an effulgence, an overflow of Reality. And while the overflow as the poet describes it is not the main stream, it is fulsome and delightful in its own way. The bountiful earth, Rúmí says, contains "a hundred thousand impressions of the Unseen World . . . waiting graciously and kindly to spring forth from non-existence" (V, 4214).[20] "The four elements of this world obtain a hundred supplies from a City beyond space," and "the water and seeds" we find in our cage have appeared "from that Garden and Expanse" (III, 3971-2). The whole world is the form of Universal Reason, and if one is in harmony with that Reason, it will show itself to be Paradise, filled with water and greenery and constantly revealing new forms and beauties (IV, 3259-70). To him who is able to perceive nature as a manifestation of the Unseen, it is ever fresh, always changing, dynamic, "moving swiftly" so that it "appears anew and anew . . . like a fleeting picture" (IV, 2382):

> One by one, the atoms of the universe momently open their doors to him, like tents, in a hundred diverse ways.
> The door becomes now the window, now the sunbeams; the earth becomes now the wheat, now the bushel.
> In men's eyes the heavens are very old and threadbare; in the eye [of such a one] there is a new creation at every moment. (VI, 4641-3)[21]

Even the human body, when properly perceived and employed, is a positive part of the universe and divine plan. To begin, the body is from a practical point of view a necessary instrument for the working out of salvation. The purpose God has in mind for history, that being the manifestation of faith and unfaith, can be carried out only by marriage of the body and spirit. Neither can function without the other, and even a revered saint such as Báyazíd is undeniably both spirit *and* body (V, 3419-28). The bodily appetites, for example, exist as a test of temperance, for "there can be no restraint when you have no desire; when there is no adversary, what need for your strength?" (V, 576). But more than this, the body when properly understood will be seen to be intimately linked to the divine, just as the spirit is. The body is the microcosm, created in the image of God; it is, according to the *Masnaví*, an "astrolabe" which, when read by the saint, points to the meanings in the heavens (VI, 3138-43). Body and spirit have a close connection with and action on each other: "Though the spirit cannot be seen [while the body is tangible and can be seen], body is not veiled from soul, nor soul from body" (I, 8). Thus repairing the spirit also repairs and transfigures the body:

> The spiritual way ruins the body and, after having ruined it, restores it to prosperity:
> Ruined the house for the sake of golden treasure [buried within it], and with that same treasure builds it better [than before];
> Cut off the water and cleansed the river-bed, then caused drinking-water to flow in the river-bed;
> Cleft the skin and drew out the iron point [of the arrow or spear]—then fresh skin grew over it [the wound] (I, 306-9).

The proximity of body to spirit is most evident in the saints.Their bodies are literally luminous with divine light; they are made of a special material to contain that light, which would blind if one were to look directly upon it.[22] Since the spirit of the saint "fares to the Kaba at every moment," since "in a single moment, the caravan is going from Heaven and coming here," his body "assumes the nature of the heart"—that is it is "transmuted" (n. *tabdíl*) so that time and place are no longer material to it (IV, 521 ff).

The key to achieving such productive, transformative harmony with nature, body, and world is holistic understanding—a vision of what Rúmí calls the Whole (*kull*) or Unity (*tawhíd*).Nature should be understood as a system and process, with an overall meaning and end in which all parts have their place, without exception—whether they might be considered from a more limited point of view beneficial or deleterious, good or evil. The vision desired is, in a word, *ecological*—an ecology that includes not only biology and physics, but also metaphysics.

The metaphysical process of the universe according to Rúmí is similar to that described by Heraklitus and perhaps Anaximander before him. For both Miletians and for Rúmí, nature is a product of the opposing forces of strife and harmony, its matter endlessly changing; just as Heraklitus says that "the sun is new each day," for Rúmí, nature is constantly fresh and new. The universe, Heraklitus says, is always igniting and extinguishing, death turning over into life and life into death. Just so, Rúmí says:

> If [a drop of water] enters into non-existence or hundred non-existences, it will return in headlong haste when You call it.
> Hundreds of thousands of opposites are killing their opposites: Thy decree is calling them forth again [from non-existence].
> There is caravan on caravan, O Lord, [speeding] continually from non-existence toward existence. . . .
> In autumn the myriads of boughs and leaves go in rout into the sea of Death,
> [While] in the garden the crow clothed in black like a mourner makes lament over the [withered] greenery.
> Again from the Lord of the land comes the edict [saying] to Non-existence, "Give back what you have devoured!
> Give up, O black Death, what you have devoured of plants and heal*ing herbs and leaves and grass!" (I, 1887-95).*

Heraklitus considers day and night, winter and summer, war and peace, satiety and hunger to be all different aspects of the same One, out of which all things come. And this is in fact the same dialectic described by Rúmí, who names in various places in the *Masnaví* the very same sets of opposites. The waves of the sea of this phenomenal world, he says, continually "dash one against the other," the collision being due to the "mingling of the spirits in peace and war" as they are confined to bodies:

> The waves of peace dash against each other and root up hatreds from [men's] breasts.
> In other form do the waves of war turn [men's] loves upside down.
> Love is drawing the bitter ones to the sweet, because the foundation of [all] loves is righteousness.
> Wrath is carrying away the sweet one to bitterness: how should the bitter sort be suited to the sweet?
> The bitter and the sweet are not visible to this [ocular] sight, [but] they can be seen through the window of the latter end (I, 2576-83).

There is, however, a crucial difference between the Heraklitean dialectic and Rúmí's worldview. Heraklitus's scheme is cyclical; "beginning and end are common." Thus his universe exists in a state of "dynamic permanence."[23] But Rúmí's universe moves, on balance, forward toward the Good. According to Rúmí and other Sufi theosophists, the world came into being as the manifestation of God's Attributes; and this included Attributes both at the pole of Mercy and at the pole of Wrath, so that He might be fully manifested. Existence is sustained by tension between the two: "By means of these two wings the world is [kept up like a bird] in the air . . . to the end that it may be [always] trembling like a leaf in the north-wind and simoom of resurrection and death" (VI, 1853-4). Mercy and Good, however, are necessarily predominant. For, as God is reported to have said[24] and as is so often repeated and illustrated in the *Masnaví*, "My Mercy preceded my Wrath."

> Although the filthy commit foulnesses, (yet) the (pure) waters are intent on purification.
> Though the snakes are scattering venom. . . .
> (Yet) in mountain and hive and tree the bees are depositing a sugar-store of honey.
> However much the venoms show venomousness, the antidotes quickly root them out. (VI, 32-5)

The true mystic, who sees through to the process of the Whole and is at the same time confident of and trustful in God's Infinite Mercy, shall be like the Sufi who fell into ecstasy at seeing the empty food wallet (III, 3013 ff); evil and penury can only remind him of the good and bounty that is sure to follow. For the work of God in the sensible world is nothing but "the transmutation of essences," a "continual alchemy" in which countless states of existence are incessantly exchanged for better (V, 780 ff). Thus, while Rúmí's worldview is certainly closer to Idealism than Materialism, here is an Idealism that does not lament the state of the world or reject matter, but carries them instead entirely upward.

As for anthropocentrism, it is certainly true that in the Islamic tradition, including Sufism, the universe is created for and around *Anthropos*. The natural world functions as the setting for human salvation history. Nature points to

God's existence and displays His provident Mercy;[25] but in the end, when it has served its purpose, it shall be completely overturned.[26] Added to this, Sufi cosmology is constructed *around the personalities* of those exemplary human beings, the prophets and saints, in order to place them as exalted intermediaries between this world and the divine. The whole world, it is said by Rúmí and other Sufi theosophists, is a display of the Attributes of God through the Logos-like figure of the chief saint, the "perfect man." Any value of nature and natural things, it would seem, must derive from Humanity.

We have already seen how the impact of anthropocentrism is blunted in the *Masnaví* by the suggestion that the things of nature are also alive, that they have their own special relation to God, and that they teach humankind by their example. But how to reconcile living nature with the imperative that Man, in order to free his soul, must ultimately leave the world behind? Is nature, with the Soul it contains, to be abandoned while Man is saved? Or, if it must, as by the rule of Mercy, also move toward perfection, how is that achieved? One possible answer, consistent with the linear scheme of Islamic salvation history, is that nature shall continue to exist in Paradise, but more fully. There is a faint suggestion of this idea in the *Masnaví*. In comparison, says Rúmí, to the "gates and walls and pitchers and fruits" of Paradise in the Next World, this living world would seem a "dead carcass" (V, 3591). "*Every* atom of that World," says Rúmí, "is living and able to understand discourse and eloquent" (V, 3591):

> God says that the wall of Paradise is not lifeless and ugly like (other) walls;
> Like the door and wall of the body, it is (endowed) with intelligence; the house (Paradise) is living since it belongs to the King of Kings.
> Both tree and fruit and limpid water (take part) with the inhabitant of Paradise in conversation and discourse (IV, 472-4).

Here is also a suggestion that, in the next world, the disjunction between human beings and nature bridged in this world only by the mystic shall disappear altogether. Intimacy with nature, it seems, is one of the realized conditions of Paradise.

This is not, however, the answer on which Rúmí ultimately settles. Instead, he turns to the emanationist aspect of his system to offer a solution for nature and for Man's relation to nature in the present time and through human endeavor. This he does by making humankind the gate to salvation for matter. According to the *Masnaví*, it is ultimately Man, the being on the earth most endowed with Spirit, toward whom all matter strives. Then, through assimilation to him, it is finally released upward toward the spirit world:

> Water goes from above to below; then from below it goes up above.
> The wheat went beneath the earth from above; afterwards it became ears of corn and sprang up quickly. . . .

> The source of all blessings descended from Heaven to the earth and became the nutrient of the vital spirit.
> Forasmuch as it came down from Heaven on account of humility, it became part of the living and valiant man.
> Hence that inanimate matter—rain and sunlight—was turned into human qualities and soared joyously in the skies,
> Saying, "We came at first from the living world, and have now gone back from below to above." (III, 457 ff.)[27]

The same idea is expressed by Rúmí in the homely story of the housewife who admonishes the chickpeas, beating them down with her ladle as they try to raise themselves up out of her boiling pot: "I boil you," she says, "not because you are hateful to me," but so that "you may become nutriment and mingle with the vital spirit."

> "If you have been parted from the garden of water and earth, (yet) you have become food in the mouth and [thus] have entered into the living. . . .
> By God, you grew from God's attributes in the beginning: go back nimbly and fleetly into His attributes. . . .
> You were a part of the sun and the cloud and the stars: you became soul and action and speech and thoughts."
> The existence of the animal arose from the death of the plant. . . .
> And when that morsel became the food of Man, it mounted from the (state of) inanimateness and became possessed of Soul (III, 4159 ff.).

Thus, though certainly still above nature, humankind does the work, in effect, of freeing the soul entrapped in it. This doctrine resembles in some ways the thought of the Manichaeans,[28] who believed that the Elect among them had the capacity to purify the Soul imprisoned in vegetables and grains—the same foods that figure most prominently in Rúmí's narrations—so as to release it upward.[29] A direct influence is, in fact, quite possible, as Rúmí's birthplace was located in Khorasan at the gates of Central Asia, where Manichaeism had some success and may have held out until his time in the thirteenth century.

It is the differences between the two worldviews, however, that are most instructive for us here. To begin, the Manichaeans held that soul indwelt only in certain kinds of foods—vegetables and grains—while other foods and matter, such as meat and decayed organisms, were dead and hence not to be consumed. Rúmí, in contrast, takes care to emphasise that *all* nature is living. Everything has Soul; everything is salvable—and, of course, in accord with Islamic norms, everything is consumable. The Manichaeans also considered the ensouled world to be sensitive to suffering, so that trampling, reaping, and digging were viewed as harmful activities (unless, that is, the produce was redeemed by being offered to the Elect).[30] According to Rúmí, however, the earth, vegetables, and animals, far from being harmed, sacrifice themselves gladly to Eros in order to ascend the ladder of Being. Just as the eater loves the food, so does the food love the eater: "Just as you are pitiably enamoured of the daily bread, so the daily bread is enamoured of the consumer,"[31] through whom it gains life:

> If there had not been Love . . . how should bread have attached itself to you and become (assimilated) to you?
> The bread became you: through what? Through (your) love and appetite; otherwise, how should the bread had had any access to the (vital) spirit?
> Love makes the dead bread into spirit: it makes the spirit that was perishable everlasting. (V, 2012-4)

The Manichaean discipline intended to separate its practicants from matter also included a prohibition against sex, at least for the Elect. There is no trace of such a negative attitude toward sex in Rúmí's work—and indeed, this is foreign to the Islamic tradition in general. [32]

Thus, placed against the worldview of the Manichaeans, the following characteristic of Rúmí's world is thrown into relief: While for Manichaeans Soul is strained out of matter and the dark remnants left to damnation—along with, even, very weak vestiges of soul—for Rúmí, *all* of nature, without exception, is to be transformed, redeemed, and saved. *Every* living and apparently non-living thing has its necessary and useful place in the great cycle that is God's plan for universal salvation, in which it participates knowingly, actively, and fully. Nothing is without use, and nothing is lost.

This view is surely facilitated by the positive, natural realism of the Quran. The Quran is cited and expounded throughout the *Masnaví* and, along with the sayings (*Hadíth*) of the Prophet, is the source of much of the poet's inspiration. In the Quran, nature is Real in itself. It is not merely the overflowing of a greater reality. Rather, it is the place we are, in our bodies, experienced not in a time that is eternal or reoccurring but in the Now. Nature is also inherently good. Just as, according to the revelation, Man is naturally noble and good, unstained by sin and exalted even above the angels,[33] so is nature a sign of God's Providence and Mercy, a blessing from Him to be fully enjoyed and utilised, as the Quran testifies in the following verse and in many other places:

> In the creation of the heavens and earth, in the alternation of Night and Day, in the sailing of ships through the Ocean for the profit of Mankind, in the rain which God sends down from the skies, and the life He gives thereby to the earth that was dead; in the beasts of all kinds distributed in the earth, in the shifting of the winds and the clouds they trail like their slaves between heaven and earth—here indeed are signs for those who are wise.[34]

Of course, our relation to nature, as good and fulsome as nature is, must be correct. The "adornments" (*zínah*) of this world are to be enjoyed as they are (e.g. Q. 10:87 & 18:7), not coveted and hoarded as an end in themselves (e.g., Q. 28:66 & 33:28). This is also one of Rúmí's central lessons.

V

Other Sufis before Jalál al-Dín Rúmí had declared the universe to be alive. The noted twelfth-century mystic and systematizer of practical mysticism Abú Hámid al-Ghazálí states, consistent with the verse of the Quran (17:44) quoted above, that all the atoms of heaven and earth praise God. According to Ghazálí, however, only the mystics are able to hear that praise.[35] Ibn `Arabí, the first great theosopher of Islam, who died in Damascus in 1240 while Rúmí was still flourishing in Konya, taught that minerals, plants, and animals all naturally know and worship God—while Man, being most bound by consciousness and intellect, often fails to do so.[36] Rúmí's father and teacher, the mystic theologian Bahá' al-Dín Walad (also known as Bahá'-i Walad) expounded a system in which all existents (*mawjúdát*) are percipient (*bi-`aql'and*)[37] servants and knowers (*`árif*) of God.[38] "The inanimate things (*jamádát*)," says Bahá'-i Walad, "the trees, rivers, and fruits of this world, are under God's command and act according to His command;"[39] "water and fire are His slaves."[40] These ideas are recorded in his *magnum opus*, the *Ma`árif* or "Gnostic Perceptions;" the text of the *Ma`árif* in general indicates that a significant part of Rúmí's thought was formed around the kernel of his father's ideas. Rúmí's important contribution is to amplify and systematize these insights of his predecessors.

What meaningful understanding can be extracted from Rúmí for the ecology movement today? We are no longer in a position to adopt thirteenth-century metaphysics; but a metaphysics, however developed, is initially inspired by and then built upon an unmediated perception of Truth. The significance of the *Masnaví* for ecology thus lies, I believe, in what it has to say about our experience and perception of the world around us. This is communicated not entirely explicitly, but rather within the poetic expression itself, the better to be received by intuition—for the first principle of mysticism is that true knowledge is acquired through intuition awakened by experience, and not through rational enquiry.[41]

What shines through the *Masnaví* is an exuberant optimism in relation to nature—an optimism crushed, perhaps, by our present anxieties. Several more precise inferences, however, can be drawn from the text that give us further hints of how to experience and understand nature. We are told, first, to maintain a direct—or, as Emerson would say, "original"—relation with nature. If each thing is animated directly by the divine (a proposition we can accept at least metaphorically), then that thing demands our immediate attention as an individual. We are also told that we need not consider ourselves alone in the world. Nature is our companion. For all its parts are living exactly as we are; and if we are properly attuned to them, they speak to and instruct us—and may, indeed, speak more truthfully than our own kind. Rúmí remythologizes nature so that we regain the sense of a world full of personalities who have their own particular, even affective, relations with each other and with us. Nature, in fact, is entwined with our world even to the point of possessing morality and judging over us. These are things, I believe, that we feel instinctively even today when we stand alone with nature. But those feelings are obscured by the notion that our relation to nature must be scientific and efficient. It is as if we have become shy of speaking our relationship to nature. Rúmí's work is a call to listen to our instincts and take them seriously—to reject the veil of *`aql* or false rationality.

Further, Rúmí acknowledges that we have a spiritual (today we would say "psychological") affinity with and yearning for our origins in nature, as in several passages cited above and the following:

> The heart is eating a [particular] food from every single companion…
> You eat [receive] something from meeting with any one, and you carry away something from conjunction with any associate. . . .
> As from the conjunction of earth and rains [there are produced] fruits and greenery and sweet herbs;
> And [as] from the conjunction of green things with man [there is produced] joy of heart and carelessness and happiness (II, 1089-95).

The phenomenon Rúmí is speaking of here is exactly that which Wilson terms "biophilia."[42]

We are told by the *Masnaví* also to regard nature as full of hidden potential, and to know that discovery of this potential is part of the process of our own enlightenment. We cannot make spiritual progress without understanding nature and our place within it—even if we are inclined to consider that place to be exceptional, as the Islamic tradition clearly does. Ultimately, we will understand that we should behave instinctively, as nature does, unencumbered by false rationality and the anxiety that produces. At the same time, we are to know that nature is—again as Emerson says—"a continuous creation." Nature is necessarily dynamic. Far from dead, inert, or mechanical, it is always surprising and new, a series of epiphanies for those who know to expect them. This also means, of course, that nature cannot be efficiently predicted or controlled (even though false rationality may tell us otherwise). We should not, however, perceive it to be capricious or without purpose and end—even when it appears, in particular moments, to be maleficent. The laws and action of nature have their own moral sense, even if that is hidden from us. For the most essential intuition of all is that, when viewed as a Whole, the universe reveals itself to be constantly evolving, moving always toward the necessarily dominant good.

Notes

1. Though the three mysticisms display apparently similar characteristics, beginning with dependence on emanation and soul-psychology, there has been no extensive work of comparison. This remains a major task in the study of Western religion.

2. "Leave the part," says Rúmí, "and fix your eye upon the Whole . . . smell all the way from the part to the Whole, smell all the way from opposite to opposite." Thus shall you realise that "the angers of Mankind are for the sake of Peace; restlessness is ever a snare for Rest." The whole is perceived through Universal Reason (*`aql-i kull*), the part through Partial Reason (*`aql-i juz*). Citations from the *Masnaví* follow the numbering of R.A. Nicholson, as well as his translation, with minor emendations. Original edition *The Mathnawí of Jalálu'ddín Rúmí*, E.J.W. Gibb Memorial Trust, 1926, reprinted in various editions and places several times since. The quotation above is from volume III, lines 988 and on, thus: III, 988 ff.

3. *Tim.* 30 D.

4. *Tim.* 30 D.

5. See III, 1020 ff., where the metaphorical interpretation of living nature (the poet likely refers to exegesis of Quran 17:44, cited further on in the text) is condemned as being of the rationalism of the Mutazilites.

6. Referring to the pillar against which the Prophet used to lean while speaking, which moaned out of longing for him after he abandoned it in favor of a pulpit.

7. When the sun, it is said, enters the sign of Aries, the earth warms and the plants stir and grow.

8. The soil, similarly, is "faithful to its trust," having "derived this faithfulness from that [Divine] faithfulness, inasmuch as the sun of Justice has shone upon it." Yet "His wrath makes blind the men of understanding"; that is humankind, who was given understanding, fails to do as much as even the earth does (I, 509-13).

9. See also IV, 2818-32 and 3532-5.

10. The tribe of `Ád, according to the Quran (e.g., 5:95) were destroyed by the windstorm for their obstinate unbelief.

11. Cf. III, 1009 ff.

12. Cf. Mt. 6:25 ff. & Lk. 12:25 ff.—the "fowls of the air" who "neither sow nor reap" and the "lilies of the field" who "neither toil nor spin."

13. Referring to the legend of the Seven Sleepers of Ephesus, which also has a place in Islamic lore (see Quran 18:17-21).

14. Because they were able to recognise unmistakeably that Majnún, the famous lover of Laylá who took to the desert, was filled with Love, the animals did not devour him (V, 2721-5; see also 2005-7). Majnún was reproached for kissing and stroking a dog—dogs being unclean according to Islamic law. He explained that a being is to be measured by its "heart, soul, and knowledge," that is love and devotion, rather than apparent form. The dog, who frequented the lane by the house of Majnún's beloved, was perfect in both (III, 567 ff.).

15. Cf. the lines of one of Rúmí's ghazals (lyric poems) from the Díván-i Shams:

> Since straw moves not save by a wind, how shall the world move without desire (havá, also meaning wind)?
> All the parts of the world are lovers, and very part of the universe is drunk with encounter;

> Only they do not tell you their secrets—it is not proper to tell a secret save to one worthy. (Furúzanfar ed. of Díván-i Shams, #2674).

The ideas explained in the Masnaví emerge everywhere in Rúmí's lyrics; this example is cited because a complete translation is available to the reader: Mystical Poems of Rúmí 2. Second Selection, Poems 201-400 (University of Chicago Press, 1979), #342.

16. De Generatione Animalium 3.1.731b30-33.

17. Cf. V, 800-3:

> From inanimateness did you move unconsciously towards vegetal growth, and from vegetal growth towards animal life and tribulation;
> And again towards reason and goodly discernment; again toward what lies outside these five senses and six directions.
> These footprints extend as far as the Ocean [that is of Gnosis or Divine Being]; then the footprints disappear.

18. V, 833-43. For another extended comment on the body see I, 1735-45.

19. See also III, 3964-70 and I, 791-3.

20. See also III, 3405.

21. See the comments following on Heraklitus.

22. VI, 3008-13; it is for this reason that blessing may be gotten from physical contact with the graves of saints.See also VI, 3059 ff.

23. Hans Regnéll, *Ancient Views on the Nature of Life* (Lund: CWK Gleerup, 1967), 87 ff. and passim.

24. Pronounced in a famous *hadíth qudsí*. Certain reported sayings (*hadíth*) of the Prophet—even though they are not considered part of the revelation—are called "Holy" (*qudsí*) because they were communicated to him by God. Many hadíths qudsí are favourite texts of the Sufis.

25. E.g., Quran 3:164, 6:99, 2:164 (quoted in the text below), and in many other places in the Quran.

26. E.g., Quran, chapters 99 and 101.

27. This section of the *Masnaví* is headed "The diverse modes and stages of the creation (*khilqat*) of Man from the beginning."

28. Note also a similarity to the *Masnaví*'s view of body: The Manichaeans believed Soul and Body to be intertwined, and that perfected souls resulted in perfected bodies, "not differing from each other . . . [luminous] like similar lamps" (al-Bírúní, tr. By Eduard Sachau, *Alberuni's India* [London: K. Paul, Trench, Trubner, 1888], cited with further discussion in Jason David BeDuhn, *The Manichaean Body in Discipline and Ritual* [Baltimore, Md.: Johns Hopkins University Press, 2000], 223). Not only does Rúmí describe the perfected body of the saint as luminous; he also uses the image of lamps, all the same and lit from the same light (IV, 1842; VI, 3069 ff.).

29. The story of the "fool" who cried out against a man overturning the soil (IV, 2341 ff.) may refer to this Manichaean stricture. The fool was unable, comments the Masnaví, to recognise the difference between cultivation and devastation and that the soil could not become "crops and leaves and fruit" until it was "turned upside down."

30. V, 2400.

31. See for instance V, 574 ff., a passage expounding the Prophet's famous saying "There is no monkery in Islam."

32. So that the angels were commanded to bow down to Adam, the father of humankind: Quran 2:34 ff.

33. Q. 2:164. The heightened realism of the Quran results in this difference between it and Rúmí's thought: for Rúmí, the meaning of nature is apparent only to those with mystical insight (although, as always with mystical truths, it is "obvious but not perceived"); whereas according to the Quran, the evidence of God contained in the "signs" (ayát) of this world are readily perceived by any who simply "reflect," "remember," "listen," or use "reason" or "common sense" (`aql). These processes are linked with the ayát in many places in the Quran; see for example 16:11-69, where they appear together.

34. Ihyá' `ulúm al-dín, Book Five of the Munjiyát, Kitábal-tawhíd wa-al-tawakkul ("the speech of the atoms is without word and without end"); for translation and commentary, see Richard Gramlich, *Muhammad al-Gazzalis Lehre von den Stufen zur Gottesliebe* (Wiesbaden: F. Steiner, 1984), 526-7.

35. Fusús al-hikam, translated as Bezels of Wisdom by R.J.W. Austin (New York: Paulist Press, 1980), 103 ff.

36. Cf. *Masnaví* IV, 2821-2: "Out of kindness, God created intelligence (*`aql*) in lifeless things (*jamádát*) . . . by His grace an intelligence appeared in lifeless matter."

37. *Ma`árif*, ed. Badí` al-Zamán Furúzánfar, 2 vols. (Tehran: Tahúrí, 1333 H.Sh), I, 293.

38. Furúzánfar, *Ma`árif*, 293.

39. Furúzánfar, *Ma`árif*, 37. For a discussion of Bahá-i Walad's living universe, see Fritz Meier, *Bahá'-i Walad. Grundzüge seines Lebens und seiner Mystik* (Leiden: E. J. Brill, 1989), 201 ff. (chapter "Die Religiosität der Dinge und Atome").

40. Rúmí lays out this didactic strategy many times in his writings, as in this line near the beginning of the *Masnaví*:

> In expounding love, intellect lay down helplessly like an ass in the mire: it was love alone that uttered the explanation of love and loverhood (I, 115).

41. Bahá-i Walad also proposes that the mazah or "sensation of enjoyment" we experience in this world from various phenomena, including natural things, is a reflexion of our attraction to God and the bliss we shall experience in heaven. See Meier, *Bahá'-i Walad*, 222 ff. (chapter "Das Lustgefühl [Maza]).

I am indebted to Ms. R. Ftaya, graduate student of the Department of Religion, for reading drafts of the paper and contributing numerous valuable suggestions and emendations; the paper was presented in a colloquium of the same department, and the remarks of my colleagues also helped to clarify my thoughts. The clue that led to investigation of a Manichaean connection was provided by Professor Madonna Adams, one of the participants in the conference on which this volume is based; comments by graduate student Mr. Hosseinali Houshmand prompted me to focus on the problem of extracting ecological thought from Rúmí independent of his particular metaphysics.

IV. Medieval Judaism

14

MAIMONIDES AND NACHMANIDES ON SENDING AWAY THE MOTHER BIRD

Edward Halper

> If a bird's nest happens to be before you on the road, on any tree, or on the ground—young birds or eggs—and the mother is roosting on the young birds or the eggs, you shall not take the mother with the young. You shall surely send away the mother and take the young for yourself in order that it will be good for you and prolong your days (Deuteronomy 22:6-7)

I

This prohibition against taking a mother bird along with its young appears in a list of other injunctions in *Deuteronomy*. It clearly does not fall among those commandments that, like the prohibitions against murder, theft, and degrading parents, are widely accepted by different societies and are, according to some accounts, rational. Instead, it belongs among the commandments that are recognized as such only because they appear in the Torah, the so-called traditional laws or revelatory commandments.[1] Though we may not be able to discover or justify commandments of the latter class, it would be a mistake to suppose that they are without reasons. Inasmuch as commandments of both types are commanded by God, and God is rational, all *must* be rational. Our human rational abilities are simply too puny to grasp their reasons fully.

Nonetheless, it is widely held by Jewish Torah commentators and philosophers that we are enjoined to seek to discover reasons, even for the "traditional" commandments. It was the great project of Jewish philosophy in the middle ages—that most *rational* of ages—to uncover the reasons for all the commandments (*ta`amei ha-mitzvot*). There is an extensive literature on the reasons for the commandment to send away the mother bird. In this essay I shall limit myself to the treatments of two of the most influential accounts, those of Maimonides and Nachmanides. Born in Spain in the twelfth century, Maimonides (or Rabbi Moses ben Maimon) commented on the Talmud and codified Jewish law (*Mishneh Torah*) before undertaking his most significant philosophical work, *The Guide of the Perplexed*.[2] This book had an impact on all subsequent Jewish philosophy and was also important to Scholastic thought. Nachmanides (Rabbi Moses ben Nachman), also born in Spain, lived mostly in the thirteenth century; he is mainly known for his Commentary on the Torah and other writings; he defended Judaism in the Great Debate at Barcelona in 1263. Nachmanides presents himself as a Biblical interpreter rather than a philosopher, but this fact ought not to prevent us from considering his philosophy. We must understand that Maimonides had been criticized because he was openly influenced by Aristotle and other non-Jewish philosophers; and this may partly account for Nachmanides' not calling himself a philosopher. Then, too, Nachmanides often makes a point of stressing his disagreement with Maimonides—some have said he exaggerates it—but one cannot disagree with a philosophy without oneself espousing an alternative philosophy.

Nachmanides' commentary on the commandment to send away the mother bird is one place where he emphasizes his disagreement with Maimonides.[3] My reasons for focusing on this particular commandment are, first, that it is paradigmatic of both the Torah's view of how human beings ought to treat nature and the attitude toward the natural environment of medieval Jewish philosophers and, second, that the disagreement between Maimonides and Nachmanides seems to echo a dispute among current environmental ethicists. I shall propose that, properly understood, their disagreement can enrich current discussion and that some current distinctions might help us to see precisely where their disagreement lies—not an easy task, as we'll soon see.

It need hardly be said that neither thought of himself as engaged in environmental ethics. But they cannot consider the reasons for the commandment to send away the mother bird without doing environmental ethics. Where other birds will fly away when a person approaches, the mother stays to protect her young; her maternal instinct makes her an easy target. And when young birds or eggs are removed from a nest within her sight, the mother bird appears to suffer distress. Forbidding the removal of her young in her presence, the Torah aims to prevent both her maternal instinct's being used to capture her and her suffering. But what precisely is the objection to the mother's capture in such circumstances or to her suffering? Would her suffering be something intrinsically bad or, rather, something bad because of its effect on the person causing her suffering? Or, to put it another way, should a person send the mother bird away because her life and feelings, and by extension all of nature, are intrinsically valuable or because causing her suffering would be detrimental to him? We face here in the middle ages the question of whether to endorse the intrinsic value of nature, that is, so-called deep ecology, or a more moderate instrumental environmental valuation. Both Maimonides and Nachmanides recognize that this is the issue though neither, of course, poses it in these terms.

In fact, Maimonides speaks about preventing the mother bird's "being pained by seeing the young taken away" (III, 48); Nachmanides criticizes what he takes to be Maimonides' suggestion that the Torah is concerned with bird's intrinsic value, and he goes on to insist that this and all other commandments serve to perfect the character of man (268). However, it would be rash to conclude that Maimonides is the "deep ecologist" and Nachmanides the instrumentalist; for in another passage Maimonides also insists that all the commandments serve to perfect man (III, 35), whereas Nachmanides offers still another reason for this commandment, a reason that seems to affirm the bird's intrinsic value. Hence, each of them would seem both to affirm and to deny the bird's intrinsic value. Maimonides' apparent lack of consistency on the explanation of this commandment has been discussed in the literature. Although, in his codification, he denies that the commandment is for the sake of the mother bird (*Mishneh Torah*, "Tefillah" ix, 7), in the *Guide* he suggests that the commandment's purpose *is* to diminish the suffering of the mother bird (III, 48); and he supports the former by citing a Mishnaic text whose relevance he denies in the latter.[4] In short, though it is clear that Maimonides and Nachmanides are both concerned with whether the mother bird has intrinsic value and, thus, is worthy of mercy from God and us, neither seems, at first glance, to give a consistent account.

To summarize, the Torah gives no reason for a commandment that bears directly on the value of nature, and two important explanations of that commandment seem confused and contradictory in themselves. In the next two sections of this paper, I shall look closely at Maimonides' and Nachmanides' discussions. The issues they address are more complex but also more interesting than they first appear. In the final section, I shall consider their differences and diagnose the reason why we have difficulty deciding whether they accord nature intrinsic or instrumental value; namely, that their conceptual distinctions are richer than ours. Exclusive attention to contemporary formulations could entice readers to neglect distinctions that they make, distinctions that could, I suggest, enrich contemporary environmental discussions and, indeed, contemporary ethics in general.

II

Let me begin with Maimonides. His account of the commandment to send away the mother bird comes in the third part of the *Guide* in the lengthy discussion of the different kinds of commandments and their reasons (III, 35-49). Like everything in the *Guide*, this discussion is brief, ambiguous, and, possibly intentionally misleading—Maimonides had said in the *Guide*'s introduction that he conceals some matters that the "vulgar" cannot handle. He opens this discussion by dividing all the Biblical commandments into fourteen classes and proposing a general reason for each class. The commandment to send away the mother bird falls under the thirteenth class, a class that aims to "put an end to lusts and licentiousness" that manifest themselves in food and drink; or so he says in III, 35. Surprisingly, however, in the actual discussion of instances of this class in III, 48, he does not mention human lusts. Instead, he connects the commandment to send away the mother bird with another in the same class, the commandment not to slaughter a mother and her young on the same day. The latter he explains by referring to the pain that the mother experiences at the sight of her offspring's slaughter: "the love and tenderness of a mother for her child is not consequent upon reason, but upon the activity of the imaginative faculty, which is found in most animals just as it is found in man." That is to say, any animal that has imagination feels pain at the suffering of its offspring. (It is well known that the Torah allows certain types of domesticated animals to be slaughtered for food only in accordance with ritual specifications that render the animal fit [kosher] for consumption; according to the traditional explanation, these rituals allow the animal to be slaughtered with the least possible pain and suffering. Thus, a dull knife would increase the animal's suffering and, thereby, render it unfit.) Apparently, Maimonides thinks that the mother's witnessing the death of her young increases her suffering beyond the threshold minimum.

Maimonides claims, in III, 48, that the commandment to send away the mother bird has the same reason. We expect him to mention the bird's suffering as her young are taken from her; but he remarks, instead, that "in most cases" the eggs and the young over which the mother sits are not fit to be eaten; so that sending her away has the practical effect that nothing at all is taken. What he means is that eggs the mother is sitting on are likely to be fertilized and thus not kosher; and the young birds would need to be ritually slaughtered and examined for illness—difficult and hardly worth the trouble for so little. But Maimonides does not say that the commandment's purpose is to protect the life or prevent the suffering of the birds. Rather, immediately after mentioning these effects of the commandment, he asks: "If the Law [the Torah] takes into consideration these pains of the soul in the case of beast and birds, what will be the case with regard to individuals of the human species as a whole?" Though the Law has the effect of sparing the mother the pain of witnessing the taking of her offspring and returning to an empty nest—if she has imagination, then she has memory, according to the Aristotelian account that Maimonides supposes here—Maimonides stresses that we are supposed to infer that the Law does even more to spare human beings pain, a rather surprising assertion given that sending away a mother bird is apt to be a painful forgoing of a good meal.

Maimonides concludes his brief discussion of this commandment by answering a possible objection. There is a Mishnaic passage which recounts that a person who claims that God's mercy extends to a bird's nest is silenced. Maimonides says that this passage should not be brought as an objection to his account of the commandment because it reflects the opinion that there is no reason for the commandment whereas he subscribes to the opinion, stated earlier, that "all Laws have causes and were given in view of some utility" (III, 26).

At first glance it might seem that since Maimonides is objecting to silencing the person who gives divine mercy as the commandment's reason, he must himself suppose that this *is* its reason. However, this would directly contradict the Mishnah, a text that approaches the Torah in authoritativeness. Besides, attributing the commandment to divine mercy here would contradict his own *Mishneh Torah* ("Tefillah" ix, 7) where he cites the same Mishnah to deny that God's mercy extends to birds and goes on to argue that if this and other such commandments did aim at mercy, God would not have permitted the slaughter of animals at all. Of course, Maimonides could have been of different minds in the two works, but there is no need to suppose this because he is not actually advancing his own interpretation of the Mishnah here in the *Guide* but merely objecting to one interpretation it *could* have. Maimonides is concerned that someone would cite this Mishnah as an objection to *any* reason for the commandment to send away the mother bird, and he rejects the opinion it would *seem* to support, "the opinion of those who think that there is no reason for the Law except only the will [of God]." Though he does not explain here how else to understand this Mishnah, we can see from his *Mishneh Torah* that he thinks the person who proposes divine mercy as the reason for the commandment to send away the mother bird is silenced not because he proposes a reason when there is none but because he proposes the wrong reason.[5] In the *Guide*, then, Maimonides affirms only the possibility of giving reasons for the commandment, not the particular reason that the Mishnah rejects, mercy for the bird.

This last point is important because someone who read only *Guide* III, 48 could easily suppose that Maimonides did think that the commandment's purpose is to spare birds' suffering; he talks of little else in this chapter. His claim in the *Mishneh Torah* that if divine mercy were the issue, God would have prohibited all animal slaughter would seem besides the point because (we might say) the commandment to send away the mother bird, like the commandment not to slaughter the mother and its young on the same day, is concerned to prevent an the animal's suffering *excessively*. Just as the laws of kosher slaughter are supposed to minimize an animal's pain, so, too, sending away the mother bird avoids unnecessary pain to the animals. Or so we might suppose. But the question remains, why should we worry about *any* pain that the animal experiences? The Torah sanctions the slaughter of animals for eating and it commands their slaughter for sacrifice. In these circumstances, the animal's pain is justified either because the animal serves a higher purpose or because it is necessary for human survival or perfection. If the Torah regarded the birds as intrinsically valuable, it would not allow them to be used for human ends. And if the birds have no value in themselves, how can their suffering be of any consequence or concern? Hence, Maimonides would seem to have a legitimate point: given that the Torah allows birds to be slaughtered for other ends, it cannot regard their suffering as intrinsically bad. The conclusion we should draw is that if the Torah prohibits their excessive suffering, it must do so for our sake rather than theirs. Thus, the commandment to send away the mother bird must aim not at sparing her pain but, somehow, at perfecting human nature.

There are at least two more reasons to reject the idea that Maimonides thinks the commandment is for the sake of the bird. The first is his claim, elsewhere in the *Guide*, that God's providence extends to humans but not to other species (III, 17).[6] All species have the means to preserve themselves in nature, but were Divine law formulated for the sake of birds, it would be a protection over and above nature and, thus, in effect, providential. The last and most important reason to deny that Maimonides thinks the commandment is for the sake of the bird is that this would be at odds with what he gives earlier (III, 35) as the general reason for the thirteenth group of commandments, the group to which it belongs, namely, the moral perfection of man's lusts and desires.

Why should we accept the general reason of III, 35 over the animal suffering emphasized in III, 48? The apparent contradiction between the *Guide* and the *Mishneh Torah*, discussed earlier, is mirrored by an apparent contradiction *within* the *Guide* by III, 35's insistence that sending away the mother bird and other such commandments are for the sake of man and III, 48's discussion of the suffering of the bird. Why affirm the one text over the other? I shall argue now that we can explain III, 48's discussion of the bird's suffering if the commandment's ultimate purpose is the perfection of man, but not III, 35's insistence that the commandment perfects man's lusts if its purpose were to prevent the bird's suffering.

The sight of a mother bird sitting on her nest and, therefore, easily captured evokes, in most people, a desire for meat. At the same time, we can imagine the intense distress of the mother bird being taken from her young or viewing an intruder taking her young from the nest. The person who follows the commandment to send away the mother bird must hold in check his desire to eat her. Obeying the commandment provides him with the opportunity to moderate his desires, and, like Aristotle, Maimonides thinks that through the repeated practice of virtuous acts a person acquires virtue in his soul. But sending away the mother bird is more than just one virtuous act because the person who follows this commandment or, perhaps, even just learns about it, stands to learn something crucially important for the virtue of moderation: he realizes that had he gratified his desire for meat, he would have caused the bird intense suffering and that the Torah's commandment specifically protects the bird from this suffering. In other words, the commandment serves to teach the potentially destructive consequences of desire as well as an important limit to desires: those desires that cause special pain and suffering to other beings ought not to be gratified. Consider again Maimonides' words in III, 48: "If the Law takes into consideration these pains of the soul in case of beast and birds, what will be the case with regard to the individuals of the human species as a whole?" If we are to hold in check our desires when they cause excessive pain to the mother bird, how much the more should we check those desires that would cause pain to people. In becoming sensitive to the feelings of the bird, one becomes even more sensitive to the feelings of other people. This sensitivity makes one more capable of moderating desires for pleasure that may harm others. Conversely, the person who takes the mother bird, despite her evident distress, becomes inured to the suffering of others. His desires will not be deterred by the pain their gratification could inflict. In this way the thought that the commandment to send away the mother bird serves to prevent her suffering contributes to the purpose of the thirteenth group of commandments, "to put an end to lusts and licentiousness." That is to say, Maimonides' remarks on *animal* suffering in III, 48 contribute to an explanation of how the *human* purpose of the commandment, described in III, 35, is attained.

It is important to realize that Maimonides' explanation of this commandment is not supposed to be a motivation for performing the commandment. One ought to perform the commandment simply because it is Biblically commanded. Maimonides' point is, I am proposing here, that the person who does perform it will himself benefit from it with increased sensitivity and a consequent reduction in desire. Of course, we can imagine especially callous individuals who perform the commandment and fail to derive this lesson, but that is no argument against Maimonides' account of its purpose. More common are people who do not need actually to perform the commandment to learn from it how to limit their desires, for merely from studying the commandment one recognizes that acting on one's desires can have painful consequences.

This analysis of the benefit of the commandment supposes that the person who benefits from it recognizes the special suffering of the mother bird and thinks it important to prevent this. However, we just saw that Maimonides denies that the suffering of the mother bird is a matter of consequence. Let us, for the moment, accept this point and try to imagine someone aware of it performing or learning about the commandment to send away the mother bird. Could he possibly "put an end to [his own] lusts and licentiousness"? He cannot learn from the commandment to limit his desires when they cause pain to other beings, for he realizes that the pain of the bird is not important. Even if he performs the commandment perfectly, he does not derive its intended lesson. His knowledge of the ultimate value of the bird inures him to its suffering and, likely, to the suffering of others. Moreover, it could be very difficult to perform the commandment; for, imagining the tasty meal he is missing, the person who sends away the mother bird will be keenly aware of the pain he himself feels in fulfilling the commandment. Even if he supposed that the Torah regarded preventing the bird's suffering as more important than his suffering, it would be hard for him to fulfill the commandment. How could he fulfill it if he realized that for the Torah the bird's suffering is unimportant and the commandment is, rather, for his own good? There are very few people who do not see their own good as getting what they want. Ironically, then, the commandment to send away the mother bird has its intended benefit for the human soul only when the agent does *not* properly understand its purpose.

This last point is crucial for understanding what Maimonides is keeping from the vulgar and why. Most people are governed by their desires and have little concern or even awareness of the desires of others. These are the people that I think Maimonides has in mind when he speaks of the "vulgar." The commandment to send away the mother bird is designed to teach the vulgar that gratifying one's own desires could cause other beings' suffering. Learning the lesson diminishes or even removes lusts and perfects the soul. Once the soul has been perfected, it is safe to understand the real reason for the commandment. Whereas a person governed by lusts will not be convinced that it is in his own interest to refrain from gratifying his lusts, the person who is governed by his intellect easily recognizes the value of a commandment designed to diminish lust. Hence, the former must be led to think that the suffering of the bird is important, the latter that it is not. Indeed, for the person governed by intellect, the Torah's concern with the suffering of the mother bird, and much else besides, will seem trivial unless he can come to understand that it functions to perfect human nature and how it performs this function.

Let us put these results more generally. Despite appearances to the contrary, Maimonides' explanation of this commandment does not depend on the intrinsic value of the bird or, by extension, any other part of nature as such. Although the environment has its own value—as do all things (III, 13)—as far as human conduct governed by the Torah is concerned, it derives its value from us just because it is valuable to us. However, in order to use it to perfect our character, we must preserve the illusion that the environment is valuable in itself. To put all this in more modern terms, it is not the destruction of the environment that is to be feared but what such an act does to the perpetrator—inflames lusts most dangerously. It has this effect because of his *perception* of the suffering he inflicts even though this perception is not justified because, after all, nature's value to us is instrumental, not absolute. Likewise, his acts of restraint will only have the desired moderating effect on his passions if he keeps in mind the suffering that his acts would have caused, something that we—from a more philosophical perspective—recognize not to be intrinsically bad.

Maimonides' idea that people who inflict pain on animals are corrupt is corroborated by recent psychological studies showing that people who torture animals are more likely to be a danger to other people. In the past year there was a move in Georgia to make inflicting pain on animals a felony with a severe punishment, but this proposal was unsuccessful at least partly because of the difficulty of excluding the slaughter of animals for food. Interestingly, Maimonides is distinguishing, in effect, the necessary pain involved in slaughter for food from the animal's unnecessary pain by distinguishing their effects on our passions. There is no way to determine whether the mother bird does feel distress, but anyone looking at her behavior cannot help but think that she does. The concern of the Torah, as Maimonides understands it, is to diminish lusts so that a person will not risk being governed by them or, thereby, inflicting harm on others, and it attains this end by keeping people from becoming hardened to the suffering of other sentient beings.

One final question remains. Though it is now clear that the main function of sending away the mother bird is the perfection of the person performing or studying the commandment, since Maimonides recognizes that the bird and other animals have some intrinsic value, why does he not regard this as a further justification for sending away the mother bird? Why not explain the commandment by mentioning the value of the bird in addition to human perfection? Though this approach would have made his account simpler, it would have raised at least two new problems. First, because we cannot see the mother bird sitting on her nest without picturing the cooked hen before us at the table, the command to send her away is a difficult and painful one to fulfill. This pain is, Maimonides must suppose, good for us because it helps us to keep our desires under control. Still, the question immediately arises to the agent, why is the bird's pain more important than mine? This question is reminiscent of a famous Talmudic dictum that if one were to find oneself part of a group of people whose lives were all threatened, one would have a duty to save his own life first. In general, where there is a conflict one ought to seek his own benefit. (This is obviously very different from Christian attitudes!) In short, if Maimonides granted the intrinsic value of the bird as a motive for the commandment, he would have needed to explain why the bird's value trumps that of the person who has come upon her. Second, Maimonides thinks that inasmuch as we are rational, we are far more valuable than any other sublunar thing. For us to act for the sake of the bird or any other bit of earthly nature is for the higher to serve the lower, just the reverse of the proper order. Hence, any benefit that accrues to birds from the commandment to send away the mother can only be a subsidiary consequence of a law whose purpose is the perfection of our nature.

III

This understanding of Maimonides helps greatly to put Nachmanides' remarks in perspective, for we will see that, despite his sharp criticism of Maimonides, he actually accepts Maimonides' justification but seeks to add to it another one. At the very beginning of his brief discussion of this commandment, Nachmanides mentions two justifications for it (*Commentary*, 265): one is that a person should not have a "cruel heart and be discompassionate," the other I will discuss later. He then turns to argue against what he takes to be Maimonides' concern for the suffering of the bird. He cites Maimonides' claims that the commandment to send away the mother bird is connected with the commandment not to slaughter a mother animal and her offspring on the same day and that both aim to avoid the animal's suffering. But Maimonides cannot be right about this, Nachmanides reasons, because then the Torah would prohibit only slaughtering the offspring *before* the mother; as it is, slaughtering either first is prohibited (265-66).[7] It must be, then, that the commandment's purpose is the perfection of our character; and here Nachmanides cites, with approval, Maimonides' remarks to this effect (266-67).

It would seem from this part of Nachmanides' remarks, that he takes Maimonides to advance *both* the suffering of the bird and the harm to the person causing this suffering as reasons for the commandment, whereas Nachmanides himself accepts the latter and rejects the former. However, we have seen reason to think that, despite his remarks in III, 48, Maimonides actually rejects the suffering of the bird as the reason for the commandment. It is possible that Nachmanides realizes this, for he speaks only briefly about the bird's suffering. In any case, despite his remarks against Maimonides, Nachmanides is, in fact, advancing the very same reason for the commandment—at least, so far.

Nachmanides next refers to the concealed reasons for the commandments and the great reward for uncovering them (267-68). Now, on the one hand, it is hard not to think that the person who has revealed the reasons and is worthy of the reward must be Maimonides, and this surmise is strengthened by Nachmanides' next remark, a rather lengthy expostulation on the purpose of this and other such commandments as the perfection of human character and thought (268-70). Apparently, Nachmanides is endorsing Maimonides' reason for this commandment, praising Maimonides, and explaining that the commandments cannot be for God's sake but only for ours.

Yet, this praise of Maimonides has a double edge. On the positive side, Maimonides does give an account of the commandment. On the negative, we have seen that that account is anything but straightforward. He speaks of the pain of the mother bird even while he suggests that the feelings of the animals are not important, and he holds, if my interpretation is correct, that the agent who is to benefit from the commandment must remain in the dark about its true purpose. So in praising the person who uncovers the truth of the commandments, Nachmanides is implicitly criticizing Maimonides' obscure and paradoxical account. Maimonides' reward for discovering the reason for the commandment is limited by his lack of candor about it.

Maimonides, though, must obscure the reason for commandment because, again, he thinks that the agent must not only be ignorant about this if he is to attain the character state that is the commandment's goal, but must also suppose, falsely, that the bird's suffering is important to prevent. At first glance, Nachmanides seems to be oblivious to the problem of motivating the agent's concern for the bird's suffering. However, there are two details of his discussion that suggest otherwise: the first is a second reason he advances for the commandment at the beginning of his discussion, the second is his reference to all the commandments as "decrees" near its end. His second reason for sending away the mother bird is that a person who slaughters the mother on the same day as her young or who takes the mother bird with her young is regarded "as though he cut off that species" (265). Now it is obvious that merely taking a mother and her young does not destroy a species, and even many people doing the same would be unlikely, in most cases, to endanger a species. The issue here is not the actual outcome of the act, but the intention behind it. Nachmanides' point is that someone who takes the mother bird and her young on the same day acts *as if* he would destroy the species for the sake of his own hunger and desire. Since the species of birds has been created by God, the person who acts as if to slaughter the species aims to negate the work of God.

Nachmanides is, I think, providing, in effect, an alternative to Maimonides' account. Whereas Maimonides faces the formidible task of explaining why inflicting pain on animals is prohibited when their pain is not intrinsically bad, Nachmanides rejects the notion that the commandment aims to prohibit inflicting pain and insists, instead, that it prohibits acting so as to destroy a species and that the person who would take the mother bird and leave her young to die would do just that. Since there is no reason to think that we have the capacity actually to make an entire species extinct, Nachmanides' point must be, rather, that the commandment makes us aware of the conditions needed to sustain creation and gives us an opportunity, by sending away the mother, to affirm them.

He makes the same point, I think, when near the end of his discussion, he claims that all the commandments are "decrees," that is, laws enacted by God to express his sovereignty (271-72). We might be tempted to suppose that he means to say that the commandment to send the mother bird away has no reason but the sovereignty of God, but this would run counter to his vigorous insistence here that the commandments do have reasons, namely, their benefits to us.Rather, in sending away the mother bird, a person affirms the sovereignty of God because he affirms, as it were, God's creation. A person who would take the mother and expose her young denies God's sovereignty by undermining the means God has provided for nature to sustain itself. Again, Nachmanides is not speaking about the actual effect of an action (how could anyone actually undermine God's sovereignty?), but what the agent intends.

Recall that Maimonides thinks that a person governed by his desires will derive the intended benefit from sending away the mother bird only if he supposes, falsely, that his act serves to prevent her suffering. On Nachmanides' account, he does not need to suppose anything about the bird's feelings. He need only bear in mind that the bird, and all of nature, is a divine creation. Then his act becomes one of respect for God by respecting his creation. In this way, Nachmanides avoids Maimonides' dialectical turns and provides a much simpler account. He shows how the commandment can benefit us without supposing a false belief in the agent.

Though no proof is possible, I think it very likely that Nachmanides understood Maimonides' account fully. One sign of this is, perhaps, his double-edged praise of the person who reveals the reasons for the commandments, mentioned earlier: we can now see that this as criticism of Maimonides' notion that the reasons for the commandment must remain hidden from the agent. Another sign might be Nachmanides' discussion here of the benefits that we derive from the commandments. He puts particular stress on their freeing us from "the dross of evil thoughts and blameworthy character traits" (270). Recall that Maimonides had mentioned only the blameworthy character traits, not the "evil thoughts." The person who sends away the mother bird rids himself of "evil thoughts" if he performs the commandment as a way of preserving the species and, thereby, acknowledging God's sovereignty over nature: he rids himself of the thought that he controls nature. Where Maimonides sees the commandment's purpose as refining and moderating desires, Nachmanides sees it as refining beliefs.

This latter is not, however, its only purpose; for Nachmanides also speaks of its "teaching us the trait of compassion and that we should not be cruel" (271). The question now is whether we need to imagine the suffering of the bird and to suppose its suffering wrong in order to derive this benefit, as Maimonides thought. Nachmanides clearly thinks we do not; for, immediately before the claim that the commandment serves to teach us compassion, he *denies* that it is for sake of the bird on the ground—by now familiar to us—that if God's mercy extended to animals, He would have forbidden animal slaughter altogether, and he follows the claim by speaking of the cruelty of butchers and of laws as divine decrees. The sequence of thought implies that the compassion we are supposed to have does not spring from awareness of the bird's suffering but from the decree to send her away and other such commandments.

He means, I take it, that we learn from the decree that the suffering of the mother bird is important to avoid and this *idea* arouses our compassion for her plight. What we need to understand is that God created the bird and gave it the means to preserve itself. To use those means of preservation to destroy the bird, as does the person who takes her while she sits over her young, is cruel. Where Maimonides sees the faculty of imagination refining the faculty of feeling by being directed toward the bird's suffering, Nachmanides seems to think that reason will refine both imagination and feeling. Ironically, though Nachmanides criticizes Maimonides for his concern with the bird's suffering, it is really he who relies on the value of the bird.

Whether reason can play the regulative role in moral psychology that Nachmanides requires of it has been a large question in the history of philosophy; I cannot pursue it here. Of more immediate concern is the apparent conflict between Nachmanides' claim, on the one hand, that the slaughter of the mother bird would make one cruel and that the commandment aims to prevent this trait, and, on the other, that though the suffering of animals should not be a concern because the Torah allows slaughter, butchers are, in fact, extremely cruel. Why, then, does the Torah permit butchers to slaughter? Perhaps Nachmanides' point is that if butchers, who are not permitted to slaughter a mother and her offspring on the same day, are cruel, how much the more cruel and compassionless would they be if they could slaughter mother and offspring together. Along these lines, the commandment to send away the mother bird prevents only an extreme cruelty and lack of compassion; it has less of an impact on our character than Maimonides had supposed, but it is only one of many decrees that aim to refine character. Our character is shaped, Nachmanides explains at the end of his discussion, first by accepting God's sovereignty and, then, by following His decrees.

IV

A central question in contemporary environmental ethics is whether other species and the environment in general have intrinsic or instrumental value; the assumption is that either we alone are valuable or other species are also valuable. Until now I have been speaking of Maimonides' and Nachmanides' views on the value of other species as if they could be fit, more or less, into this scheme. I have said little about the theological issues that were, in fact, the overriding concern of each. Let us return to the two discussions with their theological concerns in mind. We will see that their thoughts on the mother bird and the environment in general derive from their theological notions, and we will also see that the options under consideration in contemporary discussions are not sufficiently rich.

Maimonides spends nearly the entire first book of the *Guide* considering terms that seem to characterize God. Bodily parts, like God's hand, are clearly metaphors as are all other expressions suggesting that God has a body. Maimonides explores the range of usage of these expressions, but he has a more radical point to make: absolutely no attribute can be ascribed to God. Instead, what we can grasp of God must be gleaned from understanding what He is not and from his actions in the world. The giving of the Torah is one of those actions, and its commandments tell us something about God, but only indirectly. Since the commandments cannot provide us with knowledge of God, it is important for Maimonides to show that they serve a human purpose, that is, that they are beneficial to us. Now God cannot be benefited by us—not just because it would denigrate His present state if He could somehow *become* good but also because He cannot be understood to *be* good or have any attribute at all. It is thus because of the character of God—or should we rather say, because God can have no character at all—that the commandments must be human centered. This is why Maimonides must understand the sending away of the mother bird to be of human benefit. Why, though, does he not also ascribe some value to the prevention of suffering in the animal world? Part of the answer, I think, is that he sees suffering as intrinsic to the animal world and to our own Biblically sanctioned relation to it. Animals pursue and destroy each other; their very existence is fraught with fears at approaching predators. Maimonides' nature is not the idyllic peace that sometimes appears in current discussions of the environment. The mother bird's distress at the loss of her young is nothing that is not intrinsic to nature. The reason it matters to us is that the perception that we have caused her distress could inure us to her suffering and, ultimately, to human suffering. It is important for *us* to understand the potentially painful consequences of our desires, but just because the physical world is created and governed by God, our actions can have no real impact on it.

The opposite view is that just because the world has been created by God and continues to be governed by Him, we must do our part to preserve and respect it. This, I think, is Nachmanides' approach, and his real complaint against Maimonides is that the latter discusses the suffering of the mother bird rather than her continued existence. In fact, both agree that her suffering is not intrinsically important, but Nachmanides avoids the need for the agent to believe in its importance by understanding his sending away the mother bird as an affirmation of God's authority. To capture her sitting over the nest is to use the species' means of preservation as a means of its destruction.

What is particularly interesting about Nachmanides' approach is that it cuts down the middle between the two modern alternatives. Is nature intrinsically valuable or valuable to us, we ask. Nachmanides proposes a third possibility: nature is valuable as God's creation. Strictly speaking, it is not intrinsically valuable; it derives its value from the same source that we do, the divine creator. Were animals intrinsically valuable, we would not be justified in slaughtering them for food. On the other hand, because animals have some value as divine creations, they deserve some respect—this and other commandments make clear just what that respect should be. To be sure, the Torah allows animals to be slaughtered for food: human beings, created in the divine image, are more valuable than plants and animals. Nachmanides explains—and here, at least, Maimonides agrees—that humans utilize plants and animals to produce the energy for moral and intellectual acts. Yet, as divine creations, plants and animals should be allowed to preserve themselves, and this we learn from the commandment to send away the mother bird.

This idea of a scale of value, so fundamentally medieval, introduces shades of gray, a middle ground, into environmental discussions that in our time are disturbingly black and white. There is no need to say that the environment has as much value as humanity in order to respect it; Nachmanides thinks that we respect God by respecting his creation, and commandments like sending away the mother bird spell out the degree of respect due the environment

Maimonides agrees with the scale of value, but he sees nature as further removed from its divine source: creation is an "act" of God, and "all His acts . . . are an absolute good; for He only produces being and all being is a good" (III, 10). Even those beings whose matter makes them subject to generation are good "in view of the perpetuity of generation and the permanence of being through succession." Unlike Nachmanides, Maimonides is not appealing to God's goodness to support our calling nature "good"; rather, he uses the goodness of nature, its fulfilling its own purpose, as a way of learning what we can about its cause, God. Thus, he seems to think that we cannot properly worship God without knowledge of nature. Moreover, we realize our human ends by recognizing the divine source of nature—looking up rather than down, as it were—and such is the structure of the universe that beings lower on the scale thrive when a more sublime being acts for its own nature (III, 13). Hence, we need only seek to realize our own end, and lesser, created beings will benefit. The sort of stewardship of nature that Nachmanides has in mind is unnecessary.

At bottom, then, the disagreement between Maimonides and Nachmanides is theological and metaphysical. The latter thinks that God's goodness is an *attribute* that manifests itself in creation, the former that we cannot properly ascribe goodness or any other attribute to God—references to God's goodness in prayers are concessions to human needs, and we ought to reflect on their necessary inadequacy—but that nature is a divine *act* with its own intrinsic goodness. Nachmanides thinks we are obliged to preserve created species; Maimonides that creation is best preserved when we turn our attention to fulfilling our human nature by seeking knowledge of our creator. Thus, their understandings of the commandment to send away the mother bird differ significantly, but both agree that it calls for some type of respect for the environment.[8]

Notes

1. Saadia Gaon, *The Book of Beliefs and Opinions*, trans. Samuel Rosenblatt (New Haven, Conn.: Yale University Press, 1976), ch. 2, distinguishes the rational from the revelatory commandments; but he declares that though the latter are not intelligible to us, "I find for most of them also some minor and partial motives of a useful character." Maimonides, *Eight Chapters*, in *Ethical Writings of Maimonides*, edited by R. L. Weiss (New York: Dover, 1975), 80, objects to calling the first class "rational." He maintains that only the first two of the ten commandments—the commandments to believe in the existence and unity of God—are fully rational for human beings; the rest are either generally accepted opinions (his Arabic word translates the Greek *endoxa*) or traditions—see Moses Maimonides, *The Guide of the Perplexed* (*Dalālat al-Ha'irīn*), trans. Shlomo Pines (Chicago: University of Chicago Press, 1963), II, 33 and I, 2. (All quotations in this paper are from this translation.) In *Guide* III, 26 he identifies these latter types with the Hebrew terms, *mishpatim* and *ḥuqqim*, and he insists that there are reasons for commandments of both types.

2. See previous note. The Mishneh Torah appears in English as: *Maimonides*, *The Code of Maimonides*, Yale Judaica Series (New Haven, Conn.: Yale University Press, 1949-72).

3. *Ramban (Nachmanides), Commentary on the Torah* (*Perush ha-Torah*), trans. Charles B. Chavel (New York: Shilo, 1971-76), 265-73.

4. Isadore Twersky, *Introduction to the Code of Maimonides* (*Mishneh Torah*) (New Haven, Conn.: Yale University Press, 1980), 448, proposes in a footnote that these two Maimonides texts may be an instance of a blatant contradiction. Accepting that the two texts are contradictory, Roslyn Weiss, "Maimonides on *Shilluah Ha-Qen*," *The Jewish Quarterly Review* 79 (1989): 362-63, argues that Maimonides' fear of "antinomianism," the rejection of the authority and truth of Torah law, led him to disguise his views in the Mishneh Torah. According to Weiss he was afraid to speak of compassion for animals lest some people be led to vegetarianism and, thereby, fail to fulfill properly the obligation to eat meat on festivals and to seek the return of animal sacrifice. Josef Stern, *Problems and Parables of Law: Maimonides and Nahmanides on Reasons for the Commandments* (*Ta'amei Ha-Mitzvot*) (Albany: SUNY Press, 1998), 51, argues, as I understand him, against there being a contradiction by finding middle ground: in the Mishneh Torah Maimonides refers to the silencing of the person who claims divine mercy as the reason for sending away the mother bird to indicate that that is the wrong reason, whereas in the Guide he anticipates and rejects an attempt to use the silencing of this person as a ground to reject all reasons for the commandment. Stern thinks Maimonides understands this commandment as a "precautionary measure" instituted "to teach us to be merciful in every situation" (64), but he finds this explanation "problematic" because it seems to undermine Maimonides' distinction between the Written and Oral Laws, according to which the latter alone contain "precautionary measures" instituted to protect the former. Since this distinction is important for Maimonides' argument that the Torah will never be replaced, Stern thinks he hides the implication of the commandment to send away the mother bird by referring to it in the Mishneh Torah as a "decree of Scripture" (*gezerat ha-katuv*), a phrase that could be thought to mean that the commandment has no reason even if it need not have this meaning (65).

While there is no doubt that Maimonides is concerned in general about antinomianism and while Weiss and Stern's readings are both ingenuous, I find neither solution adequate. Maimonides warns readers in the *Guide's* introduction to expect contradictions because he has hidden his real views from the vulgar, but Stern and Weiss hold that he covers up his real views in the Mishneh Torah. Weiss's account requires that we dismiss a good bit of Maimonides' texts as merely for the vulgar, and she does not consider his remarks on the purpose of this commandment in III, 35, a passage that will figure prominently here. Stern, on the other hand, helpfully reconciles the two texts of Maimonides and emphasizes the commandment's human benefit, but he does not explain why the Guide seems to assign intrinsic value to the bird and his claim that Maimonides fears his real explanation would undermine, for the "multitude," the distinction between Written and Oral Law and confidence in the eternity of the Torah strikes me as unlikely: the issue is too abstract for the multitude, too inconsequential for Maimonides' concern, and one that Maimonides would himself need to address, were it real. Both Stern and Weiss explain Maimonides' antinomial fears quite generally; on the account that I shall propose, the antinomial concern is specific to this commandment. Part of the appearance of contradiction between the Mishneh Torah and the Guide stems from the former's referring to sending away the mother bird as a "decree of Scripture" and the supposition that this phrase means "without reason." Stern argues that the phrase need not have this meaning (55-61), but he still needs to explain why Maimonides would use it (65-66). I suggest that the phrase implies that the proposed reason for the commandment, Divine mercy for the mother bird, would be too apparent; a "scriptural decree" must have less obvious reasons.

5. See the preceding note.

6. See Stern, *Problems and Parables*, 54.

7. Is the imagination of the mother bird sufficient for her to feel additional distress at her own capture or death because she pictures her young, now defenseless, being taken and killed? If so, Nachmanides' argument would be wrong, but the degree of the bird's imagination is unclear.

8. I am grateful to the audience for their questions and comments and to Josef Stern for excellent comments on an earlier draft.

Bibliography

Moses Maimonides. *The Code of Maimonides*. Yale Judaica Series. New Haven, Conn.: Yale University Press, 1949-72.

———. *Eight Chapters*. In *Ethical Writings of Maimonides*. Edited by R. L. Weiss. New York: Dover, 1975.

———. *The Guide of the Perplexed* (*Dalālat al-Ha'irīn*). Translated by Shlomo Pines. Chicago: University of Chicago Press, 1963.

Ramban (Nachmanides). *Commentary on the Torah* (*Perush ha-Torah*). Translated by Charles B. Chavel. New York: Shilo, 1971-76.

Saadia Gaon. *The Book of Beliefs and Opinions*. Translated by Samuel Rosenblatt. New Haven, Conn.: Yale University Press, 1976.

Stern, Josef. *Problems and Parables of Law: Maimonides and Nahmanides on Reasons for the Commandments* (*Ta'amei Ha-Mitzvot*). Albany: SUNY Press, 1998.

Twersky, Isadore. *Introduction to the Code of Maimonides* (Mishneh Torah). New Haven, Conn.: Yale University Press, 1980.

Weiss, Roslyn. "Maimonides on *Shilluaḥ Ha-Qen*." *The Jewish Quarterly Review 79* (1989): 345-66.

15

THE THIRD AND FIFTH DAY OF CREATION VERSUS THE TIMELESS NOW

Emilie F. Kutash

In the narrative of creation in *Genesis*1:1-2:3, each unit is marked off as a day. On day three the earth and vegetation are created, on day five the swarm of the water and the flier in the sky and all the living creatures.This creation ex nihilo commanded by the word of God gives the greatest attention in detailing a bringing forth of the generation of species "each of its kind." In Plato's dialogue on creation, the *Timaeus,* no commands are given and there is no mention of a single act of creation. The physical world unfolds in a discursive or successive manner according to intervals that are determined by the ratio structure of magnitude and of number, as it is determined in turn by geometrical proportions. Creation in time on analogy with the cutting of the canon in music in accordance with geometrical patterns is a process that recurs continually as the world in time follows its course of endless becoming. "*Gegonen,*" Plato answers, to the question "whether the world has existed always, having no beginning of generation or whether it has come into existence having begun from some beginning." "It came to be." A plethora of literature has followed upon this enigmatic utterance. It has been interpreted to refer to everything from continuous creation to the juxtaposition of the unstable material world to the stable invisible world of form. While in *Timaeus* to discover the Maker and father of this universe is a difficult task, in the Hebraic culture he is omnipresent and makes his voice totally known through his commands. Thus in Isaiah 55.10, God says, "For as the rain . . . comes down from heaven and returns not thither but waters the earth making it bring forth and sprout. . . . So shall my word be that goes forth from my mouth." Nature is God's creation in its particularity: rain, wind, grass, trees and creatures. This contrasts with the Demiurge of *Timaeus*'s careful geometry, based on ratio and proportion as he contrives the continuous creation in time carefully imitating the paradigm.

The God of Israel uses no preexisting plan in the same sense as does the Demiurge, he creates singly and by uttering the words that bring forth creation. Rather than copy a paradigm like the Demiurge of *Timaeus* He creates each thing individually and with a purpose of its own, out of nothing. The Hebrew idiom (*Ha) Me-Ayin* is comparable to the Latin ex nihilo.[1] This phrase, used in discussions by the Sages of the issues involved in Creation, can be translated "from what is not." In fact, the Hebrew word for creation, the second word in *Genesis*, "Borah," is used exclusively of Divine activity.Man is spoken of as "making" or "forming" but never as creating, i.e., producing something out of nothing.[2] In Classical Greek thought, on the other hand, the idea of creation from preexisting chaotic matter presupposes the imposition of form from preexisting paradigms. In the Hebraic view creation out of nothing means just that, it is God's will to produce each thing after its own kind and out of its own purpose. There is a singularity in creation that is discontinuous with any form of material or intellectual continuity. It is a radical willing. There is no before and no preexisting formless matter. The injunction, which follows from this, that this is God's creation and man cannot destroy it, is perhaps best stated in the following Midrash:

In the hour when the Holy one, blessed be He, created the first man, He took him and let him pass before all the trees of the Garden of Eden and said to him: "See my works, how good they are. Everything that I have created, I created for you. Think upon this and do not corrupt and desolate my World. For if you destroy it, there is no one to set it right after you." (*Ecclesiastes Rabbah* 7:28)

Man is clearly created on top of the food chain, but with injunctions to act with restraint when tempering the environment according to his needs.

Those thinkers who are considered the Jewish Philosophers, with the exception of the Platonist, Philo, for the most part date from the eleventh century and adapt Kabalistic, Aristotelian, or neo-Platonic themes. The more appropriate contrast, therefore, with Ancient Greek thought, is the essentially Hebraic thought and spirit of the Torah-Midrashic and Talmudic literature that predates and/or is outside of the Greco-Roman philosophical tradition. Ibn Gabirol, who represents a later Jewish philosopher's approach, for example, has a doctrine of matter as an intelligible entity deriving from the first principle. As John M. Dillon[3] points out, this is very reminiscent of Proclus, a late neo-Platonist's, view in proposition 72 of *Elements of Theology*, as it might have been transmitted in the Arabic *Liber de Causis*. For Hebraic thought, there is no such thing as matter and form but rather a very radical kind of "beginning" of the creation out of nothing. Thus Ephraim Urbach concludes that there is a great difference in both style and presentation in ideas prevalent in the contemporaneous Hellenistic world and the world of the Sages who commented on *Genesis*. (213) The various "doctrines of creation, from that of Plato to those of the neo-Platonists, including the cosmogonic dramas of the Gnostics," he contends, do not seem to have influenced the sages. "God himself and alone—without the help of Demiurge, angels, or forces-created the world . . . by an utterance." (213) Maimonides, too, interprets the creation out of nothing doctrine as more true to the words of *Genesis* than Greek influenced interpretations regarding a preexisting matter.[4] In Hebraic doctrine, therefore, there is no presumed continuity between the creation of the material substance of the world on the first and second day and the creation of the living creatures.The radical discontinuity between God and his creatures and between the types of creation is marked by the separation of original days. Each form of life occurs on separate days and separateness is a hallmark of the creation of each in its kind. Neo-Platonic procession and reversion, with continuity between matter and form on both extremes of the continuum, make this view of creation fundamentally irreconcilable with the Hebraic approach.

Let us look now at the source material for the injunction, following from *Genesis,* that Mankind must preserve and at the same time subdue nature for his own ends. Biblico-critical theorists have noted the two different themes in the creation story. There seem to be two types of Adam, and two different manuscripts within the Pentateuch have been identified. One does not have to be Harold Bloom to note the discrepancy between the two distinct types of Adam in *Genesis.* The first type of Adam follows from the passages in *Genesis* concerning the creation of man in God's image: "male and female created He them" and "God blessed them and God said unto them, be fruitful and multiply and fill the earth and subdue it, and have dominion (*vekivshuha*) over the fish of the sea, over the fowl of the heaven, and over the beasts and over the earth." The second Adam is to be found in *Genesis II,* where God formed man of the dust of the ground and breathed into his nostrils the breath of life . . . planted a garden eastward in Eden and instructed man to preserve it and keep it (*Lotashchit*). Adam the first, as Joseph Dov Soloeveitchik,[5] a famous contemporary Rabbi who does not himself subscribe to the dual manuscript theory of the Pentateuch, points out in *The Lonely Man of Faith*, received the mandate from the Almighty to fill the earth and subdue it. Adam the second was charged with the duty to cultivate the garden and to keep it. The first Adam's mandate (*vekivshuha*) has always been construed by commentators as a command to engage in technology as he subdues nature for his own needs.[6]

Lo tashit, the command of the second Adam passages, enjoins upon mankind that as part of nature he should conserve his resources and not destroy nature unless there are strong overriding considerations. Purposeless destruction is a prohibition that follows from this commandment, and is very much a part of the canon of the succeeding generations in both Midrashic and Talmudic literature. The Torah (*Devarim*: 22:6) teaches that one may not take the mother bird with the young or the eggs, while Rabbi Charina reports in Pesachim 50B of the Talmud that his son died because he had cut down a fig tree. The Ramban, Nachmonides, explains that killing the bird and its young together is the moral equivalent of destroying the entire species. Deuteronomy (*Devarim:* 20:19) also contains the injunction "When you besiege a city for many days to fight and conquer it, do not destroy its trees, because you eat from them, and do not cut it down, for is the tree of the field a person, that it should fall before you in siege?"

According to Rashi this prohibition exists because trees do not belong to man: mankind has no right to inflict damage on vegetation. Among those who will never see a blessing from their activity in their lifetimes, the Talmud (*Bava Bathra*: 91b) lists people who destroy good trees. The prohibition of destroying fruit trees then is more stringent than any other biblical laws; thus while *vekivshuho* (subduing nature) is a right and a privilege, it is also a responsibility limited by *Lo tashchit* (preserving nature) (47).[7] The mitzvah of *Bal tashchit* reminds a man that he is part of nature and must be careful to guard the world's resources and not squander them. The Talmud states (*Shabbat* 67a) that one should even pray for a sick tree in addition to taking care of it physically. These prohibitions apply even when the property being destroyed is ownerless (*hefker*). The destruction of wildlife, Rabbi Turkel concludes, through oil spills, industrial pollution or similar catastrophes, are all prohibited by this law. The biblical proof text for proenvironmental commentary is to be found in the First Book of *Genesis*—the Hebraic account of creation.

Timaeus, the archetypal text for the Greek account of creation, identifies God and reason, unity and the good in the creation of the "all perfect living being." Diversity, which is fabricated by the Demiurge, is subsumed by ratio and proportion as he applies the geometry of Pythagorean physics, creating differentiation and variation but within parameters commensurable to the whole.This allows a basis for continuity in creator and created. In the ontology of the *Timaeus* the only substance, in effect, is the cosmos itself and its soul, whereasin *Genesis* the celestial bodies, the earth and the various species of animal and plant life are all separately created substances, organic and singular in their kind. Both accounts have a beautiful vision of the cosmos, but of an entirely different kind. The Garden of Eden abounds with natural life, and man is placed immediately within it and enjoined to manage it and at the same time not to destroy it. The *Timaeus* vision is of a perfectly spherical whole, ageless and unailing, to which man must assimilate by being intellectually circular in the revolutions of his soul. *Timaeus*'s famous vision of the whole is as follows: "And he gave to it (the universe) the shape fitting and akin to it. Now for that Living Being which is to hold in itself (*periechein*) all living beings the fitting shape would be that which holds within itself all shapes. Therefore it is spherical (*sphairoeides*) and equal in all directions from the center to the extremities, all most perfect and selfsame (*homoiotaton*), since the selfsame is infinitely more beautiful than that which is not."

The language of this account of creation is one that could have been devised by Euclid. A language of shapes, spheres and self-identity contrasts with the Biblical account of swarming creatures and herb-yielding seed and fruit-yielding trees. When Plato discusses the creation on the part of the Demiurge of the material cosmos he describes his activity as a technical fabrication. The Demiurge is one who has "fabricated" the cosmos (33a6-b1). The construction of a model is carried out with the precision of an engineer or geometer producing on paper what he knows only in formula.[8] Aristotle, too, seems quite used to the idea of "coming to be" as a geometrical construction within the Academy tradition.[9]

For Plato a demiurge (creator), whether human or divine, produces on two levels; originals or real objects and imitations or images that can only more or less approximate the reality of their models. Fabrication of the universe is a technology; and the cosmos comes into being through *techne* on the part of the Demiurge, who tries to emulate an eternal paradigm. The analogy with architecture, in terms of blueprints and model building or cartography and astronomical models, is evident, and Proclus notes Plato's use of a vocabulary of technology. Hebrew providential creation requires no craftsmanship, no model and no rendering of a raw material. Things do not "become" but are immediately being created from nothing, and God creates every last of the beings, down to the lowliest, with a purpose. Among Jewish authors the Gaon Saadia, one of the First Talmudic commentators, of the generation of Scholars immediately following the Amoraim (the redactors of the Babylonian Talmud), is the first one who systematically taught the dogma of the creation out of nothing (ex nihilo) possibly laid down already by Karaitical theologians. He refuted all systems contrary to this dogma, and maintained that the sole will of God was active at the creation. The universe, then, is the result of the sole act of God and not the dominion of man, although he can be commanded to make technological alterations if they serve an end such as the maintenance or preservation of life.What follows from the idea of creation out of nothing is the grounding of the sanctity of all living things in the fact that they are works of an omnipotent creator. Rav Saadiah Gaon enumerates at great length the rights of man under the rubric of "conquest of nature." He includes using animals and fish for food and medicine, pearls from shells, constructing dams for power, extracting metals from the earth. The Talmud and the Midrash teach that everything in the world was created with a purpose. Even field wasps and other insects can be used for medical purposes or are messengers of God. Again, the Torah view towards the environment stipulates that although the world was created for man's benefit, mankind must take into account that it is God's creation and not his own.Everything is created with a good purpose, and thus we should not change or pollute our surroundings in any arbitrary way. V*ehivshuho* is a privilege granted during the first days of creation, and this privilege comes with a prohibition against wanton destruction (*bal tachchit*). In fact the command in *Deuteronomy* that no fruit tree was to be destroyed (D*euteronomy* 20:20) is still followed today among Orthodox Jews. An Orthodox Jewish colleague of mine, when he was renovating his house, had to consult with Rabbinical authorities to determine if it was acceptable to cut down a cherry tree in the back yard.

The differences between the two creation theories are made even more apparent in the contrasting views of time and eternity within the two traditions. A cyclical nature of creation and destruction is a very different kind of infinity than the Hebrew *olam*, that unknown mystery "from eternity to eternity." In the former recurrence is built on mechanism; while in the latter there is no necessity ruling the eternal existence of any created entity. *Genesis* starts off with a notion that "in the beginning" there was the creation of time, which was as much a creation as light and darkness. (See, for example, Maimonides, *Guide for the Perplexed*, 171.) Another author (Boman) has pointed out that for the Hebrew "time is the notion of occurrence; it is a stream of events"[10] The idea that life is sanctified grows out of this kind of radical beginning of time, since there is occurrence in the Hebraic view, but there is no necessary recurrence either, as there would be in a cyclical view of Time. God takes two of everything on the ark knowing that the same conditions will never recur for the creation of this universe, and all has to be preserved in the seed and egg. In neo-Platonic logic of creation, there seems to be a perpetual dance wherein becoming reverts to being and then proceeds again. The main intention of the activity of genesis is to further the tendency to wholeness and perfection of the universe which must ensue after the diminution of essence which comes about through the dissipation of infinity. Completion is a continuous event, as is stated in Proclus's commentary on the *Timaeus* in a very typically neo-Platonic reading of Plato's creation story.

Generation, therefore, must be said to be the formation of bodies, being a motion (or tendency) to the wholeness and perfection of the universe. For that which is composed from parts has a preconceive production of the parts. Hence the formation which takes place between matter, the whole orderly distribution of things and the one completion of the universe, must be called generation in order that it may be a path to the whole in which fashion is intermediate between the absence of *kosmos* and *kosmos* (arrangement).[11]

According to this view, destruction comes about when individual singular entities pass away while preservation is of form and species assimilating to eternal paradigms. One can see this in the following extract of Philoponus's work *Against Proclus on the Eternity of the World*. "He (Proclus) says that qualities and all material forms derive their subsistence, according to Plato, from non-being and again perish by returning into non-being, when the composite is dissolved."

The Monad of time is analogous to Eternity, which does not move or change, and Eternity is under the command of Being. Destruction, on the other hand, partakes of not-being, for Plato through Proclus, and entails transference to another form of all perishable things. "Not-being is hardly less real than being" is how Plato puts it in the *Sophist* (*Soph.* 258a)." Corruption contributes hardly less than Generation to the make-up of the universe.[12] In the *Philebus* (16e1-30) Plato makes the following remark: It is after being mediates and is finished with becoming that things can pass into infinity unmediated. For the Platonist/neo-Platonist Time corrupts all but what is eternal in paradigm, but thanks to the realignment of the celestial arrangements with every recurring "Great Year" all is restored in time.

In the Hebraic way of regarding things there is no guarantee, on the part of a fecund Eternity, that things will renew themselves, as there is in a cyclical view of time. As radically as they are created from nothing, so can they disappear. While God giveth and taketh away, he does so on an individual basis and it is singular living entities that are born and which perish. The preservation of any form of life is not guaranteed by the fact of any formal paradigm which itself could disappear should the last individual of that species disappear. Man must intervene to help prevent the passing away of any of the forms of life. This is not just an abstract idea but one that is put into practice. An illustration of this is the practice of the Sabbatical year, something enacted even today in the land of Israel, which dates from Biblical times. This is the year, occurring every seventh year when the land is not cultivated. Destruction is not taken for granted, man must use the following injunction to make absolutely sure that the soil replenishes itself, namely, "The Land shall enjoy its Sabbaths." (*Leviticus* 26.34.) Thus, according to the Torah, the following types of work are prohibited during the year of *Shemittah*: Sowing ("you shall not sow your field"), pruning, reaping, harvesting the vine and ploughing. All fruits of the tree which grow in the year of *Shemittah* are permissible as food, but they are invested with the sanctity of the Seventh year, the reason given by the Torah for the celebration of the jubilee Year, "For the earth is Mine, for thou art strangers and sojourners with Me." For the Torah Jew man does not really own anything in the world, for all is the property of the creator, and the right to work the land and eat of its fruits does not give authority over the crops that grow of their own accord during the sabbatical year.

Conclusion

Both Hebrew and Greek revered the Universe as a unique creation expressed each in its own way, a reverent view of the environment. In the *Timaeus* tradition it takes the form of respect for the cosmos as an orchestrated whole, while in the biblical view it appears as a reverence for the singularity of mundane creations. For Plato in *Timaeus* God constructed the universe "to be one single whole, compounded of all wholes, perfect and ageless and unailing." In *Genesis* God deems his creation Good. Respect for this cosmos as an orchestrated whole, however, with eternally existing cycles of recurrence and perfection and destruction, does not rely on man's role in preservation except for the fact that moral perfection is attached to ideal societies. Spiritual and intellectual assimilation to the cosmos as a whole is seen as a spiritual or intellectual ideal. The Jewish view of creation, on the other hand, leads to very specific Halachic injunctions concerning permissible acts in regard to the environment. At 31a4-5 of *Timaeus*, Plato declares that "that which contains all intelligible living creatures cannot have any second to it." The receptacle, nurse of all Becoming, yields in time to the domination of reason as the Demiurge molds all things according to geometrical principles. The revolutions of the Same dominate the better part of becoming, while that which exists through all eternity and time provides its living image. Every 26,000 years, or whatever the Great Year is calculated to be, all things align, all is restored in the eternal recurrence of perfection. The God of the Hebrews, on the other hand, creates only Once, deems His universe Good and gives it up for man's use with a label on it which is removed only at the risk of total destruction. The label, while giving a clear mandate for the use of nature for man's purposes, at the same time warns that there are severe prohibitions upon the uses of God's world.

Notes

1. See Ephraim E. Urhbach, *The Sages* (Cambridge, Mass.: Harvard University Press, 1979), 190.
2. *The Soncino Edition of the Pentateuch and Haftorahs*, ed. J. H. Hertz (London: Soncino Press, 1969), 2, n.2.
3. John M. Dillon, "Solomon Ibn Gsbirol's Doctrine of Intelligible Matter," in *Neoplatonism and Jewish Thought*, ed. Lenn E. Goodman (Albany: State University of New York Press, 1992), 43-59.
4. Moses Maimonides, *Guide for the Perplexed* (New York: Dover, 1956), 212 ff.
5. Rabbi Joseph Dov Soloveitchik, "The Lonely Man of Faith," in *Tradition* (summer, 1965): 5-65.
6. Rabbi Eli Turkel, "Judaism and the Environment," in *Journal of Halachah and Contemporary Society* XXII (fall, 1991).
7. Rabbi Eli Turkel, 49.
8. Proclus, *A Commentary on the First book of Euclid's Elements*, trans. with introduction by Glenn R. Morrow (Princeton, N. J.: Princeton University Press), 207.4 ff.
9. Aristotle, in a comment upon whether the creation myth in Timaeus should be taken literally, mentions a tactic employed by "some" who speak of the universe as a coming to be but who want that discounted. "For they say that they have spoken of coming to be in the way that (mathematicians) draw diagrams, not as if it ever did come-to-be, but for the sake of teaching, so that they will more easily gain knowledge, just as those who behold the diagram coming to be." (*De Caelo*, A 10, 279b33-280a2)
10. Thorleif Boman, *Hebrew Thought Compared to Greek* (Philadelphia: Westminster, 1960), 139.
11. *Proclus, In Platonis Timaeum Commentaria*, ed. E. Diehl (Leipzig: Teubner, 1903), vol. I: 358, 18-25.
12. Proclus, *Commentary on Plato's Parmenides* (Princeton, N.J.: Princeton University Press, 1987), 1012.

V. Then and Now

16

REUNITING SCIENCE AND VALUE IN THE NATURAL ENVIRONMENT

Daryl M. Tress

The Greeks of the Classical period knew about environmental pollution and the need to safeguard nature. Evidence of their awareness of pollution's dangers comes in part from the discovery of the ancient stele that Prof. Rossetti presents in this volume. The inscription on this stone tablet from fifth century B.C.E. records the Athenian legislature's call for an end to the poisoning of the river Ilissos from leather tanning. While we today are concerned, too, about the misuse of our water, land and air, I suggest that our situation differs significantly from that of antiquity, in two respects. First, the material perils facing the planet obviously are vastly more extensive and complex. At our juncture in history, global industrialization and technology, increases in population around the world, depletion of resources, and other such developments pose highly serious threats, as all informed people know. Second, the intellectual circumstances of our era differ importantly from those of the Classical Greek world. We are modern, scientific thinkers. The Scientific Revolution in Europe and changes in philosophical orientation roughly in the seventeenth century replaced the principles of classical thought with scientific thinking and its methods as the new model for looking at the world. In short, we inhabit the same planet as the ancients, but the world has changed drastically, both materially and mentally, from theirs.

A good deal of attention is now routinely paid by a wide range of people to the material conditions dangerous to the environment. Governmental agencies, concerned citizen groups, and scientists from many specialties, especially those biologists who are experts in the interconnections among organisms and their environments, namely "ecologists," follow these matters closely. I wish to supplement their valuable efforts by discussing the intellectual outlook of our time, to consider how it, too, presents a particular environmental hazard, namely in science's *value-free* or *value-neutral* character. This feature of scientific thought emerges clearly in the contrast with classical philosophies of nature: modern science insists on the separation of value and scientific knowledge, whereas philosophers like Plato and Aristotle integrate *value*, or reference to the good, within their studies. That is, modern science conducts its inquiries and develops its technologies without a requirement that it evaluate or take into account the good of the objects it studies or makes, maintaining that such considerations are distinct from science proper and not part of its charge, but Plato and Aristotle regard the good as central to explanations of nature.

While the value-neutrality of modern science was freeing in some respects, it has come to be seen in the twentieth and into the twenty-first centuries as more and more of a problem. It is now a fairly common observation, not only that our planet is imperiled by scientifically generated technologies (e.g., the dangers of contamination from nuclear power facilities or genetically altered farm animals and crops), but by value-free scientific thinking itself. The general public has become more ambivalent about the preeminence granted to science. We are pleased with its benefits but skeptical of the nearly unqualified sanction given to scientific research and technological development, no matter what the cost of or the readiness for what they yield. We have become wary, too, of the type of response science commonly makes to ethical concerns expressed about its endeavors, namely that some designated set of "experts in ethics" or "the people" will have to make the decisions about how to permit access to or use of new discoveries and developments[1] The public has begun to suspect that such experts might not exist, and to sense its own growing inability to understand or control what goes on in the scientific world.

Despite these misgivings, it is very hard to see what controlling science could *mean*. To remain objective and thus value-free, modern science requires freedom from external authority. The implicit contract of modern science is that it pursues its inquiries unencumbered with the need to assess value or good, so that the responsibility for ethical evaluation and consequences, if there be any, lies elsewhere. This mandate has allowed it spectacular growth and impressive results (e.g., in medical treatments), which only an advanced and highly complex science could achieve. But it has also brought great worries. Thus the current predicament: on the one hand, the public's fearful ambivalence about an unfettered science, and on the other, the apparent impossibility—both in principle and in practice—of limiting new scientific and technological developments in any significant way. Applied to the environment, the situation may be put this way: first, to insure our survival and the health of the planet into the future, a science is needed that is capable of effectively coping with the enormous complexities of environmental degradation. This can only be a modern science; a program of replacing standard science with "alternative sciences," is, realistically, quite out of the question. And secondly, for science to cease its involvement with practices and technologies that endanger the natural environment, and to become a force for repairing and defending nature against further assault, seems to demand that science become more self-aware and value-sensitive—which modern science, by definition empirical and value-neutral, cannot do. These incompatibilities seem to amount to an impossible situation.

There are, however, two encouraging signs that this divide between science and value might be narrowed. The first is the growth of the science of ecology, the second is the environmental philosophy of Laura Westra. Both involve principles or insights of ancient Greek philosophy. Ecology makes interdependencies in nature the object of its scientific inquiry and in this way, value, or "the good" is integral to its study. Westra's vision of global environmental integrity makes plain how the presence and absence of value already actively operates in the environmental domain, and her work has deepened this awareness among scientists and policy makers. This paper begins with modern science at its inception, looking at how it came to jettison the category of value. It then traces several historical ideas of nature and its value that contribute to the science of ecology, to see how ecology retains a value dimension. Finally, I turn to Laura Westra's contributions. Working within the contemporary context of environmental science, economics, and politics, Westra demonstrates how and why value belongs in all such deliberations. Thus, there is progress in reuniting science and values occurring both from the side of science in the case of ecology, and from the side of value in Westra's introduction of philosophy into the science-policy domain. Reuniting science and value helps to reduce the hazards to the environment in our modern thinking.

Ecology is a bona fide biological science (as distinguished from "environmentalism," the activist movement on behalf of the earth) that is fundamentally engaged in establishing the minimal survival requirements and optimal flourishing conditions of organisms and, more broadly, nature as a whole. It emerged from Darwin's nineteenth-century theory of evolution, a theory that changed biological study into a modern science. Thus, ecology has full scientific credentials, yet it violates the value-free criterion of modern science. How ecology manages to be science *and* value-laden is a story traceable through the history of "biology," from its roots as natural history in antiquity through its progression into evolutionary biology. But before telling that story, it is useful to recall the beginnings of modernism for science, and how science distanced itself from value in the sixteenth and seventeenth centuries in Europe.

Hannah Arendt remarked in referring to the seventeenth century that "the Modern period begins with the loss of the world." She might have had in mind the cosmic and psychic shift produced by Copernicus's astronomical findings of a heliocentric system: our planet was not the center of it all, nor perhaps were we. But the Scientific Revolution altered not only our idea of our place with respect to the heavens but our relation to things on earth as well. The enormous success achieved in astronomy by Copernicus, Kepler, Galileo, and Newton was due in large part to the new way of regarding celestial phenomena mathematically. This led to mathematical applications in many more local areas of investigation, for example optics, harmonics and chemistry.[2] Philosophy not only participated in but played a significant role in this turn to mathematization; Descartes was among the leaders and champions of the intellectual revolution in

Europe that made quantitative and mechanical analysis the centerpiece of the human attempt to know the world. And while the achievements of the new scientific method were impressive, they were of a piece with a loss that perhaps Arendt had in mind as well, namely the loss in the Modern era of the familiar and meaningful world of human experience. One way to see how this happens is to notice that mathematics describes things abstractly. When that abstract description is taken, as it generally is by science, to be *the* true one, it leads to a neglect or rejection of those aspects of the world that do not yield to quantification. For example, musical sounds that we might hear as melodic and touching are, scientifically speaking, *really* waves of vibrating air the lengths of which can be measured. Music is redefined as, or reduced to, sound waves, and hence the pleasantness of the music, and its meaning and value (or we might say, its *goodness*) do not have scientific standing because these features are not objectively quantifiable. The world of human experience—what we see with our own eyes, experience, and enjoy or not—was replaced as the truth by the measurable and mechanized world that science offered.

Science in this period did not set out to become value-free, to jettison all moral recognition. Rather, the separation of science from values was an important but indirect consequence of several factors, chief among them being the overthrow of classical substance metaphysics. By the time of the Scientific Revolution, the new scientists and philosophers were eager to put behind them Aristotelian scholasticism, the dominant institutional philosophy during the later Middle Ages. The new science's opposition to Aristotelianism is a complex story, but involves several points pertinent to our discussion: (i) The strong drive towards a materialist and quantitative science, and the consequent need to eliminate formal and final causality from the scientific explanation. These basic Aristotelian causes involve the essences and aims of things that are neither measurable nor subject to experimental treatment. (ii) The need to establish the new scientific method of controlled experiment to replace Aristotle's procedure of observing things in their ordinary settings, a method consistent with his substance philosophy that takes the essences of things to be best actualized and exhibited in their natural places. And (iii) the need to guarantee the freedom of scientific investigation, apart from the authority of the texts of Aristotle, whose physics was proving to be incorrect, and the authority of the Church which supported it. But among the salient ideas in Aristotle's substance metaphysics is the principle that things strive naturally for their proper good by virtue of their essences or form. Thus, with the rejection of Aristotelianism and the idea of essence, came the disappearance of the "good" is something inherent in things themselves. Religion represents another outlook that integrates the value of things in their very nature, as an effect of the divine creator. But science was defining itself during this period as distinct from religion and religious explanation, determined, as Newton put it in his First Rule, "to admit no more causes of natural things than such as are both true and sufficient to explain their appearances,"[3] and so the religious route to inherent value was blocked. Once the new scientific method of experimentation established itself on a materialist and quantitative basis, it was impossible to conceive of the presence of immaterial, nonquantifiable values that would be integral to the things science studies.

Once this course was set, modern science hardly departed from it. The natural sciences progressed rapidly, and the new scientific methodology extended into many other areas of inquiry. But some domains were not obvious candidates for a scientific makeover, notably the world of natural things, that is, the flora and fauna, field and mountain, air, sea and sky that man encounters daily. Why didn't this surrounding world succumb immediately to the scientific worldview? For one thing, plants and animals were not a simple fit as subjects for the new scientific method. They seemed most naturally and easily to be grasped via observation rather than controlled experiment, and to prompt observations that were qualitative rather than quantitative. There was already in place a long tradition of the study of flora and fauna, namely "natural history." Natural history emphasizes the collection and cataloging of the observed features of animals, vegetables and minerals, most often for practical purposes.[4] There is a second reason that nature study did not immediately submit to the new, value-free model of science, having to do with the unique character of living things, Although Descartes and some other philosophers and scientists of the early modern period were proposing mechanist models of living organisms that interpreted living bodies as machines, thereby making them more amenable to scientific methodology, there was strong resistance to this reductionist view. It was held, on religious and on philosophical grounds, that life is something unique and irreducible, that it involves some vital principle. Living things are different from machines and somehow valuable. And third, in connection with the previous point, a theme of appreciation and wonder at the remarkable beauty and order of nature, great and small, is still heard at this period of history, as it is heard from naturalists throughout history. Some such appreciation indeed seems an *appropriate* response to the natural world, compared to which the objective, value—neutral outlook of modern science looks like an alienated attitude that had to be imposed on the human response to flora and fauna. For these and other reasons, then, two more centuries were needed after the scientific revolution in physics for the modern science of biology and ecology to commence.

In the nineteenth century, Charles Darwin furnished a materialist basis necessary for the new science, which biology then rapidly became by the turn of the twentieth century. Darwin accomplished this transformation, interestingly enough, not through the modern route of experimentation but rather through the "unmodern" method of years of observations as a field naturalist. This mixture of the old and the new characterizes the science of ecology that Darwin inaugurated. Certainly, his evolutionary theory upheld the new science's disavowal of metaphysics and mystification, dismantling not only the Biblical story of the origins of the earth and its living inhabitants, but remnants of philosophical essentialism as well. But Darwin did not repudiate all earlier traditions. He himself acknowledged the importance of Aristotle's biology, and his methods, as noted, reflect the persistence of the old natural history tradition. Several earlier conceptions of nature and its study come to play a role in the new biology. We might consider three: (i) Aristotle's philosophical biology, with its theoretical intentions; (ii) the natural history tradition, with its emphasis on practical applications; and (iii) the Romantic view, with its emotional response to nature.

(i) G. E. R. Lloyd, the distinguished scholar of ancient science, makes the point that the Greeks invented the concept of "nature" as explainable.[5] Within this explanation-seeking attitude were competing accounts of the principles thought to be at work in nature's regular operations. If we let Aristotle be our guide, he tells that many of his philosophical predecessors and the physicians who were his contemporaries favored materialist explanations of things, that is, they thought that all the causes of things lay in the basic elements or material parts of the thing, and that the presence of these parts was enough to explain the composition and behavior of complex, natural entities. Aristotle rejects this approach, arguing that we never see materials simply organize themselves (wood and iron will not combine themselves to form an ax, for example). These materialist thinkers, he says, have failed to specify the needed, nonmaterial cause that organizes and shapes living things, and acts in such a way that the results are highly regular. Aristotle specifies that the responsible causes are the form and the *telos*, or end purpose, intrinsic to natural things. Aristotle does not exclude matter and motion as causes, but insists that the immaterial form and *telos* of the thing must be included in the account as well. And at the heart of his philosophy is the notion that the *telos* or actualization of the natural object is its *good*. Aristotle's several important treatises on animals (such as *History of Animals*, *Parts of Animals*, and *Generation of Animals*) are rich and striking compendia of facts that include his own and others' detailed observations on animal structure, parts and behavior, all of which is a means for his fuller inquiry, ultimately, into the form and *telos* and the good.[6] Aristotle's biology is theoretical rather than practical, which Darwin appreciated and favored. But more importantly, it is philosophical in that its empirical dimension serves his interest in understanding the essence and good of nature.

(ii) We might contrast Aristotle's theoretical study of an internal, causal good in nature with other ways in which nature's value was recognized, coalescing in "natural history."[7] From the natural history point of view, nature is seen as capable of a range of valuable activities, such as teaching, entertaining, healing, predicting the future, and so forth. So, for example, early in Greek history, Aesop's popular fables reflect the generally accepted principle in antiquity that nature has moral lessons to teach.[8] A similar attitude is found in Pliny, the natural history writer of the first century C.E. in Rome.[9] Medieval bestiaries constitute a later part of this tradition, combining edification and entertainment in their sometimes arcane depictions of animals. In ancient times, soothsayers scrutinized animals, plants and various natural phenomena, watching for messages for human fate; such practices continued covertly for many centuries. And the herbal manuals of healers from early and medieval history were collections of facts about plants and other natural substances with medicinal properties. When we add to this list the unwritten know-how of farmers, herders, foresters, and hunters, it is plain that nature lore had considerable practical value, easily overshadowing the theoretical interests of a thinker like Aristotle.[10] Indeed, the practical mentality of natural history came to dominate shortly after Aristotle's death, and the Aristotelian research program in biology disappeared for over 1700 years, only to be discarded yet again, after a brief resurgence, with the demise of Scholasticism.[11]

(iii) The third view, nature Romanticism, arose in part at least as a reaction against the quantitative and experimental program of modern science and its denial of a role for value in its inquiries. The Romantic attitude developed in the eighteenth and nineteenth centuries in Europe and the United States and found wide expression in the arts, philosophy and politics of the time. Romanticism encouraged the full engagement of the senses and sentiments, and these pictured a world that was vibrant, alive, majestic and vitally interdependent, a vast holistic community.[12] Not only did nature romanticism reject the emotional aridity of the new science, it also reacted against the industrialization associated with it.[13] During this period, a number of talented and passionate amateurs appeared who studied and wrote about the working of the natural world with a dedicated focus on the grandness of nature. Perhaps the most notable among them was Henry David Thoreau.[14] Thoreau's deeply felt response to his own locale of Concord, Massachusetts, led to a profound naturalist's involvement, such that he came to hold that it was only through love of and identification with nature that we could really understand it. His was an Arcadian ideal in which man would live simply, in harmony with nature. Thoreau was well aware that his holistic attitude towards nature, which gave primacy to the interdependence of all things, was subversive to many of the values of both science and capitalism in the modern world.

Darwin, too, was at work in the nineteenth century, and his new biology retains aspects of these three older approaches to nature. The theoretical thrust of Aristotle's science, natural history's methods of observation in the natural setting, along with a dark, "reverse" version of the Romantics' idealization of nature can all be detected in his new science of the natural world. What Darwin appreciated in Aristotle was his broad and theoretical interest in nature.[15] Darwin, like Aristotle, simply wanted to know how nature works. And like earlier natural historians (including Aristotle) and the Romantics, Darwin was deeply engaged by nature and was a premier naturalist. But there are important differences, too. Unlike Aristotle and Thoreau, Darwin was a modern, materialist scientist who rejected essences and divine design as ways of explaining the workings of nature, positing instead the mechanisms of natural selection and the survival of the fittest. Missing in Darwinian science are the essences that in Aristotle's philosophy convey the intrinsic good of natural things; gone, too, is the creator's hand ordering the character of nature and natural things. It is no accident that with Darwin's elimination of both intrinsic ordering principles in nature and the divine creator, the highly ordered *and inherently good* world of nature, associated with Aristotle as well as with some religious outlooks, is replaced with a turbulent nature, ridden with competition, strife and randomness. His picture of the intensity of nature resembles that of the Romantics, but it is more ominous.

Evolutionary theory arguably represents as disturbing a shift as did the Copernican heliocentric displacement of the earth, yet it is not so utter a break with the past.[16] Darwin does not preserve the classical way of recognizing value (i.e., through an immaterial essence that conveys the good, as in Aristotle). But unlike the modern physical sciences that fully separated themselves from value, Darwin's science of ecology necessarily retained a role for values. It did so by virtue of its object of study, namely nature's interdependencies, in that "dependency" and "interrelation" carry ethical implications—even within the ethically attenuated framework of modern evolutionary biology. That is, even if the sole criterion is survival rather than a more robust conception of the good, ecology's recognition of interdependencies in nature—many of which it now tests for and precisely measures—ushers in questions of obligation and prohibition. And the basis for obligation and prohibition is desert or entitlement to something good, such as continued existence. Because of the vital character of natural objects, their vulnerability, the irreversibility of certain effects they suffer and the risk of extinction, inquiry about the good is inescapable for ecology.

But which values does nature imply? Donald Worster's superb book, *Nature's Economy: A History of Ecological Ideas,* recounts the tensions involved in establishing and stabilizing values within the new ecological science. In twentieth-century ecology, two major competing answers emerged, one from the manager ecologists, the other from the nature-romantic ecologists. Early in the century, the conservation movement encouraged ecologists to see value in resource and wildlife "management." The aim was to benefit man through maximizing desirable natural output (such as crops or irrigated farm lands) and eliminating species of predators and pests. The background for this vision of control was Darwin's picture of a turbulent nature which needed subduing, along with a materialist, mechanical conception of nature that allows for the very possibility of it being "run" by man, like a machine. By the 1950s, however, Rachel Carson and others saw value in protecting nature that was under assault both from pollution and the environmental managers. At that time, conceiving of nature as a machine fell into disfavor as ecologists emphasized organicism, i.e., nature as a living system or entity. Reviving ideas derived from Romanticism, some environmentalists in the 1960s and 1970s adopted a "naturist" attitude that gave nature moral supremacy, so that nature in its perfection and goodness became the ethical model for man to imitate. These competing visions, nature as a machine to be controlled or nature as a superior living entity to be served and emulated, have produced the ethical conflict with which all educated citizens are by now familiar, that is, the collision between nature's usefulness and service to man, on the one hand, and the demand that nature, as holistically simple and peaceable, be served by man.[17]

Thus we arrive at this remarkable instance of a modern science incorporating value within its study, only to encounter an impasse in the conflict between subordinating nature to man's goods, on the one hand, and elevating the goodness of nature above man, on the other. Here we may turn to the second of the two positive developments on this score, namely Laura Westra's philosophical work on ecological integrity.[18] She detects that the impasse is best resolved through a third alternative, one based on principles derived from ancient philosophy, that retrieves nature's own intrinsic value. The management and the romantic models are both faulty. The management model falsely regards nature as good and valuable because it is a good producer *for us*; like pre-Copernican astronomy, it mistakenly makes man the center and purpose of nature. The Romantic model falsely anthropomorphizes and sentimentalizes nature as pure and gentle, and then attributes value to it based on this dubious ideal.[19] The principle of environmental integrity, instead, acknowledges the intrinsic value of nature and its integral relations, especially living nature, along the lines of Aristotle's "form" and *telos* and nature's overall orderliness. On the Integrity model, nature does not need to earn its value, either by being useful or by being glorified. Rather, the value or goodness of nature belongs to it by virtue of itself, as an interdependent system supportive of ongoing life cycles. Indeed, the continued health of nature is the foundation upon which value is realized.

Westra works out this thesis in detail that does not lend itself to simplified summary. Clearly, though, her resolution does appeal to the holism of nature. Modern sciences find this idea unacceptable because intrinsic order and value cannot be quantified and demonstrated via experiment. So the notion of environmental integrity may at first appear suspect to scientists. Nonetheless, on the integrity model inspired by Aristotle, value is ascertained through the intellect. At its best, then, it avoids the self-interest and the emotionality that ground the management and romantic models, and thus has a rational basis that scientists can respect. The Integrity Project, through major grants and meetings in the 1990s, has engaged scientists, policy makers and philosophers, both in Canada and internationally, in discussion of the rational basis of value. Indeed, the most promising and heartening aspect of the Integrity Project is that it shows in the details of ecological science and policy, just how we can—and already do, in fact—"see" nature's own value. The Integrity Project actively and practically brings an Aristotelian dimension directly into the center of ecological science and policy making, helping to resolve the difficulties connected with the presence of values in ecology.

About the Contributors

Madonna R. Adams is assistant professor of philosophy at Caldwell College, Caldwell, NJ. In 1999, as director of the Center for Applied Ethics at Pace University, New York, she organized the first, national interdisciplinary conference on the Ethics of Parenting. She has published articles on ancient philosophy, ethics, women's studies, and spirituality.

Giovanni Casertano è professore ordinario di Storia della filosofia Antica nell'Università di Napoli "Federico II" dal 1980. Si è occupato principalmente dei pensatori presocratici e di Platone. Tra le sue pubblicazioni più importanti: Il piacere, l'amore e la morte nelle dottrine dei presocratici, Napoli 1983; Parmenide il metodo la scienza l'esperienza, Napoli 1989; L'eterna malattia del discorso, Napoli 1991; Il nome della cosa. Linguaggio e realtà negli ultimi dialoghi di Platone, Napoli 1996.

Lynda Clarke is professor of the history of religions and Islam at Concordian University, Montreal. Her interests include *Shiite Heritage*, a volume of edited essays (Global Press, 2001) and *"Hijàb According to the Hadíth: Text and Interpretation"* in *Veiling and Dress Codes in the Diaspora*: *Muslim Women's Voices* (Scholars' Press, 2002).

Edward Halper, Professor of Philosophy at the University of Georgia, is the author of _One and Many in Aristotle's Metaphysics: The Central Books_ (Ohio State University Press, 1989), _Form and Reason: Essays in Metaphysics_ (SUNY Press, 1993), and numerous papers that have appeared in philosophy journals. His is currently in Germany on a Fulbright working on the metaphysical nature of friendship, family, and other relationships.

Michael W. Herren is Distinguished Research Professor of Classics and Humanities at York University, a Member of the Graduate Programme in Medieval Studies at the University of Toronto, and Editor of *The Journal of Medieval Latin.* His main area of expertise is the Latin Literature of Western Europe, particularly the British Isles, in the period ca. 400–ca. 900. His earlier research concentrated on the edition and translation of challenging texts. More recently, he has worked on theological issues; his book, written with S. A. Brown, *Christ in Celtic Christianity* will appear shortly. He has also undertaken projects on medieval mythography and the history of exegesis of classical mythology. He has been a recipient of the Killam Fellowship and the John F.

Simmon Guggenheim Fellowship, and is a Fellow of the Royal Society of Canada.

Alan Holland is Professor of Applied Philosophy in the Institute for Environment, Philosophy and Public Policy at Lancaster University, UK, and editor of the journal Environmental Values.

Helen Karabatzaki is Assistant Professor of Philosophy at the University of Ioannina, Greece. She is specialised in ancient Greek Philosophy, especially Plato and Hellenistic Philosophy. She is the author of a monograph on Posidonius and the Ancient Stoa, Ioannina 1998, as well as of many articles on a wide range of subjects in classic, hellenistic and graeco-roman philosophy.

Emilie F. Kutash currently holds a Research Fellowship for the Boston Colloquium for History and Philosophy of Science. She holds a PhD in Ancient Philosophy from the New School for Social Research and a Doctorate in Psychology from Rutgers University. She has published in the Graduate Faculty Journal, Journal of Neoplatonic Studies, Philosophy and Rhetoric, American J. of Semiotics, American Imago and others.

Teresa Kwiatkowska, originally from Poland, is Professor at the Philosophy Department of the Universidad Autonoma Metropolitana-Iztapalapa in Mexico City. Main interests: environmental ethics, aestetics, moral dilemmas of genetic and environmental engineering. Author of various articles published in Mexico, Argentina, Poland, USA and Australia. Co-author of the book *Naturaleza y mundo antiguo* (Nature and the Greek World), Plaza y Valdes, Mexico, 2001. Co-editor of the first environmental ethics textbook published in Mexico. (Los caminos de la etica ambietal, Plaza y Valdes, Mexico, 1998, with Jorge Issa.) Co-editor (with Ricardo Lopez Wilchis) of the collective book *Ingenieria genetica y ambiental: problemas filosoficos y sociales de la biotecnologia.* (Genetic and Environmental Engineering: Philosophical and Social Problems) Mexico, 2000, Plaza y Valdes. Co-editor (with Manuel Medina) of the book published in 2001 in Spain: Ciencia, tecnologia/Naturleza, cultura, en el siglo XXI. ed. Anthropos.

Parviz Morewedge earned his Ph.D. at UCLA and has taught for over forty years at several universities in the United States, including Cornell, Columbia, UCLA, Fordham, NYU, and in the State University of New York system, as well as seminars in the United Kingdom, Canada, Iran, Turkey and Malaysia. He was employed as a computer specialist for several years, including as a Senior Research Engineer at General Motors. His publications in the University Presses of Oxford, Cambridge, Columbia, NYU, Fordham and SUNY, and elseware include twelve books and over forty articles and reviews. Currently, Morewedge is a Senior Resarch Fellow at Binghamton University, and an editor for Board

College. Additionally, he is an active editorial board member of over twenty scholarly journals in the history of philosophy.

Rosmarie Thee Morewedge is Associate Professor of German and Chair of the Department of German, Russian and East Asian Languages at the State University of New York at Binghamton. Upon receiving her Ph. D. at UCLA with a dissertation on the Grotesque in Wolfram von Eschenbach's Parzival, she has published widely in German literature, pedagogy and folklore, but has specialized in medieval studies. She has edited a collection of essays on the Roles of Women in the Middle Ages and has writtten essays and articles on the German medieval lyric (Burkhard von Hohenfels), Parzival, the narrative and narration, medieval wisdom literature, and orality and literacy.

Lorina Quartarone is Assistant Professor of Classics and Liberal Studies at the University of Montana. She has also taught at Whitman College and Loyola University Chicago. Her research interests include ancient literature on nature and the environment and Augustan poetry. She has recently co-edited, with W. S. Anderson, *Approaches to Teaching Vergil's Aeneid* (MLA 2002).

Thomas M. Robinson is Professor of Philosophy at the University of Toronto. His best known work is *Plato's Psychology* (University of Toronto Press, 2nd edition, 1995), which was recently designated one of the "hundred most influential and important books" published by the University of Toronto Press in the century 1901–2000. Winner of the Aristotle Award in 1998, he has served as President of the Canadian Federation for the Humanities (1988-90), of the Society for Ancient Greek Philosophy (1993–1995), and of the International Plato Society (1995–1998), and is currently Honorary President of the International Association for Greek Philosophy.

Livio Rossetti is a professor of Ancient Philosophy in the University of Perugia since 1983. He served as convenor of the Symposium Heracliteum (Chieti 1981) and of the II Symposium Platonicum (Perugia 1989: the International Plato Society was established on that occasion). Among his books is *Plato's Euthyphro* with diskette (Rome 1995) and *Introduzione alla Filosofia Antica* (Bari 1998).

Daryl M. Tress is Associate Professor of Philosophy at Fordham University in New York City. She was a Fellow at the Radcliffe Institute for Advanced Study at Harvard University in 2000-01. Her main field of study is ancient philosophy, with special attention to the intersection of ancient philosophy and science. She has also published philosophical work on environmentalism and feminism.

Laura Westra is Professor Emerita at the University of Windsor, presently working on a second Ph.D. at Osgoode Hall Law School. She has authored and edited fourteen books, and the one arising from her thesis is under contract (details at www.ecointegrity.net). She has been funded by SSHRC from 1992 to 1999 and from NATO. She has written over eighty articles and chapters and has lectured in Europe, North and South America and Australia. She has been a consultant with the WHO. Most of her work is on environmental and justice issues.

Hideya Yamakawa is Professor of Philosophy in St. Andrew's University, Osaka. He is the author of *Greek Philosophy and the Modern World*, the International Center for Greek Philosophy and Culture, Studies in Greek Philosophy Series, Athens (1998) and many other books on Greek philosophy including *Zeno's Four Paradoxes*, Kodansha (1996).